The All-New and Expanded
SCHOOL ADMINISTRATOR'S
PUBLIC SPEAKING PORTFOLIO
with Model Speeches and Anecdotes

Also by the authors:

*Educator's Lifetime Library of Stories, Quotes,
   Anecdotes, Wit, and Humor*

Encyclopedia of School Humor

New Encyclopedia of School Letters

*101 Pupil/Parent/Teacher Situations and How
   to Handle Them*

School Administrator's Encyclopedia

*School Administrator's Public Speaking
   Portfolio: With Model Speeches and Anecdotes*

*The All-New
and Expanded*
SCHOOL
ADMINISTRATOR'S
PUBLIC SPEAKING
PORTFOLIO
with Model Speeches
and Anecdotes

P. Susan Mamchak
and
Steven R. Mamchak

*Illustrations by
Charlotte Kindilien*

PARKER PUBLISHING COMPANY
West Nyack, New York 10995

© 1992 *by*

PARKER PUBLISHING COMPANY
West Nyack, New York

10 9 8 7 6 5 4 3 2 1

Library of Congress Cataloging-in-Publication Data

The all-new and expanded school administrator's public speaking
portfolio
    p. cm.

   ISBN 0-13-031436-6
   1. Public speaking —Handbooks, manuals, etc. 2. School
administrators—United States.
PN4192,S35A74   1991
806,5'1—dc20   81-29867
                                               CIP

ISBN 0-13-031436-6

Parker Publishing Company
Business Information Publishing Division
West Nyack, NY 10995

Simon & Schuster, A Paramount Communications Company

Printed in the United States of America

We gratefully dedicate this book to

Dolores Recupero,
exhorter and encourager,

Connie Barber,
helper and friend,

and

Carole DiSalvo,
Joanna Neuenhaus, and
Andrew Newfeld;
educators without equal.

What a privilege it is to know and work with you!

ABOUT THE AUTHORS

P. Susan Mamchak has been active in education for over 20 years and has served in a variety of positions ranging from substitute teacher to school disciplinarian. She is also a past member of *Toastmistress International* and has lectured extensively on teacher effectiveness and interpersonal relations.

Steven R. Mamchak is an educator with over 29 years of experience in the New Jersey public school system. He has lectured widely before both educators and community members, has hosted his own weekly radio show on education, and is the recipient of the *New Jersey Governor's Excellence in Teaching Award.*

The Mamchaks are deeply involved in education and are the authors of 15 books on education and effective communication techniques.

INTRODUCTION
How This Book Will Help the School Administrator

In our introduction to the original *School Administrator's Public Speaking Portfolio with Model Speeches and Anecdotes* we stated that the administrator's first priority was to be an educational leader. This book holds to that statement. In fact, it is obvious to anyone who is vitally a part of American education today that the statement is even more relevant now.

The problem then, and now, remains the same. The demands of the position are so intense, that there seems hardly enough time in a day to handle the demands of the modern school, let alone attend to those peripheral demands for our time and our person that are put upon us at every turn. The question becomes, "Where are we going to find the time?"

Yet, those demands are real and must be met if we are to become an essential part of the educational scene. Yes, it *is* important to address the PTA and that group of parents of incoming students. Yes, it *is* important that you take part in that panel discussion on drugs in the school. Yes, it *is* important that you serve as chief speaker at the retirement dinner of the Assistant Superintendent. Yes, *of course* you will not turn down the request to speak at the memorial service for the teacher who died last year. Yes, *certainly* you will represent the school's contributions to the community at the civic awareness luncheon. Yes—of course—certainly . . . .

Now, where do you find the time?

The school administrator needs to find material that may be used either as is or with a few adjustments that will meet his or her needs for every public speaking occasion. The administrator needs a source that is highly relevant to education, which presents American education as it really is, and covers a myriad of topics on which an administrator may be asked to speak. This material should be entertaining, accurate, and dynamic. In terms of public speaking and the sheer weight of the task of administration, what a time and effort saver this source becomes!

If we are to judge by the sales of the original *School Administrator's Public Speaking Portfolio* as well as the many positive comments that we received on that book, then a source of public speaking aid exists for you.

Educators everywhere have told us that our book has helped them to cope successfully with their public speaking demands by providing the kind of relevant, thought-provoking, dramatic, and dynamic speeches, anecdotes, and commentaries that they can use in all their public speaking tasks; material that not only is appropriate and tasteful, but which reflects familiarity with the educational scene that only decades of active participation could possibly provide.

It is precisely this type of response that has occasioned us to write *The All-New and Expanded School Administrator's Public Speaking Portfolio*. As the title implies, all the speech material in this book is new. None of it appeared in our original book. Yes, we have kept the same format, especially with the "Special Data" section following each entry in which we provide times and tips for the speeches. Yes, many of the topics are the same as in the original, because some of the concerns of education have remained the same. And yes, the brief guidelines in Part Two are repeated because it seemed right to make this useful "Blueprint for Preparing and Delivering a Speech" available to educators who may not possess the original. Nonetheless, there is not a single speech, poem, or accompanying commentary in this book that may be found in the original. The speeches are truly all new.

We have also expanded the volume, adding a section on speeches that cover the "troublesome" situations that school administrators often face. In this section, you will find speeches to combat rumors, rebut negative editorials in the local paper, and deal with the issue of using live animals in science class as well as tough speeches on drugs in school, the abused child, sex education, and the AIDS tragedy—topics that are at the forefront of controversy and concern.

Throughout the book, you will find topics that are as relevant to the modern school as today's attendance figures. There are speeches on the settlement of negotiations, handling parental conferences, the role of the middle school in the development of the child, "roasting" an educator, eulogies and memorials for teachers, students, and administrators, homework, testimonials, the legality of supervision, and speeches that inspire, along with stories and anecdotes that break the ice to establish almost instant rapport with any audience.

In short, here is a treasure chest of *useable, relevant,* and *highly effective* public speaking material that was written by educators specifically for educators, which stands ready to meet your every educational speaking need.

This volume, like the original book, is complete in and of itself and stands ready to meet those public speaking needs. Together, the original book and this all-new version form a storehouse of invaluable speaking materials for the school administrator that will truly meet every speaking challenge.

From what we have been told by others and seen for ourselves, the original volume was used far too frequently to have ever gathered dust on any shelf. This book too, may never see the shelf in your office, because it will be right there beside its companion—well within your arm's reach!

We wish you success and joy in your every speaking task.

P. Susan Mamchak
Steven R. Mamchak

TABLE OF CONTENTS

CLOSING SPEECHES

SECTION FOUR: NEW SPEECHES BY ADMINISTRATORS FOR THE LAY AUDIENCE 87

SECTION FIVE: NEW SPEECHES FOR EDUCATORS 111

SECTION SIX: ALL NEW SPECIES THAT INSPIRE 135

SECTION NINE: NEW SPEECHES FOR SPECIAL EVENTS 207

SECTION TEN: ORIGINAL SPEECHES FOR HOLIDAYS AND OTHER JOYOUS OCCASIONS 231

SECTION ELEVEN: SPEECHES THAT DEAL WITH TROUBLESOME TOPICS 355

PART TWO
AN ADMINISTRATOR'S BLUEPRINT FOR
PREPARING AND DELIVERING A SPEECH

Part One

EFFECTIVE MODEL SPEECHES FOR ALL OCCASIONS

Part One of this book contains model speeches and anecdotes specially crafted for the school administrator. Here, you should find the right speech for the occasion you have in mind.

This part is divided into eleven sections covering general areas of speaking that affect the school administrator. Check the one appropriate to your wants, then look in the Table of Contents for more exact listings. Finally, check the locatomatic index *for convenient listings by topic.*

May these speeches serve you as well as they have us.

A COLLECTION OF ALL-NEW ICEBREAKERS FOR SCHOOL ADMINISTRATORS

Few things can be more stressful or upsetting than rising to speak and facing a sea of stony faces with their eyes and jaws set, and the corners of their mouths pointing at the floor. The very thought of speaking to this type of audience is enough to cause a week's worth of nightmares.

Fortunately, this audience is the exception rather than the rule, and the vast majority of the speeches you will give will be before people who are, if not thrilled, at least politely receptive to what you have to say. *That* is a blessing.

Nonetheless, an audience does not automatically respond to a particular speaker. Indeed, the speaker is expected to set the tone for the speech and guide the audience in their reactions to its content.

That's why the anecdotes in this section are called "icebreakers." That's exactly what your task is at the beginning of every speech; a successful speaker understands that he or she must "break the ice" that exists between audience and speaker, to establish rapport early on. A speaker who begins with hard, factual material (*in media res,* so to speak) without laying a groundwork of understanding and rapport is considerably *less likely* to have his ideas remembered and appreciated than the speaker who took the time to craft a speech that does break the ice, establish rapport, and gently and logically flows to the substantive matter, ending in an upbeat fashion, and leaving a smile on their lips or a point of reflection in their mind. This is the type of speech that will be remembered and earn you a reputation for speaking that will keep you in demand.

On the following pages, you will find a collection of "icebreakers" that may be used for a variety of occasions in order to establish that rapport of which we spoke, facilitate that transition, or even end your speech on that positive, warm note. Although the majority of them are humorous, you will find several of a reflective nature as well. We are certain that they will suggest many uses to you.

Finally, when you use these icebreakers, laugh along with your audience, because if you enjoy yourself, your audience will enjoy you. That's a fact!

$$\boxed{1}$$

TOPIC: **Cleverness; ingenuity; overlooking the obvious.**

AUDIENCE: **Appropriate for all audiences.**

Recently, I had the honor of attending an educational workshop with our superintendent, Dr. Smith, and the president of our Board of Education, Mr. Jones. Dr. Smith took his car and drove Mr. Jones and myself to the affair which was held in a nearby town.

It was really an excellent workshop; we learned a great deal, and we had a really great time. In fact, it seemed that it ended all too soon, and we headed to Dr. Smith's car for the drive back.

Dr. Smith dug around in his pockets for a few moments and then uttered those words dreaded by all motorists, "I think I locked the keys in the car . . . ."

Sure enough, as we approached his automobile, we could see the keys hanging from the ignition, and every door on the car was locked tight.

"Perhaps we should call the police," Dr. Smith ventured.

"No need for that," volunteered Mr. Jones. "We can go over to that gas station, borrow a crowbar, and pry open one of the doors."

"That would cause too much damage," I remarked. "Why don't we go back inside and borrow a coat hanger and see if we can "fish open" the door lock?"

"I don't care whether you use a crowbar or a coat hanger," said Dr. Smith, "as long as you hurry up. After all, the top is down; it's starting to rain; and I don't want the seats getting wet."

Special Data: *Time of anecdote: about one and a half minutes. This could be used as a "roast" for someone who was being honored, or it could be used to expand upon the point that we often overlook the obvious when trying to solve a problem. As with all the anecdotes in this book, try to personalize them by putting in the names of actual people and places with which your audience is familiar.*

$$\boxed{2}$$

TOPIC: Clever analysis of human nature.

AUDIENCE: Adult audience; particularly effective with workers (aides, PTA volunteers, etc.).

It seems to me that we can learn a great deal from anatomy, especially the study of the skeletal system. I think this is true, because people are so much like bones.

Some folks are *tailbones;* they sit around a lot and are always "behind" in everything they do.

Many people are *funnybones;* the moment you come near them, they get touchy, because they're so easily hurt.

Others are *jawbones;* they certainly manage to talk and talk, and they can tell you exactly what's wrong with everything, but they are not too hot on doing anything about it.

Still others are *wishbones;* they "wish" they could help out, but somehow they never get around to it.

And, finally, there are, thank God, the *backbones;* strong and untiring, they work to support the entire body. Without them, the structure would fall apart.

What a delight it is to be surrounded by an audience of backbones!

Special Data: *Time of anecdote: about one minute. This is extremely effective before any group composed of people who "volunteer" or do the "thankless" jobs around a school. PTA workers, class mothers, cafeteria servers, volunteer aides, and the like are often overlooked or feel that they are overlooked, which amounts to the same thing. Therefore, a clever opening such as this can do a great deal to set the tone of support for the "supporters" which will reap dividends throughout your school.*

$$\boxed{3}$$

TOPIC: Quick thinking; delicate situation; honesty.

AUDIENCE: Suitable for all audiences.

My wife had been nagging me about the way I tend to exaggerate. In fact, one day, she exacted a promise from me that from then on I was to tell the truth and nothing but.

Everything went fine, until the mother of one of our students arrived at my office carrying a huge pie which, she proceeded to inform me, she had baked personally.

"It's for you and your family," she told me. "I'll call you tomorrow to see how you liked it."

I took it home that night, and we cut into it for dessert.

Now, the woman who gave me that pie might be the best mother in the world, but she was undoubtedly the world's worst cook. My son kept looking around for an empty flower pot, and even our dog took one nip and ran away to chew on his rawhide for three hours. Under the circumstances, we did the only sensible thing we could—we threw it in the garbage!

I spent the rest of the night wondering what I was going to say to this person when she called the next day. How was I going to be honest and still not offend this woman who had, after all, offered the pie in honesty and in love.

Sure enough, she called the next afternoon and asked, "Well, how did you like the pie?"

"Ma'am," I said, taking a deep breath, "I want to thank you for that pie. Not only is the entire thing gone already, but I can assure you that food like yours will never last long at our place!"

Special Data: *Time of anecdote: about two minutes. This could be a plea for honest communication between, let's say, the faculty and administration. The point could follow that we all like compliments, but if real progress is to be made, we also need honesty. In other words let's strive to communicate in order to make the best "pie" (school) we can.*

$$\boxed{4}$$

TOPIC: **Trust; faculty meeting; left-handed compliment.**

AUDIENCE: **Adults; particularly teachers.**

Once I called a faculty meeting to discuss a very important change in our educational setup. I had really done my homework for this one, and by the time the end of the day came around, I was ready for that meeting.

In highly impassioned tones I described the many benefits attendant to the proposed changes. I believe I even traced the history of education, showing the proposed program as the next logical step in its evolution. I was really fired up, and, deep inside, I knew that I was doing a wonderful job.

It was then that I spotted a teacher who was one of the most respected members of the faculty. He was seated with his hands folded across his stomach, his head back, fast asleep!

What a letdown for me! I finished my speech, but my heart wasn't in it anymore, and I decided that I just had to say something to this person whom I respected and whose opinion I valued.

At the conclusion of the meeting, I sought him out and invited him into my office.

"Harry," I said, "I couldn't help noticing that you were asleep through most of my speech this afternoon. Now, I'm not angry, but please tell me what I did. Was I boring? Was I confusing? What?"

"Not at all," the gentleman replied. "From what I heard of it, you were quite good, and I'm sure the new program will be wonderful."

"I don't understand," I continued. "If it was so good, why did you go to sleep?"

"Because," he answered, "I have the greatest confidence in your judgment, and I knew that whatever you proposed would be fine. Look at it this way—if I didn't trust you, I wouldn't have gone to sleep, now would I?"

Special Data: *Time of anecdote: a little over one minute. This gets a good laugh from teachers, and it can be used to lead into a speech about trust; remembrances from faculty members; the importance* *of confidence; the need to study and test new ideas—just to name a few. Certainly, other uses will suggest themselves to you.*

$$\boxed{5}$$

TOPIC: Kindergarten; misperception; a child's view of life

AUDIENCE: Adults; parents in particular like this one.

One of the mothers of the kindergarten class was visibly pregnant when she stopped by the classroom to help out with a special project. It wasn't long before the woman's son announced to all present that his mother was going to have a baby, and that the baby was inside her, even as he spoke.

"No, he's not!" protested one of the tykes.

"He is, too!" protested the precocious kindergartener. "Come on, you can hear him!"

And, with that, the lad ran up to his mother and placed an ear on her abdomen and scrunched up his forehead as if listening intently. Soon, two or three other kindergarteners had joined him, and the small band listened with all their might.

Mother and the kindergarten teacher smiled to each other at the children's antics, when suddenly one child's eyes grew wide and he stepped back with a start.

"He *is* in there!" shouted the boy. "I can hear him!"

"What's he doing?" asked another child.

"You won't believe this," replied the boy, placing his ear once again on mother's stomach. "He's making coffee!!!"

Special Data: *Time of anecdote: about one minute. The woman who told us this story has a wealth of tales from elementary school days. Parents and teachers are always pleased with these anecdotes, and they never fail to bring a smile or a laugh. You might use something like this just for laughs, or for a reflective child's view of the world, misunderstanding, or even a speech on making certain that we interpret data correctly—i.e. on the value of informed knowledge. You* *will also find that you can get more mileage out of it if you deliver the children's lines with wide-eyed enthusiasm, particularly the punch line. Enjoy this one.*

$$\boxed{6}$$

TOPIC: **Self-evaluation; how others see you; a child's view.**

AUDIENCE: **Suitable for all audiences.**

> My little girl came running up;
>   With twinkling eyes, she said,
> "I love you best in all the world;
>   You're prettier than Fred!"
>
> And all the while, upon her hand,
>   Her pet, named Fred, just sat;
> His whiskered jaw chewed noisily;
>   His scaly feet were flat;
>
> His gray-white fur stood out in scruffs;
>   His beady eyes were pink;
> And I can tell you this, my friends,
>   That really made me think!

Special Data: *Time of anecdote: less than one minute. This might be used as a steppingstone to a discussion of how others view us or our school system, or as a self-evaluation in which we look at various strategies and techniques and ask ourselves how well they are working. We're positive you will find other uses for it as well.*

$$\boxed{7}$$

TOPIC: **One-line commentaries on human nature.**

AUDIENCE: **Suitable for adult audiences who can appreciate them.**

A lot of people are very much like footballs; you can never tell which way they are going to bounce.

* * * * *

There are some people who remind us of balloons; full of hot air and just looking for the chance to blow up.

* * * * *

Some people are like canoes floating aimlessly down a stream; what they really need is a good paddling to set them straight.

* * * * *

I know people who are like wheelbarrows; if you're going to get any work out of them at all, you are going to have to lift them up and give them a push.

* * * * *

There are people who remind you of kites; unless you really tie them down, they'll fly off in all directions.

* * * * *

Thank God, there are also people who are like an excellent pocket watch; filled with good works, well-regulated, with pleasant faces and busy hands.

Special Data: *Time of each commentary: a few seconds. These can be used anywhere in a speech, or you might want to just read the* *whole list, saving the positive one for last. That way might be effec-tive when speaking before a volunteer group, referring to them all, or at a special affair where one person, known for his or her good works let's say, was being honored. The commentaries are not laugh-getters, but are pleasant and leave heads nodding in agree-ment. As such, they can be useful.*

$$\boxed{8}$$

TOPIC: **Children; misperception; pride; patriotism.**

AUDIENCE: **Suitable for all adult audiences, especially parents.**

The political leader from a foreign country had just been released from exile and prison for his political views. He was currently touring the world, espousing the benefits of freedom and reform for his country and the world. At present, his itinerary had him touring the United States.

On his tour through our state, he was slated to visit one of our elementary schools, and this is just what he did. Choosing to visit the kindergarten class, he smiled broadly as the children flocked about him, hugging him, and climbing on his knee.

"Oh, Democracy! Democracy! How wonderful you are!" the man intoned as photographers' flashes glowed.

Then the gentleman threw back his head and began to laugh with the sheer joy of being surrounded by these happy and buoyant children.

One little girl, startled by the man's outburst, placed her hands on her hips and asked, "How come you're so happy?"

"I am happy," replied the man, "because I'm free! Free!"

"Big deal!" replied the child. "*I'm* five!

Special Data: *Time of anecdote: about one minute. For some reason, this story goes over extremely well. It is all but guaranteed to get a big laugh. Certainly, this could be used on any patriotic occasion. It also contains the idea of misinterpretation of what has been said, so it can be used anywhere that that would apply. Rather than analyz-*

ing the story, however, just use it, and see the positive results it brings.

$$\boxed{9}$$

TOPIC: **Three outrageous puns.**

AUDIENCE: **Suitable for an audience who would appreciate them.**

There was a young man who was engaged to be married to a young lady named Kate. In the month prior to the marriage, however, he met a young lady named Edith who lived in a nearby town. Soon, he began seeing Edith regularly, although he still felt amorous about his fiancé. Finally, he went to the minister who was to join himself and Kate in marriage and explained the whole thing.

"I can't decide," said the young man. "I want to marry both of them!"

"Son," replied the minister, "you know that's impossible. Surely, you must know that *you can't have your Kate and Edith, too!* (. . . can't have your cake and eat it, too . . . .)

*   *   *   *   *

A young man named Benny and his girlfriend went to a carnival where Benny decided to visit the fortune teller. The old woman told him that he must grow a mustache and never, never, *never* shave it off.

"If you do," she said, "something terrible will happen to you."

So, Benny grew a mustache, but his girlfriend hated it on sight and nagged him steadily to shave it off.

Finally, Benny relented and went to shave off the offending mustache. As he swept away the last whisker, a lightning bolt came through the bathroom window and incinerated him on the spot. All that was left was a little pile of ashes which his girlfriend swept up and, overcome by grief, placed in an urn that stands on her mantlepiece to this very day.

Which just goes to show you the truth of that old adage, 'A *Benny shaved is a Benny urned.*' (. . . A penny saved is a penny earned . . . .)

*   *   *   *   *

Mr. and Mrs. Smith were visiting Russia, and, like all visitors, they were assigned a personal tour guide. Their guide was a young man who introduced himself as Rudolph, a member of the Communist Party and very proud of that fact. In fact, he took every opportunity to expound on the doctrines of Karl Marx.

One afternoon, as the party of three was about to leave the hotel, Rudolph said, "You had better bring umbrella, because is going to rain."

"No it's not," answered Mr. Smith. "The sky is clear; it's not going to rain."

"I am expert on weather," the guide asserted. "I say is going to rain!"

Mr. Smith was about to continue the argument, when Mrs. Smith placed a hand on his arm and intervened.

"Now, darling, don't argue with him," she said. "He has to be right, because everyone will tell you that *Rudolph, the Red, knows rain, dear!*" (. . . Rudolph, the red-nosed reindeer . . . .)

Special Data: *Time of each pun: less than one minute each. That last one is good for a holiday speech. The others may be used wherever the truth of the adage would apply. People always groan loudly when they are told puns, but they always remember them and are quick to tell them to others. Moreover, people enjoy the cleverness that went into the twisting of words and situation. If you want to try some of your own, just make certain that they are short, to the point, and not so convoluted or far out that the audience cannot follow the storyline. Tell each pun with a merry twinkle in your eye and with great enthusiasm, and the results will be as enjoyable for you as they will be for your audience.*

$$\boxed{10}$$

TOPIC: **Failure to grow; complacency; great music.**

AUDIENCE: **Suitable for all adult audiences.**

I heard this fantastic story on the news recently.

It seems that over in Germany, they were clearing some land to make room for a new building, when the workers chanced upon an old grave with a small headstone. When they cleaned off the stone, it very clearly read "Ludwig von Beethoven."

With great enthusiasm, they began to dig down into the grave itself, where, at the very bottom, instead of a coffin, they found a door, a very ornate door. They pried it open, and inside was a long staircase that they followed to another door which they also opened.

Inside was a room lit by candlelight. There was an antique harpsichord in the center of the room, and on the bench sat Ludwig von Beethoven himself! Before him was a stack of handwritten sheet music. They watched as Beethoven took a sheet of the music and picked up a large, pink eraser. Slowly, he began erasing the notes from the ancient manuscripts.

"Herr Beethoven!" shouted one of the workers who had discovered the room, "What, in Heaven's name, are you doing?"

"What does it look like I'm doing?" Beethoven replied. "I'm *de*-composing!"

Special Data: *Time of story: about a minute and a half. Besides being a clever play on words, this could be a natural lead-in to a speech along the lines of making certain that we don't lose ground; ie., let's constantly reevaluate what we do: let us not become complacent; we must grow, or we will, indeed, decompose. Any speech along these lines could be enhanced by this story.*

$$\boxed{11}$$

TOPIC: **Progress; getting started; moving ahead.**

AUDIENCE: **Suitable for all audiences.**

Older brother was going to teach younger brother how to ride a bicycle. After showing the younger lad the various parts of the vehicle, the older brother announced that the only way to learn was to ride, and it was time for his brother to get on board the machine.

The young lad got on, and with a push from his brother, he was off. The bike wobbled and shuddered, threatened to collapse in a heap, and, finally, as the boy picked up speed, righted itself with the boy perched on top proudly.

In fact, there was only one problem. The younger brother, wide-eyed with triumph, had frozen the handlebars into a permanent, leftward angle, so the bicycle continued to make large and lazy counter-clockwise circles in the back yard.

"Look at me! Look at me!" shouted the youngster. "I'm doing it! I'm moving!"

"There's only one problem that I can see," shouted the older brother as he observed the circular patterns in the soil of the back yard. "You might be moving as fast as you can, but you're sure not going anywhere!"

Special Data: *Time of story: slightly over one minute. This is not a "funny" story. Rather, it is a reflective one that may touch on some memories of audience members, but its main purpose is to make a point. Certainly, we won't belabor you with it, since the point is so obvious, but we all have a tendency at times to run around like mad and not seem to make an inch of progress. This story is good for a speech of that nature.*

$$\boxed{12}$$

TOPIC: **Preparedness; looking toward the future; wisdom.**

AUDIENCE: **Suitable for adult audiences.**

The principal of the elementary school was walking on the playground one day, when he observed a first-grade boy doing something curious. As the principal watched, the boy began to use his books and the books of others to create a pile in front of the door that connected the school with the playground. The stack was growing higher and higher as the principal watched.

"Little boy," the principal intoned, "what do you think you're doing there?"

"I'm making a big wall," replied the boy, "so that when the elephants attack the school, they'll see it and get scared and run away."

"Don't be silly," continued the principal, "there are no elephants within 500 miles of here!"

"See how good it works," said the child.

"Son, you don't understand. Even if the elephants decided to attack the school, they're so far away that it would take them weeks and weeks to get here, so you don't have to build that wall now."

"Aha!" said the boy. "And if I waited for them to get here, it would be too late to start!"

Special Data: *Time of anecdote: just over one minute. This story has two climaxes. "See how good it works" (bad grammar intentional) is the first punch line and will bring a laugh. The second punch line "too late to start . . . " is more reflective and is the point made by the story. Don't forget to pause after the first climax to wait until the laughter begins to fade before going on. The second climax with its message about being prepared may then be used to flow into any speech where that is one of the themes. You might want to personalize the story by telling it in first person narrative, or by using the name of an actual elementary school within your district.*

$$\boxed{13}$$

TOPIC: Humorous responses to introductions of yourself.

AUDIENCE: Suitable for all audiences.

WHEN YOU HAVE RECEIVED GENEROUS APPLAUSE:

I feel like the farmer up in New England who got up one winter morning and went out to the barn to milk his cow in the twenty-below dawn. When he was finished, the cow turned to him and said, "Thanks so much for that warm hand!"

* * * * *

WHEN THE INTRODUCTION HAS BEEN FLOWERY:

I'm so disappointed. A beautiful introduction like that, and it's only me!

* * * * *

IF YOUR CHARACTER HAS BEEN PRAISED:

While our chairman was giving that kind introduction just now, my wife (husband, friend) poked me in the ribs and said, "Who's he talking about? I though you were going to speak!"

* * * * *

IF YOU HAVE BEEN INTRODUCED AS AN EXPERT:

Actually, I was going to give my 'flannel night gown' speech, that's the one that covers everything, but I think that I'll give the French bathing suit speech instead and just touch on the essentials.

* * * * *

IF YOU HAVE RECEIVED A PARTICULARLY FINE INTRODUCTION:

I'd like to thank Mr. __ for that truly fine introduction. I want you to know that what he said was completely unprepared and came right from his heart. (Reach in your pocket, take out a dollar, and very obviously and broadly, go over to the MC and press the dollar into his hand. Make the "OK" sign to him, wink broadly, and say:) Just the way I wrote it!

Special Data: *Time of each comment: a few seconds. Suit the remark to the situation and the audience. The last remark with the visual bit about the dollar should be used with a group that knows you well rather than with a first-time audience. Make an effort to have these remarks sound spontaneous, and don't forget to smile openly. These are true icebreakers that will set the tone for your speech.*

$$\boxed{14}$$

TOPIC: **Equivocation; fence-sitting; looking at both sides.**

AUDIENCE: **Adults; especially an audience for a debate.**

There is a story about a famous politician who was asked to speak at a rally. At the time, the citizens of the county were about to vote on a very controversial tax issue. All polls seemed to indicate that the people were almost divided evenly on the issue.

It was no surprise therefore, when, halfway through the person's speech, someone in the audience shouted, "How do you stand on the tax issue?"

The speaker did his best to ignore the question, but soon it was being posed throughout the auditorium.

Finally, the speaker heaved a sigh, stopped his prepared speech and turned to the audience.

"It seems," he said, "that I will not be able to finish my speech until I make clear my position on the proposed tax law. Therefore, I will tell you honestly and without fear exactly what I think.

"You see, I have many good friends who are fully in favor of this tax issue, and I must tell you that I have many good friends who are diametrically opposed to the tax law. Consequently, I can answer you without equivocation.

"Yes, I stand behind my friends!"

And he continued with his speech.

Special Data: *Time of anecdote: about one minute. This is a good anecdote for an occasion where an issue is being discussed from both sides, such as a proposed change in curriculum. After you get your laugh with this, point out that the program they are about to hear will* not *reflect the politician's rhetoric; they will hear both sides of the issue and be able to judge for themselves, etc. It works effectively when used this way.*

$$\boxed{15}$$

TOPIC: **Various remarks about the length of the speech.**

AUDIENCE: **Suitable for any audience.**

"Ladies and Gentlemen," said the speaker, "I want to say something for posterity!"

"Talk any longer," yelled a man from the audience, "and you'll be speaking *to* our posterity!"

* * * * *

When I accepted this speaking engagement, I asked your chairman, "what do you want me to speak about?"

And, he replied, "Certainly no longer than fifteen or twenty minutes."

* * * * *

I'll promise you one thing, folks, I won't express a one-minute idea by using a one-hour vocabulary.

* * * * *

Once, I got up to speak after dinner, and I said, "That meal was so wonderful that if I have another bite, I won't be able to speak at all . . . ."

Whereupon some joker from the back yelled, "Give that man another piece of pie!"

* * * * *

The last place I spoke, the people were very religious. I said, "Well, folks, I'm just about finished!" And all over the place I kept hearing, "Thank God . . . Thank God!"

* * * * *

I don't like to brag, but after the last speech I gave a fellow came up to me and told me that my speech had been nothing short of miraculous. Seems he had suffered from insomnia for years, and he was cured on the spot!

Special Data: *Time of each remark: a few seconds. It is never wrong to poke fun at yourself, if it is done in a good-natured manner. These remarks should also bring home one of the essentials of all good public speaking—that a short, entertaining, lively speech is always better accepted than one that drones on and on. Use no more than one of these remarks in any given speech however, as you don't want to plant the idea in the audience's mind that you will be speaking too long.*

$$\boxed{16}$$

TOPIC: Getting the job done; ingenuity; interpreting data.

AUDIENCE: Suitable for all audiences.

Recently, a family moved in next door, and they had a son who stood six foot two, weighed three hundred pounds, and was solid muscle from head to toe. The lad didn't have too much going on in the brain department, but he was an outstanding physical specimen.

About a month after they moved in, we had our first snowfall of the season and got two feet of the white stuff.

I was standing at our door contemplating the shoveling job ahead of me, when I chanced to spot the boy in his yard, throwing snowballs at a tree. I motioned for the lad to come over. When he arrived, I asked if he'd ever shoveled snow before, and he told me that he hadn't, but he'd like to learn.

I showed him how to lift the shovel, pointed him to our sidewalk, and said, "Now why don't you practice for a while."

Then, I went inside and had a cup of coffee.

When I came out later, not only was our sidewalk clear, but the boy was four blocks away, still shoveling.

Now, you might well ask what is the moral of this story?

You might think that the moral is that if you work as hard as you can, you'll get further than you thought possible—but that's not the true moral.

The true moral is this: When you've got a hard job to do, get some muscle-head to do the work for you!

And that's why I volunteered!

Special Data: *Time of anecdote: a little over one minute. This is an effective story when you have just been given a new job or duty, such as chairing a committee. Never tell this about someone else, for then it would appear to be insulting. The joke must be on you. It has a double punch line. The first laugh comes with the line, "... to do the work for you!" Pause for a moment, and as the laughter fades, look at the audience directly and deliver the second line. You'll get results.*

$$\boxed{17}$$

TOPIC: **Overlooking the main point; the unusual; complacency.**

AUDIENCE: **Suitable for all audiences.**

A man invited his friend to join him for a cup of coffee, and they were sitting at the kitchen table waiting for the coffee to brew.

Just then, the man's cat came sauntering in, went to the refrigerator, stood up on his hind legs, opened the door and took out a container of milk.

The cat opened the carton, sniffed the milk, then proceeded to pour it in the kitchen sink and throw the empty carton in the garbage.

As the cat began walking out of the room, he turned to the man and said, "That milk was practically sour. You'd better get a new bottle when you go out."

And, with that, the cat walked out of the room, leaving the two men sitting at the table.

"Well," said the man to his friend, "did you notice anything of interest?"

"I sure did," said the man's friend. "This means we won't have any milk for our coffee."

Special Data: *Time of story: less than one minute. Besides being a humorous story, this can also be a valuable one to lead into a discussion on such topics as missing the point; not recognizing the wonder that lies before us; being so complacent we fail to recognize the good that we see every day; etc. Also, you might indicate that we shouldn't be like the man in the story, so tied up with the mundane that we fail to appreciate the miraculous that lies about us.*

$$\boxed{18}$$

TOPIC: **Jumping to conclusions; interpretation; truth.**

AUDIENCE: **Suitable for any audience.**

A man was at the race track one day, and was down a few dollars in the afternoon. As he studied the entries for the final race of the day, he chanced to look down in the paddock area, and who should he see but Father O'Malley, his own parish priest, blessing one of the horses to run in the next race.

The man's eyes grew wide, and immediately, he took all the money he had left and placed it on the horse he had seen the priest bless.

Then it was post time, and the man watched in absolute horror as the horse on which he had bet trailed the field around the track and came in dead last!

As the man was leaving the track, he happened to bump into Father O'Malley.

"Father," said the man, "you cost me some money today. I saw you blessing that horse before the last race, and I bet on him, and he lost."

"Son," said the good Father, "you shouldn't have done that; I wasn't blessing that poor animal, I was giving him the Last Rites!"

Special Data: *Time of story: about one minute. The point of this story is that we should always check our facts before acting on them. Also, it can be used to show how wrong it is to jump to conclusions; let's wait until all the facts are in; let's not go by appearance alone; and other topics along that line.*

$$\boxed{19}$$

TOPIC: **Communication; quotations; what others have said.**

AUDIENCE: **Suitable for all audiences.**

The young man was learning Morse Code. To do so, he and his friend had hooked up a line between their houses, and they were practicing and gaining speed and proficiency.

During one particular practice session, one young man tapped out the message, "SAY SOMETHING INTELLIGENT."

Just then, a gas main in the street exploded with an earth-shattering roar that shook the entire neighborhood and sent the pictures flying from the walls of the young man's room.

The young man picked himself up from the floor, shook his head, and looked at the code receiver.

"Gosh," he murmured, "I wish I had said that!"

Special Data: *Time of story: less than one minute. Suppose someone on the program has made a particularly good or incisive point. This story could be an excellent follow-up to it. Also, if you are going to quote from a report or someone else's work extensively, this is a good lead-in to it. This story is quite effective when used in this manner.*

$$\boxed{20}$$

TOPIC: **Several quick stories about parents and children.**

AUDIENCE: **For all adult audiences, especially parents.**

"Hey, Mom!" said the little boy. "Do you remember how you said you were always worrying that I'd break that fancy vase Aunt Mary gave us?"

"Yes," Mother replied.

"Well," said the lad, "you can stop worrying!"

* * * * *

"Remember," said Father to his teenaged daughter, "I want you home by eleven."

"Really, Father," said the girl, "I'm not a child any more!"

"I know," Father responded, "and that's precisely why I want you home by eleven!"

* * * * *

"I'd like to speak to you about Billy's personal hygiene," said the teacher. "His fingernails are filthy."

"I know," said Billy's mother, "but that's only because he keeps scratching his head!"

* * * * *

It was Mark Twain who remarked that when he was seventeen, he was convinced that his father was the stupidest man on the face of the earth, but when he reached twenty-one, he was positively amazed by how much the old man had learned in just four short years.

* * * * *

Mother ran into her friend on the street.

"Have I told you what Johnny did in school?" Mother asked.

"No, you haven't," replied her friend, "and I really want to thank you for that!"

Special Data: *Time of each remark: a few seconds. That Mark Twain story really strikes home with parents of older children. The last remark also never fails to get a laugh, since most of us have been in the position where we would like to have answered that way. We are certain you will find a use for these.*

21

TOPIC: **Ingenious solutions; frugality, innovative thinking.**

AUDIENCE: **Suitable for all audiences.**

A man walked into a local bank and asked the manager for a bank loan in the amount of ten dollars. The manager was about to tell the gentleman that the amount was too small for a loan, when the man added, "For this loan of ten dollars, I will repay the amount within one year at 15% interest, and as security I'll let you hold $100,000 in bearer bonds."

This set the manager to thinking that perhaps this was an eccentric millionaire who might turn a great deal of business the bank's way, so he granted the loan, gave the man the ten dollars, and took the $100,000 in bonds to hold as security.

One year later, the gentleman walked into the bank, placed down the ten dollars plus $1.50 interest, and asked for his bonds back, which the manager supplied.

"Sir, I just have to ask," said the manager, "with so much money in bearer bonds, why in heaven's name would you want to borrow ten dollars and pay interest on it? Excuse me, but that really sounds insane."

"Does it?" replied the man. "Well, sir, you tell me: where else could I go to put those bonds in a safety deposit box for a full year for only a buck and a half?"

Special Data: *Time of story: about one minute. This is a natural for any speaking occasion that involves a school budget or financial affair relative to the school. It also contains the idea of 'penny-wise and pound-foolish' and can be used to convey that concept. It might also be used as a 'roast' for someone noted for frugality, in which case you would tell it as if the subject were the man in the story.*

22

TOPIC: **Handling the situation; wrong approaches; ignorance.**

AUDIENCE: **Suitable for all adult audiences.**

A farmer decided to try his hand at raising chickens, so he ordered 50 baby chicks.

Two months later, he ordered another 50 baby chicks.

A month after that, he ordered yet another 50 chicks.

The man who delivered the baby chicks said, "You must be doing all right raising chickens, eh?"

"No," said the farmer. "In fact, I keep buying so many chicks, because none of them ever grow up!"

"Well, that's unusual," remarked the delivery man. "Do you have any idea what's causing that?"

"I don't know for certain," answered the farmer, "but I got it down to one of two things. I figure I'm either planting them too close together or too deep!"

Special Data: *Time of story: less than one minute. This one gets a laugh. Even if we have a laudable goal in mind, let's make certain that we go about accomplishing that goal in the correct manner. That would be an excellent message gleaned from this story. It might then apply to any new program or policy that was being implemented.*

$$\boxed{23}$$

TOPIC: **Quick thinking; innovative solutions; children and noise.**

AUDIENCE: **Suitable for all audiences, especially parents.**

Junior received a drum set for his sixth birthday. Thereafter, he proceeded to drive Mom and Dad to distraction by constant thudding and pounding on the drums.

One day, a friend was visiting when Junior decided to start "practicing" on his instruments.

"I must apologize for the noise," and Junior's mother, "but we simply cannot get him to stop beating those drums. We've tried everything, and he still keeps banging away."

"Let me see what I can do," said the friend who then proceeded to walk into the child's room casually and shut the door.

Less than a minute later, the thudding noise ceased, and several minutes of blessed silence passed as the friend emerged from Junior's room and rejoined Mother and Father in the living room.

"It's a miracle!" exclaimed Mother. "How did you get him to stop that noise?"

"Relatively simple," answered the friend. "I told him I was sorry I had missed his birthday, gave him a penknife as a birthday present, and finally, I asked him if he knew what was *inside* his drum . . . ."

Special Data: *Time of anecdote: a little over one minute. Make a child curious, and you have set him on the road to learning. You may use this story to amplify that point, or you may want to use it to express the need for direct action or for getting to the "heart of the matter." It may also be used for fun, as it is indicative of common parent-child situations.*

Afterthoughts

As educators, we have no need to tell you about the value of good examples. Certainly, we are all aware that examples and stories illustrative of the points we make help to clarify the issues and provide starting points for understanding. Moreover, good examples are often remembered long after the factual content of a speech has faded.

Enough philosophy! The sample anecdotes and remarks in this section provide good-natured humor on a variety of subjects that are common to the educational speaker. Don't force an anecdote to an issue, but use one that clearly has reference to what you are going to say, and you will find that not only is the "ice" broken, but you will have prepared the soil for the "seed" you wish to plant.

Have fun with these stories; enjoy yourself; and your audience will enjoy you!

MORE INTRODUCTIONS, TRANSITIONS, AND BENEDICTIONS FOR THE SCHOOL ADMINISTRATOR

While it is more or less expected that the school administrator will make a number of speeches during his or her career, it is also a certainty that not all of them will be of the full-length, formal variety. As likely as not, you will be called upon to host programs, serving as the Master of Ceremonies or coordinator of an evening's activities. Since much of the success of programs depends upon the manner in which they are presented to the audience, it is extremely important that your speaking skills enhance your presentation.

You will, from instance, be required to introduce speakers and "guests of honor" at various affairs; often, it will be up to you to effect a smooth transition from one part of the program to another, or from a procedure that is known to one that is not known; there will even be occasions where you will be expected to say deep and meaningful words, a "blessing" if you will, for an occasion or an event. Each of these will present its own particular challenge.

In this section we will cover all three of these vital areas. We offer introductions that have been proven effective for a wide variety of potential speakers, suitable for a teacher who has won an award, to a high-ranking government official; we offer organized, effective transitions for several educational possibilities, from starting a new year to the transition from a junior high to a middle school; we offer a number of "benedictions" for typical events where they might be required (and also have, hopefully, crafted them in such a manner as to be meaningful and warm without interfering with or offending anyone's religious sensibilities).

Of course, you may wish to change material here and there to suit your particular set of circumstances, and that is as it should be. These will provide you, however, with a basis for building introductions, transitions, and "benedictions" that will be remembered.

Introductions

$$\boxed{24}$$

TOPIC: **Introduction of a teacher who has won an award.**

AUDIENCE: **Adults; educators; friends, family, and community.**

When I first heard that Shirley Haddenfield had received the Governor's Award for Teaching Excellence, I will tell you quite frankly that I was shocked. I was shocked that it had taken so long for the award committee to recognize her.

Everyone who has had the opportunity to be associated with Shirley knows of her dedication to the youth of this district; we know of her untiring efforts in their behalf; we know of the quality education that she continues to provide her students day after day throughout the school year; we know that each child becomes a personal challenge to her and an individual to be nurtured with personal care and concern; we know of the long hours beyond the final bell of the school day that Shirley puts in because of her personal commitment to offering each student the best possible education; we know of her warmth and humanity and the unselfish manner in which she gives of herself, to her students, her colleagues, and the entire community; we know that to her, teaching is not merely a profession—it is a lifelong mission which she carries out with zest and verve.

And, we know as well, that there are few as deserving of recognition as this outstanding example of teaching at its finest.

Ladies and gentlemen, may I introduce this year's recipient of the Governor's Award for Teaching Excellence—Mrs. Shirley Haddenfield!

Special Data: *Time of introduction: about one minute. Think of this as a general form for the introduction of an award recipient—mention the award; outline the reasons why the person is deserving of the award; and end by mentioning again the award and the person's full name. In fact, in an introduction it is a good rule of thumb to make certain that the last words you speak are the person's name.*

$$\boxed{25}$$

TOPIC: Introduction of a controversial speaker.

AUDIENCE: All adults, many of whom may dislike the speaker.

Ladies and gentlemen, it is rare, indeed, for any group of human beings to achieve unanimous agreement on anything. That is a fact of human existence. If we cannot reach agreement, however, allow me to hope that we may at least achieve understanding.

In a certain book that is held in high esteem by a great many people, a man asked the question, "What is truth?" Later, in the same book, there is this statement: "You shall know the truth, and the truth shall set you free . . . ."

Hopefully, that is what we are all about—freedom and truth. The question of what truth *is* must, indeed, be answered within the sanctity of the individual mind. Yet every individual who cherishes that truth knows that without freedom, truth is but an illusion. The freedom of ideas, even those that we may find personally offensive, unjustified, or wrong, is an absolute necessity if we are to arrive at a truth that will enrich our lives and *perpetuate* our freedom.

We have with us this evening a woman who is noted for her original ideas and her dynamic presentation of them. To many, she presents a challenge; to many she provides great insight; to many she presents controversy. To all of us, she is a speaker who merits our thought, our consideration, and our attention.

May I introduce to you our speaker this evening, Ms. . . .

Special Data: *Time of introduction: a little over one minute. You will run into controversial speakers in your career as a school administrator. What with AIDS, sex education, and rising taxes and budgets, you are bound to face the position of introducing a speaker whom half the audience is for and half against. This introduction is a basic plea for civilized behavior and for a free and rational interchange of ideas. Naturally, you would tailor the next to last paragraph to suit the speaker you were introducing.*

$$\boxed{26}$$

TOPIC: Introduction of a school board president.

AUDIENCE: Adults; teachers, parents, and community members.

If you are with a group of people, and the conversation has fallen into a lull where you can hear each other breathing, just stand back and whisper these words—Board of Education. Within seconds the entire group will become animated, and you may not be able to hear yourself for the shouting and the screaming that is going on.

Few things seem to stir the passions of our citizenry as the doings of the local school board. Some are for; some are against; but none are indifferent.

Our speaker this evening knows that only too well. For the past ten years he has served with distinction on the __ Board of Education, for four of those years as president, the position he now holds. During that time, he has been instrumental in the building program, curriculum revision, and the transition to a "middle school" setup within our community. He has spent many long hours and several sleepless nights in this capacity, his only reward being the knowledge that he continues to serve the youth of our community.

Ladies and gentlemen, it gives me great pleasure to introduce to you a man whose dedication to excellence in education is unquestioned—the President of the Board of Education, Mr. . . . .

Special Data: *Time of introduction: slightly over one minute. School Boards or Boards of Education, whatever you may call them, have been a source of contention among the people they represent possibly from their inception. This introduction acknowledges that and then goes on to spell out the positive contributions of the president, the speaker you are introducing. Alter the specifics to the speaker, and you will have a short and appropriate introduction for any member of that particular group.*

$$\boxed{27}$$

TOPIC: **Introduction of an educational expert.**

AUDIENCE: **Adults; parents, teachers, and concerned citizens.**

It has been said that as long as there is learning, there is growth, and as long as there is growth, there is life. To learn is to live, and we all live and learn.

We also realize that there are people to whom learning is a way of life; people who will pursue a subject to its limits, convinced of its importance and dedicated to the dissemination of the knowledge they have gleaned for the betterment of all humankind.

Our speaker this evening is just such an individual. She has . . . .

(Outline the career and accomplishments of the speaker relative to the area of expertise being addressed . . . .)

I know that I look forward with great anticipation to listening and learning. Therefore, it is a true pleasure to introduce our speaker this evening, Dr. . . .

Special Data: *Time of introduction: variable, depending upon the credits of the speaker. Remember, in this and all speaking assignments, the audience is anxious to hear from the speaker you are introducing—not necessarily from you. That is why these introductions are short and to the point. Rarely should* any *introduction exceed two or three minutes. Get to the point, and get to the speaker.*

$$\boxed{28}$$

TOPIC: **Introduction of a parent (PTA worker; volunteer; etc.).**

AUDIENCE: **Adults; most likely parents and teachers.**

There are so many stories about parents and children, parents and teachers, and parents and the school, that you can just think of your personal favorite, and I won't have to tell you one.

Yes, we all like to smile at stories about the interplay between the parent and the various groups that touch our children during the formative years. Quite frankly, some of it is hilarious, but we all appreciate that it has a serious side as well. The nurturing, growth, and education of a child is one of the most important, if not *the* most important, job on earth. Nor is it one that may be taken lightly or irresponsibly; it requires tremendous outlays of time and energy; it is frequently rewarding and often heartbreaking. Certainly, being a parent is one of life's greatest challenges.

We have just such a person with us tonight; a person who not only works hard at being a parent, but who manages to find time to give of his considerable talents to help the children of other parents, to work unceasingly for the benefit of all the children of this school and this community. We have been witness to his good works these past several years, and we have also benefitted from his work with the PTA and our student population.

Children, in general, tend to take their parents for granted, and the children of this school may never fully appreciate just how much he has done for them, but we see; we know; and, we appreciate deeply.

It is with great pleasure, therefore, that I present our next speaker, Mr. . . .

Special Data: *Time of introduction: about a minute and a half. Obviously, you could add to this by detailing specific instances in which this parent has helped the school. Parents can begin to feel unnoticed and unappreciated sometimes, and an introduction such as this can go a long way toward letting all of them know just how much they are appreciated. This will work well in any situation where the audience is composed mainly of parents.*

$$\boxed{29}$$

TOPIC: Introduction of a school administrator.

AUDIENCE: Adults; professionals and community members.

It has been suggested that a good school administrator is someone who gives others credit when things go right and takes blame when they don't. While I know of many a school administrator who would agree with that statement, I think we are aware that it is only part of the picture.

A school administrator is a combination of teacher, business person, public relations expert, accountant, chief of police, counselor, handyman, educational theorist, fortuneteller, and father-confessor all rolled into one. Today's school administrator not only answers to the School Board, but to parents, students, faculty, and, quite often, the media as well.

There is so much to do and so little time. There are times when it feels that half the population of the town are waiting outside your door, with earth-shaking questions that must be answered by you now, right now! You are expected to be in twenty places at once, often at the same time that reports are due, while somehow finding time to drop by a particular classroom to see the presentation that class has been working on.

All of this takes enormous energy, great insight and understanding, and a dedication and determination that will see the person through the trying times that *will come* with the position. It is a task that few people fully appreciate and one that is often thankless. Yet it is a vital job; a job whose ramifications reach the very essence of our society; a job that truly affects all our tomorrows.

Where does one find such a rare individual? I will tell you; he is seated on this dais with me tonight. Here is a man whose twenty-six years as a school administrator have contributed to the growth of our school system and his personal growth as well. Here is a man who has met the tremendous challenge of being a school administrator, and met it with intelligence, dignity, good humor, and a deep concern for each and every student under this administration. Here is a man whose opinion is respected, whose wit and wisdom is well-known, and whose integrity is unfailing.

I take pride in presenting our speaker this evening, Dr. . . .

Special Data: *Time of introduction: about two minutes. Certainly, this type of introduction should be reserved for someone who truly merits it. Never make the mistake of praising someone whom most of your audience realizes does not merit such praise. It has been our experience, however, that you will find many school administrators who do fit this description, and this is an effective introduction for such a person.*

$$\boxed{30}$$

TOPIC: **Introduction of a "well-loved" personality.**

AUDIENCE: **Adults; a very receptive audience.**

We all know people who are not what they seem. We know of people, for instance, who are proud of being humble; we know people who talk a good game and do nothing; we know people who can run on for hours and say nothing. Yes, we all know people who are not what they seem.

And then, we know our speaker this evening. We know a man who is truly humble, always placing the needs of others before his own; we know a man of action whose deeds speak for themselves; we know a man of few words who has, over the years, spoken volumes that have enriched all who know him.

I characterize a man who is an educator in the truest sense of the word. This is someone who teaches virtue by personal example; who teaches love by giving love to all with whom he comes in contact; who teaches integrity, honesty, care and concern by living those qualities each and every day of his life.

Certainly, we are privileged to know him; certainly, we have come to depend upon his insight, kindness and compassion; certainly, we are blessed by our association with him over the years.

I am delighted to introduce to you a man whom we are all overjoyed to call our friend—our speaker, Mr. . . .

Special Data: *Time of introduction: about one minute. Every school district has its "grand old man" or "woman" who has spent a lifetime giving to the children of that community. In this case, everyone in the audience knows and respects this "well-loved" individual, and nothing less than a warm and effusive introduction is expected. Be warned, however, that whenever you praise someone, as in the last introduction and this one, you had better mean what you say, because if you don't, if you are merely "mouthing words," the audience will pick up on it, and they will not approve. Mean what you say, and your audience will feel as good as you do.*

$$\boxed{31}$$

TOPIC: **Introduction of a high-ranking political officer.**

AUDIENCE: **Adults; teachers, parents, community members, media.**

Ladies and gentlemen, we are extremely pleased and honored to have with us this evening the Governor of our state, the Honorable John J. Smith.

Ask any principal, supervisor, or superintendent, and he/she will tell you that administration is a most difficult task; he/she will also tell you that the responsibility for the students, faculty, and school workers under purview can, at times, be virtually overwhelming. The weight of that responsibility rests squarely on our shoulders, and it can be a very heavy burden indeed.

Take that burden and multiply it by thousands—no, by hundreds of thousands, and you begin to have some idea of the enormity of the task that our speaker this evening faces on a daily basis.

We are especially delighted, therefore, that Governor Smith should make time in his extremely busy schedule to be with us this evening. We all know of his record with regard to education, and of his deep concern for the students of our state. His appearance tonight is a reaffirmation of that concern, and we thank him for his graciousness in being our guest this evening.

Ladies and gentlemen, will you please join me in welcoming the Governor of the State of ___, the Honorable John J. Smith.

Special Data: *Time of introduction: about one minute. High-ranking government officials share one characteristic—they are busy people, pressed for time. They will expect you, therefore, to adhere to the schedule that has been set up beforehand. This introduction is short, to the point, and identifies you as a school administrator with the official. Please do* not *make a political speech out of the introduction, whatever your opinion may be. This is the place for brevity; it is the official the audience has come to hear.*

Afterthoughts

An introduction that is overly long or one that turns into a personal speech by you is one that will make an audience restless. Keep every introduction short, concentrating on either the reasons why the speaker is worthy of attention, the good that is to be derived from the speech, or personal qualities of the speaker. When you finally say the speaker's name, do it with enthusiasm and lead applause for the speaker. Finally, *back away* from the microphone as the speaker rises to approach. In that way you will never give the idea that you are turning your back on the speaker.

Transitions

$$\boxed{32}$$

TOPIC: **Transition to a new school year.**

AUDIENCE: **Faculty members; other administrators; staff.**

I'm of the opinion that most babies, if they could talk, would tell you that they didn't want to be born.

They'd say, "Hey, Mom! How about we forget this birthing business, huh? I'll stay right here, OK? It's so nice and pleasant in here; nobody bothers you, and you get to rest all you want. Tell you what, Mom—let me stay here until I get my act together, and in twenty or so years I'll be out, OK?"

Now, I realize how ridiculous that is, but I also think that a lot of us, (and I include myself in this) are exactly like those reluctant infants.

Just yesterday, it seems, we were in the middle of our summer hiatus. Some of us were working other jobs, some of us were soaking up the sun, and some of us were just watching TV with our feet up. Whatever we were doing, it was different; it was a change; it was a moment to be cherished. Oh, how we would have loved to languish in those days; if only we could have had a few days more, just until we "got our act together." We would gladly have returned to school . . . in twenty or thirty years!

Yet, just as we could not put off our own birth, the inevitability of time has brought us to our meeting here today. In a very real sense, we are present at a birth; the birth of a new school year. In a short time, students will flow through our doors and a new life of learning, growth, and fulfillment will begin for them and for us.

Certainly, we all have times when we would like to stand still and savor the time we have to ourselves, but just as certainly, there is an anticipation and potential to be realized. How shall the baby grow? Whom will she resemble? Will she be strong? What problems will she have to overcome?

It is you who will answer these questions. It is you who guide and cajole and raise that child who will be a different person in June than he or she is today. It is a tough job; it is a challenge; it is an adventure that each and every one of you *is up to.*

With your help, she'll grow up straight and tall!

Welcome to our new school year!

Special Data: *Time of speech: two and a half to three minutes. All transitional speeches should follow a basic pattern—acknowledge the past and look forward to the future. If, in the process, you can manage to challenge your audience, express confidence in them, inspire them to their best effort, and tell them how much confidence you have in them, then you will do just fine with all speeches of a transitional nature. Be certain to remember that if you are enthusiastic about the change, your audience will be as well.*

$$\boxed{33}$$

TOPIC: **Transition to a new policy.**

AUDIENCE: **Faculty members; administrators; those affected by it.**

If education were a stagnant pool, no one would drink from it. As it is, however, the learning process is a vital and bubbling stream from which untold numbers have come to drink. It is a stream whose waters refresh, invigorate, and give health.

But while a stagnant pool may have calm waters and an unrippled surface, every pure and flowing stream is a source of movement— splashing around rocks, turbulent at times, yet sparkling and clear in the sunlight.

If this analogy holds, then we must look upon our profession as a vital entity that grows and changes; sometimes smoothly, sometimes with turbulence, but always with an eye to the future and a willingness to adapt to changing times and changing ideas.

So it will be with the new policy that is soon to be carried out in our district. Of course there will be controversy; some offering praise while others, condemnation. Certainly, there will be those who have looked forward to its initiation, while others bemoan either its necessity or its effectiveness. Understandably, there lie trials in the days ahead.

Yet, if we are to be an integral part of a vital and changing profession, then we can do no less than try our best with new ideas and new positions; we can do no less than than give it our support and work towards its successful implementation; we can do no less than try today to build for tomorrow.

Now, let us take a closer look at what we shall all work so hard to attain. . . .

Special Data: *Time of speech: a little over one minute. Obviously, this is not a complete speech. The speaker should go on to explain the particulars of the new policy or program to be implemented, perhaps answering questions afterwards. Naturally, you would adapt this speech to the particulars of the policy in your district. It is a very good wager, however, that any "new" policy will have its advocates and its detractors in any school district. This speech acknowledges both sides while seeking an opportunity for the new policy to succeed.*

$$\boxed{34}$$

TOPIC: **Transition to new school leadership.**

AUDIENCE: **Faculty members; administrators; community.**

When Dr. Greene resigned the principalship of Rock Township High School last June in order to retire, we all had mixed emotions. Certainly, we wished Dr. Greene the best retirement possible, knowing that he had truly earned a fruitful rest. At the same time, I doubt there was anyone who did not realize that a very large emptiness had been created by his leaving. His years of tenure as principal had been such that not only was he known and respected, but all who worked with him understood how essential he was to the functioning of education within our district.

We realized, however, that every ship needs a captain or it is bound to founder in the heaviest seas. The search for a new principal began in earnest, and it was a task taken seriously by all involved. Indeed, the opinions of all who cared to comment were not only recognized but appraised and inculcated wherever possible. It was a long search; it was a hard search; it was a search where no one "settled," but made certain that they selected the best successor.

I take pride in introducing the new principal of Rock Township High School, a person who . . .

(if desired, this would be the place to detail the person's credentials, experience, accomplishments, etc.).

Finally, I would like to make clear the fact that no one is "replacing" Dr. Greene. Rather, we have a man of integrity and vision who has accepted the challenge of carrying on the tradition of excellence we have been left as a legacy; a person whose goal is to achieve the finest in education for our students; a man who will maintain the greatness of the past, accept the challenges of today, and build toward an unparalleled tomorrow for all of us.

Please join me in welcoming the new principal of Rock Township High School, Dr. . . . .

Special Data: *Time of speech: variable, depending upon inserted material. If the former school leader were such that no one really lamented his passing out of the picture, the transition should be an easy one. If, however, the former principal were admired or even "loved," then there is bound to be some resentment to whomever takes over. Notice, therefore in the example given, that every attempt is made to present the new principal as someone who is "carrying on" rather than "replacing." This is a subtle difference, but one that will surely be picked up on by the audience.*

$\boxed{35}$

TOPIC: **Transition to new leadership (School Board).**

AUDIENCE: **Teachers/ administrators; community members; media.**

There are few things that are certain in our ever-changing world, but one of the few certainties is this: No one seeks office on the Board of Education in order to secure for themselves a restful, well-paying job. Indeed, the pay is minimal (to say the least), the hours long and tedious, there is contention virtually at every turn, and the responsibility of directing matters that will affect the lives of thousands of individuals weighs very heavy indeed.

The School Board has been well aware of these problems for some time. It has worked with diligence and dedication to achieve the best for the students of this township. It has not been easy, but the School Board has performed tasks that had to be done; it did not shirk from that responsibility.

Now, with the School Board elections behind us, the same challenges remain, but several of those who have been elected to meet those challenges are new to the Board. Certainly, they have a fine legacy to sustain them as they begin to deal with the issues with which we are all concerned and in which we all play a part. Indeed, it will not be long at all before they learn first hand the enormity of the task before them.

That is why our best wishes, our hopes, and our prayers are with them tonight as they assume their new positions of leadership. We know that in the days to follow, we will all work together for the best possible education for our children.

Please allow me to introduce these men and women to you. . . .

Special Data: *Time of speech: just over a minute and a half. If there are several people to introduce, then you should introduce each one separately and then sum up by saying something like, "Ladies and Gentlemen, may I present the newest members of the Township Board of Education!" Then you would start the applause for them. You have acknowledged the old board and offered support for the new—that will work well.*

$$\boxed{36}$$

TOPIC: Transition to a new school building.

AUDIENCE: Students; faculty; parents; administrators; media.

It is a comfort to live in a town you know well. Your hometown is familiar and filled with friendly faces you have known all your life. Even so, most of us leave the towns in which we were born and head out into a larger world, because we become aware that our hometown has become too small for us, and our vision requires a greater scope that only the world at large can offer.

In a like manner, we were all comfortable at Ramsey High School. Indeed, it had stood as a beacon of our community for over fifty years. Whole generations of yesterday's students and today's parents filed through its doors and sat in its classrooms. It was a place in which we were very comfortable indeed.

Yet, time does not stand still; and with time comes change, and with change comes growth, and with growth comes the inevitability of moving on. Here we stand on the steps of our new high school, with the past at our backs and the future before us.

We shall not forget the good times, fellowship, and learning that were an intimate part of Ramsey High School. Indeed, they are part of our memories and part of the heritage we shall pass on to generations of our children yet unborn. No, we shall not forget.

But, we shall also look forward. We shall look forward to establishing new traditions, new friendships, new loyalties for our high school. We shall look forward to more and better learning due to increased capacities and better facilities. We shall look forward to building a high school second to none in our state. We look forward to the work ahead and the rewards that work shall bring us.

Certainly, we do not forget, but we *do* look forward. As we go through these doors today, it is with hope, with joy, and with the strong foundation of the past which will guide us toward the promise of the future.

We look forward to tomorrow!

Special Data: *Time of speech: about two minutes. If you are ever involved in a transition to a new school building from one that has served a community for many years, you will find that there is a good deal of emotion tied up in the process. Particularly the "old timers" in a community will be nostalgic about the school they attended. This transitional speech acknowledges that sentiment while anticipating only good things for the new location.*

$$\boxed{37}$$

TOPIC: **Transition from junior high to middle school.**

AUDIENCE: **Faculty; students; administrators; parents; community.**

Ladies and Gentlemen: I loved the first car I ever had. I washed it; polished it; changed the oil even when it didn't need changing; and rotated the tires every other week—I think it got more attention than my first child.

Even so, there came a time when that beloved vehicle simply would not go another mile. I was spending inordinate sums on gas and oil, and the upkeep began taking more and more of my time and effort. Yes, it got me from point A to point B, but the trip was becoming more and more bumpy and taking longer and longer. There came a time when I knew that I had to start looking for something else to better serve my needs.

When I got that new car, it was *not* because the other one was old, but because it no longer *functioned,* and the new one would do a much better job.

Now, that story, while quite true, can also serve as an analogy for the change of our school from a junior high school to a middle school. Years ago we were all in favor of the junior high school setup, because it met the needs of our students and functioned in our community dynamically. Now, we are changing to a middle school setup that, we are certain, will better meet the needs of today's students as they grow into tomorrow.

But, the decision was neither haphazard nor a capitulation to modern trends. Rather, like that car I mentioned before, we did not abandon the former because it was old, but because it no longer fully met the needs of our students and the community; we did not instigate the new because it was new, but because it was our feeling that it simply *worked better* and would continue to work better for our students, their parents, and our community.

The emerging adolescent today, as never before, is beset with pressures and demands that range from the academic to the social, all of which require decisions and levels of maturity that are difficult at best and often devastating. With one foot in childhood and the other in adulthood, they stand at a crossroad, and it is often here and now that decisions will be made that will lead the student down pathways to the future. Will these pathways be bright and well-lighted or twisting and fraught with disaster?

The Middle School, with its child-centered philosophy, can better help to guide the growing youth, protect some elbows and knees from cuts and scrapes along the way, and put bandaids on those hurts that are an inevitable part of the growth process.

All of this it is our goal to accomplish; all of this we actively seek to do; all of this the Middle School setup will allow by providing this unique opportunity.

We have thought and studied and polished and trained, and we are eager to begin. We are grateful to the junior high school setup for what it has accomplished, and we look forward with tremendous anticipation to the Middle School for the many benefits it will bring our way.

Like the car—not because it was old, but because it no longer worked; not because it was new, but because it will work better.

Welcome to the Middle School.

Special Data: *Time of speech: about five minutes. Notice that there is a theme to this that is repeated and acts as a powerful ending. This is an effective method of presentation. The content also bespeaks a truth about today's preadolescents and the Middle School that has emerged as one of the preeminent forces in today's educational scene.*

Afterthoughts

Look back; reflect; look forward—that is the basic outline of every good transitional speech. You say, in effect, "This is the way it was," and you describe that way or time. Then you reflect, saying, "Yes, it was good, but does it meet our needs today, or do we need something else?" Finally, we look at the new area to which we will be going and state, "Now, this will do quite well!"

Again, we must remind you that an audience more frequently than not takes its lead from the speaker. If *you* are not enthusiastic about the change, perhaps you had better think twice before making the transitional speech. If *you are* enthusiastic about what is happening, however, then by all means strike that match and watch your audience glow with excitement!

Benedictions

38

TOPIC: **The "Moment of Silence," I**

AUDIENCE: **Suitable for any audience.**

> **NOTE:** *This "Moment of Silence" would be in memory of someone (student; teacher; official; etc.) who had died recently.*

We are all aware of the untimely death of John Smith, a highly respected teacher in our school for the past eleven years.

It is natural, at times like these, that we should pause for a moment and reflect not only on his passing, but on what his life has meant to each of us.

Let each of us in his own heart and in his own way be thankful that we were privileged to know him, if only for a time.

Let that memory become a prayer within your heart as we observe a moment of silence in the memory of Mr. John Smith.

> **NOTE:** *The actual "moment" of silence should be no more than 30 seconds; any longer than that and the audience might become uncomfortable.*

Thank you. . . .

Special Data: *Time of benediction: a little over one minute, including the period of silence. Always say, "Thank you," or "You may be seated" at the conclusion of the moment, as it is essential that you give some cue for the audience to relax. Also, with all benedictions, please keep them short and to the point. An audience will easily forgive brevity, but it can become stony if you go on too long.*

$$\boxed{39}$$

TOPIC: The "Moment of Silence," II

AUDIENCE: Suitable for any audience.

> **NOTE:** *This "Moment of Silence" is appropriate for an impending event such as a decision of the state legislature regarding education, or for a tense international situation.*

There are but a few people who are *not* aware of the gravity of the situation that faces all of us today. I think we all realize that what will or will not happen seriously affects us all.

It is at times like these that we feel the need to seek a strength beyond our own; to seek the guidance of a power "beyond"—one that understands so much better than we what we are all going through.

Let us all stand, and in our own words and in our own hearts, let us seek out the care, guidance, and strength of the power that is beyond ourselves.

(Allow for the thirty seconds of silence.)

Thank you; let us please be seated.

Special Data: *Time of benediction: about a minute and a half. The reference to a "higher power" is, we feel, hardly inflammatory to anyone, regardless of religious conviction. The whole point of the "Moment of Silence" is to allow each individual to reflect on the subject presented, according to the individual dictates of his or her conscience. We think this speech allows for that.*

$$\boxed{40}$$

TOPIC: Benediction for volunteer workers.

AUDIENCE: Suitable for an audience of volunteers and supporters.

The corn, the beans, the roast, the bread,
    The knives and forks and such,
Don't fix or place or make themselves;
    That takes a "someone" touch.

It takes that special "selfless" one
    To serve with loving care;
To give her time in making that
    Which other hands will share.

Just now and then, at times like these,
    Do our assembled ranks
Begin to understand their worth
    And offer them our thanks.

Unheralded, unnoticed, and
    Ignored, or so it seems,
These volunteers give of themselves
    To help achieve the dream.

And, so, we pray with fervent hearts
    For blessings from above,
Upon these selfless souls who share
    Their lives so filled with love.

And, only they can realize;
    It's neither strange nor odd
To serve a meal or guide a child
    And know the heart of God. . . .

Special Data: *Time of benediction: about a minute and a half. Originally, this was printed on the back of the menu for a "Volunteer Workers Appreciation Banquet"—the name says it all. It was a great hit. There is no reason why it could not be spoken as a benediction as well at just such a gathering, or anywhere where "unsung heros" are being honored. You might want to begin with the second stanza if the first does not apply to your specific situation.*

$$\boxed{41}$$

TOPIC: **All-purpose benediction.**

AUDIENCE: **Suitable for any audience.**

It is altogether fitting and proper that we take a moment to pause and reflect upon our situation.

Life goes by so quickly, and often the pressures of daily life close in upon us and threaten to sap us of our strength and our vitality.

It is then that we need to pause and look within ourselves to rediscover the source of the strength that will allow us to carry on. To each of us, that source may be different, but each of us must find it and draw upon it.

We pause, therefore, to think about our purposes here tonight, our thoughts and personal reflections, and our relationships to each other. We pause to give thanks for the joy that we can draw from this union of minds and hearts.

We pause to be thankful for each other.

We pause to ask for guidance and strength.

We pause to rest for a moment and then to go on as we always have . . . together.

Special Data: *Time of benediction: about one minute. We call this an "all-purpose" benediction, because, with some slight modifications, there aren't many occasions where you can't use it. It would be appropriate for a dinner, a workshop, a special convocation, and many other situations where a benediction might be asked for. In the first line, instead of "our situation," you might want to mention the particular occasion you are addressing.*

$$\boxed{42}$$

TOPIC: Inspirational benediction.

AUDIENCE: Suitable for all audiences.

Yes, we can—but not alone.

Yes, we possess the talent and the resources to accomplish the goal we have set for ourselves—but not alone.

Yes, we can go on to achieve that which we have dreamed—but not alone.

We need each other as we begin our task—yes, that we need.

We need a vision and a purpose that reaches far beyond today—yes, that we need.

We need the guidance and the strength and the blessing of our Creator as we set upon our task—yes, that we need.

We have each other if we just reach out and take each other's hand in friendship and in love—and we are not alone.

We have the vision if we keep our eyes upon the goal for which we all strive—and we are not alone.

We have the strength and guidance each of us will find in his or her own way that flow from God to humankind, and there, as well, the blessing—and we are not alone.

Yes, we can—but not alone.

Yes, we may—and we are not alone.

Yes, we shall—as we have always done.

Yes . . .

Together . . .

One. . . .

Special Data: *Time of benediction: just over one minute. If you are going to use this, please don't "toss it off." It should be read as poetry, with appropriate pauses and feeling and with a flowing smoothness of speech. Like poetry, each listener will find something personal within the words. This can be used when a communal task is beginning or when a challenge is faced, whether internal or external. Present it with feeling.*

Afterthoughts

The root words of the term "benediction" can be translated as "good saying" or "the saying of something good." That should be your general guide for understanding their use. A benediction is to be used when you are asked to set the tone of an affair such as a dinner; when you are asked to "bless" an occasion; when you are asked to say a few final words that add dignity to an evening. In short, when you are asked to "say something good."

Again, we must remind you that sincerity is your greatest ally. If you are sincere and truly mean what you say, then it will be well-received by the hearers, and it will touch their hearts and minds—precisely the effect you wish to achieve.

If you are touched by what you say, your audience will be too.

A NEW COLLECTION OF OPENING AND CLOSING SPEECHES

Whatever the subject of the program may be, and whether it is for all educators, all parents, or a mixture of both, one fact remains true. The opening and closing speeches of the evening are a vital part of the program's success or failure.

If you are the opening speaker, then it is up to you to set the theme for the evening. In show business, the person who comes out first has the task of "warming up" the audience. Certainly we are not entertainers, but that terminology is rather reflective of what the opening speaker must do. You should establish the theme and (this is just as important) set the tone of the program. Your opening speech should prepare (warm up) the audience for the speakers to follow.

As the closing speaker for a program of speeches (or even if there was only one major speaker), your task is twofold: To sum up, and to "look forward." This does *not* mean that you must give a point by point summary akin to an outline of what has been said, but it does mean that you should hit the high points of what has been said during the evening, reminding the audience and "setting" the material in their minds. Then, you should give some sort of "forward" look, perhaps explaining what this program will mean to the audience; what could be done if its advice is taken to heart; how it is within our power to inculcate the procedures given; etc.

In effect, the opening and closing speaker says, "Look, audience, here's what's coming, and you're really going to love it!. . . . OK, this is basically what you just heard, and just think of the wonderful things that we can do with it!"

Like our first book, the first part of this section deals with opening speeches for programs on a wide variety of subjects—from a program on alcohol and drug abuse to one on the mainstreaming of special education students. The second half presents closing speeches for the same programs.

Of course, the middle of the program must be strong, but a good opening speech and a dynamic closing one go a long way toward giving an audience a memorable and worthwhile presentation.

$$\boxed{43}$$

TOPIC: **Opening speech for a program on alcohol and drug abuse.**

AUDIENCE: **Suitable for an adult audience.**

It was American poet John Greenleaf Whittier who wrote these lines: "Of all sad words of tongue or pen,/The saddest are these, 'It might have been....'"

Surely, there is no one here tonight who is not touched by those words. Each of us knows of someone or some situation that "might have been..." and wasn't—wasn't, not because of mental or physical limitations; not because of barriers of race or class; not due to poverty or lack of opportunity, no. Rather, it "was not" due to a ghoulish and horribly insidious spectre that haunts our land and strikes out at our families; our neighbors; the people we love.

I speak, of course, of the horror of drug and alcohol abuse that, according to many, has reached epidemic proportions in our country. Indeed, if I were to ask how many in this audience have been touched in some way by the tragedies associated with these two killers, it would be far easier to count the hands that would *not* go up. Each of us knows a relative, a friend, the children of friends, coworkers, and perhaps individuals within our own families who have suffered and caused others to suffer because of their abuse of alcohol and other drugs.

Yet, it is abhorrent to believe that there is no solution where such a problem exists. Certainly, there must be something that can be done, however small, to fight this crippling problem that besets us all.

The speakers who will address us this evening will tell you that they don't have a complete answer, for the magnitude of the problem precludes any single individual from offering a "magic" solution. If we say the right words, it will not go away. Yet, each of our speakers is a person with vast experience in this field, and each will tell you what cannot be done and, more importantly, what *can* be done, and what *you* can do within your own homes and within the community.

Tonight, you will learn that alcohol and drug abuse is extensive but *not* a hopeless problem; that you can take steps to recognize and help treat the problem *before* it gets worse; that *you* can make a difference.

Therefore, let us give the speakers our attention for this vital presentation; let us give them our minds as we learn and think; and, let us give them our hearts and hands, to join in the battle against the scourges of which they will speak.

For ourselves; for our neighbors and community; for our families and loved ones; for all that "might have been," we can do no less than try.

Let us begin this evening by hearing from a woman who will give you an overview. . . .

Special Data: *Time of opening speech: about three and a half minutes. What is the tone of this program? Is it to be a light evening's entertainment in which the audience can come and go, bantering lightly among themselves? Of course not! This opening speech has set the tone for the program to come and prepared the audience to deal with a very serious subject. You might want to change some portions of this speech, depending upon the content of the program you were hosting; but as an opener for a drug and alcohol abuse program, it will do quite well.*

$$\boxed{44}$$

TOPIC: **Opening for a program on AIDS.**

AUDIENCE: **Suitable for an adult audience.**

> *NOTE: You need only read the newspapers to understand how controversial a topic this is, particularly when it comes to education about it in the schools. This opening speech is, therefore, also a model of openings on controversial subjects.*

Someone gets up and says, "I remember the days when 'aids' were kids who worked in the school office." Perhaps we smile at that or even give a short laugh, but underneath the smile, we all wear a grimmer face, a face grown older with the experience and knowledge of the tragedies that life has brought our way.

If we should ask ten people at random about Acquired Immune Deficiency Syndrome, their responses would very likely reflect ten divergent views on the subject, half of which would undoubtedly be opposed diametrically to the other half.

Causes, cures, preventions, what information to give or not give, what should be taught to our children and what should not—all these seem a matter for vigorous debate, stirred and heated by the obviously deep convictions and concerns of all sides.

Yet, if there is any point of agreement, it is on the fact that AIDS remains a deadly killer; a force that will not simply go away; a force that we must deal with in strong and effectual terms.

Whatever your personal views on the subject, I hope that you will agree with me on one other point as well. I hope you will agree that it is only through the democratic process of free dialog and the free exchange of ideas and viewpoints that we can even hope to begin to form some base from which to approach, view, and deal with this menace that faces us.

Extremely necessary to that process are programs such as the one in which we are about to participate. Certainly, there are divergent views represented; certainly, you may hear opinions or points of view that may be contrary to your beliefs; certainly, all sides may come away with a deeper appreciation of opposing viewpoints.

And, just as certainly, we may learn from each other, because freedom of speech carries that benefit with it as well.

With that in mind, and with the knowledge that this evening is far from an exercise in rhetoric but rather a meaningful dialog addressing the very future of our children, let us begin by hearing from our first speaker. . . .

Special Data: *Time of opening: slightly over two minutes. If you have ever hosted a program on a controversial topic, then you will appreciate the fact that the audience for such an affair is in high gear before your speech even begins. Obviously, there will be responsible adults on both sides of the issue. We feel that the best you can hope for under circumstances such as these is an "armed truce." Consequently, your opening remarks should concentrate on the seriousness of the topic, acknowledgment of the fact that there is a diversity of opinion, and an appeal to a reasonable tolerance on all sides.*

> *You should appeal to the sense of fairness of the audience. The per-*
> *spective conveyed is that the audience may not like or agree with*
> *everything, but as reasonable and fair minded adults living in a*
> *democratic society, they have a responsibility, and duty, to hear all*
> *sides in a rational and orderly manner. That approach works more*
> *often than not.*

$$\boxed{45}$$

TOPIC: **Opening speech for a program designed for a middle school.**

AUDIENCE: **Suitable for an adult audience; mainly parents.**

The little, red schoolhouse; the little, red, one-room schoolhouse; the little, red, one-room, all-grades-lumped-together schoolhouse; the little, red, one-room, all-grades-lumped-together, 50-kids-in-a-singleroom-with-one-teacher-trying-to-teach-eight-levels-of-all-subjects schoolhouse. . . . No wonder the schoolhouse was red; it had indigestion!

We all long at times for a respite from our busy lives, and sometimes, we like to turn our minds back to simpler, less complicated, and less hectic times. Well, that's fine, and the media often helps us by painting idyllic pictures of bygone days, not limited to but usually including that "little red schoolhouse" of which I spoke.

While it is certainly relaxing to stroll for a while in that pastoral fantasy, when we return to our present, we must bring with us an understanding that the "little red schoolhouse" was a totally fitting and well-functioning educational tool—for the time and place in which it existed.

For, make no mistake, that is precisely what the school must do—fill the needs of the community it services. If an elected official ignored the needs of his constituency, there would be little doubt but that he would be voted out of office. So, too, schools change and approaches to education change. An educational system that stays the same while the community around it changes would soon take on the status of the "little red schoolhouse" but without the sentiment, for it would quickly be seen for what it was; something that no longer met the needs of the children it purposed to serve.

We are here this evening to learn about a transition that is soon to take place in our community—a transition from a junior high school setup that we have used for the past eleven years to a middle school setup that we know will serve us well for many years to come.

Certainly, the junior high school setup served us well for a long time. It more than met the promise it extended when it implemented the elementary-high school plan. However, nothing stands still, and the needs and natures of children and communities are no exception.

Tonight, you will hear how the school system of this community is endeavoring to meet those challenges of change by turning to the middle school system. You will hear how the middle school can better meet the educational needs of your children and how it is geared toward guiding the developing preadolescent through those times that are, at best, trying and hectic for parents, teachers, and, of course, the student. You will hear how the middle school stands as its name implies, as a middle ground (a "growing place" if you will) between the elementary school experience and the young adult responsibility of high school.

Finally, we will learn that the middle school concept is not magic; it will not give us anything without hard work and dedication. We will see, however, that with the application of dedicated educators and a willingness to work toward a goal together, it *will* give us *the best chance* to achieve the best possible education, both academically and developmentally, for the children of our community—for your sons and daughters.

Therefore, let us listen together and learn together in order that together we may build a school system that serves our needs with as much grace and polish as that little red schoolhouse enriched the community of its day.

Our first speaker this evening will introduce us to. . . .

Special Data: *Time of opening speech: two and a half minutes. While the middle school is far from a controversial topic, when there is a change in an established school system, there is bound to be some confusion and perhaps even resentment and resistance on the part of some members of the community to the change. That's the time when we as educators have to start educating. Notice that the previous system was not ridiculed. Never make that mistake; after all, if it was so bad, how come we used it for so long? Notice also, that the entire thrust is toward the fact that the new system will serve us better, and that's why we're going for it. The middle school concept is growing like mushrooms in a dark cellar, and throughout* *this book, you will find several speeches on various aspects of it. The very next section, for instance, has a speech on middle school and the "total" child. You might like to glance at them all, for we feel they will supply you with a great deal of material to use in your speeches when dealing with this topic.*

$$\boxed{46}$$

TOPIC: **Opening for a program on Special Education.**

AUDIENCE: **Parents of special education students; teachers; community members.**

When we speak of " special education," it is essential that we learn to place emphasis on the right word. Obviously, we are drawn to the word "special," because these children are just that—very special to you, their parents, to us, their teachers, and to our society as well. We need our "special" children, because they supply us with love and provide us with the direction we need if we are to evolve into a truly caring society where the rights and the needs of all its members are addressed to the best of our ability.

We must not forget, however, that the second half of that phrase is the word "education," which, in its literal meaning implies a "drawing out"; a leading from one state to another; a transition from a lack of knowledge to knowledge; from a lack of skill to skill; from a promise to a realized potential, whatever that potential might be.

"Special education"—without forgetting the first word, we must place emphasis on the second. For our children's sake, we must train, lead, guide, shape, and help place those eager feet on the road to that realized potential.

During our program this evening, we will be privileged to hear of the many ways in which we are striving to meet those goals. Tonight, *we* shall learn. We shall learn what our children have been doing over the past months; the activities and learning in which they are engaged at present; we shall learn of some exciting plans for the future.

We shall hear, for example, about the status of "mainstreaming" in our schools, the process whereby certain special education students are attending some regular classes during the school day. We shall learn of how the acceptance and concern of our staff have helped to make this process successful and enriching for all our students.

We shall also learn of some individual cases who have truly filled us with joy as they have stretched beyond limitations to achieve some outstanding accomplishments. These "special" students have gladdened the hearts of their parents and their teachers, and have managed to provide a glimpse of the world of promise that can await them.

Certainly, not every story is a success story. Were I to tell you that, you would have every right to turn away in disbelief. Of course we have had our failures, and we shall undoubtedly continue to have them. Yet, we know that were we to allow these failures to overwhelm us, soon there would be no successes at all.

And that is precisely what we wish to concentrate on tonight—success. That is what we want to focus on tonight—promise and potential. That is our emphasis this evening—not the word "special," but the term "education," the "leading forward" of each precious child.

Let's begin our exploration tonight by hearing from our director. . . .

Special Data: *Time of opening: about two minutes. Our "special" children are just that; very special, and nowhere is a greater need for parental involvement and close home contact more necessary than in this area. Consequently, programs such as the one this speech addresses are very common. Particularly with the parents of special students, your job as an administrator, we have observed, is to do what that old song says, "accentuate the positive." There are many wonderful advances in the special education curriculum, and an opening speech such as this, that does not ignore the negatives, allows parents to look forward to hearing positive messages filled with hope. That is no small thing.*

$$\boxed{47}$$

TOPIC: **Opening speech for a professional in-service.**

AUDIENCE: **Teachers; administrators; the building staff.**

Suppose for a moment that you had a very bad tooth that had to come out. No doubt about it—the tooth must go. So, you make an appointment with a dentist and arrive at his office one afternoon.

You are led into his office, and there you find a wooden kitchen chair next to a workbench strewn with pliers, hammers, and chisels in wild profusion. On the walls are scratch marks (from previous patients?) and several unidentifiable stains.

The dentist finally enters, eating a salami sandwich and murmuring something about never having time for lunch. He rubs one hand on his pants before he offers to shake hands, burps loudly, then scratches a sudden itch on the top of his head.

"Well," he states, "let's get that little bugger out of there; I don't have all day. Which one is it?"

As you point to the offending tooth, the good doctor begins unwinding a length of heavy twine from a ball that he has collected on the workbench. He bites off a portion, and approaches, string in hand.

"Try to think of something else," he tells you as he ties the end of the string to what you hope is your bad tooth. "That way it might hurt a little less. Oh, and when the tooth is ripped out, try not to bleed all over the place, OK?"

With that, he crosses the room and ties the remaining end of the twine to the knob on the door.

"This will be quick . . . if not painless," he grins as he leaves the room and slams the door shut behind himself with a thunderous *thud.*

Now, if you have that picture set firmly in mind, please choose which of the following applies:

A. This doctor sure is a "fun" guy!

B. Excuse me, did I stumble into an Alfred Hitchcock movie?

C. Is it too late to get a second opinion?

D. Hey, this tooth doesn't really hurt at all! I think I can live with it!

E. Somehow, I don't think this doctor has kept up with advances in modern denistry. . . .

Please excuse me, ladies and gentlemen, for this exercise in face-tiousness, and I think that I have been heavy-handed enough that we all get the point. No profession, if it is to remain a profession, can afford to stand still. We *all* need to learn and grow to keep abreast of techniques and advances developed by our colleagues. To enter any profession means to enter into an unspoken contract to continue learning and growing throughout our entire professional lives.

That is precisely why we are here today. It is at in-services such as these that we all have the opportunity to share knowledge; to learn new educational techniques and strategies that can enhance the educational process in our classrooms; to grow for our professional benefit and for the ultimate benefit of our students. Where education continues, educa-tion flourishes—and children realize potentials.

So, welcome to today's in-service. Whatever you come away with today, I know you will find it enjoyable and useful. I can guarantee you, it won't be like pulling teeth!

Our first speaker today has some really exciting insights to share with you. . . .

Special Data: *Time of opening: two to three minutes. This is a very ef-fective opening for an in-service. First, your point is made quickly and in an entertaining fashion. Second, you have given the audi-ence credit for their intelligence by not having to "explain" the moral of your story. Third, you have given a viable reason for par-ticipating in the activity. We all realize that there is teacher resis-tance to these in-services, particularly if teachers feel that the pro-gram is all theory, impractical, and that time might be better spent correcting papers. This speech, consequently, gives them a purpose for their attendance; a reason that can be grasped and appreciated.*

$$\boxed{48}$$

TOPIC: An all-purpose opening speech.

AUDIENCE: Suitable for all places, times, and audiences.

Ladies and gentlemen, it is a personal pleasure to be here today to host this program on _____.

I am no expert in agriculture, but I hope I have enough common sense to realize that any seed or any bulb that is placed on a shelf and is forgotten will never spring to life as a rose or a tree or an ear of corn.

That seed must be taken and planted in good soil; it must be nourished and watered and tended as it grows if it is to become the flower or plant we wish it to be; we must see to it that it is cultivated. It is often hard work, but that work produces a crop that can benefit us all.

Experience teaches us that it is precisely that way with life itself. Of course, we all have the potential to be hermits, to hide away in some cave where no one touches us and we touch no one, but few of us would accept such a premise as anything but a wasted life. Fortunately, we also have the potential of becoming productive members of our society; people who can make a difference and who will leave the world better by their presence in it.

We do not achieve that latter goal, however, by sitting on a shelf unattended. Like the seed and like the flower bulb, we need nourishment. For us, that nourishment consists not only of food for the body, but of sustenance for the mind as well.

That is why we attend programs such as this. Today, we will see and hear, and we will learn as well. And in that learning, we will find nourishment for our minds to take one more step in the growth that will allow us to "blossom" to our benefit—to the benefit of our community and society as well.

Therefore, let's begin by hearing from. . . .

Special Data: *Time of opening: about a minute and a half. Very obviously, you can amend his speech to fit a specific topic or a specific program. As it stands, it is a good opening for any program. It bespeaks a very basic human truth and applies it well to the situation at hand. Consequently, there are few who can argue with it. It is* *also short and gets right into the program while giving the audience credit for intelligence and providing a reason for their receptiveness. It works.*

Afterthoughts

All opening speeches have one thing in common; they set the tone for the program to follow. Again, the speaker's attitude is key in this regard. You, school administrator—do you look upon the program to follow as dull and a waste of time? You *will* convey that to your audience no matter what your words might say. You, school administrator—are you truly enthusiastic about what will happen tonight, and are you convinced of its importance? You will convey *that* to your audience along with your words, and they will catch fire from you.

The speeches in the second half of this section represent *closing* speeches for the same programs the speeches in the first half "opened." These will give you a more complete picture of how you can effectively host a program from start to finish.

Closing Speeches

$$\boxed{49}$$

TOPIC: **Closing speech for a program on alcohol and drug abuse.**

AUDIENCE: **Suitable for all adult audiences.**

It has been quite an evening.

I think I may safely speak for everyone here tonight in saying that the program we have just gone through has been an eye-opening and sobering experience. Certainly, we have learned a great deal.

And, if we have learned, we are also left with questions. I know I have several, and the most pressing are these: what can be done, and what can I, personally, do about these issues?

I remember that a while back a little girl playing in her backyard broke through a covering and fell into an abandoned well. She was trapped in there, and it soon became very clear that unless she were gotten out swiftly, she would most certainly die. When word got out, people in the community flocked to the aid of that child and her parents. Soon, teams of volunteers were digging, attempting to excavate the area. People bravely risked their own safety in the darkened interior of that abandoned well to get to the child. Outside, neighbors, friends, and strangers who had been touched by the tragedy came to volunteer, to console the child's parents, and to pray for the child's deliverance.

Soon, the entire nation was in that backyard via the mass media. Offers of help poured in from all over the country. An anxious nation watched as the drama unfolded.

After what seemed an eternity of waiting, a rescue worker appeared carrying the child who waved feebly to the cheering people. In their homes throughout the country, people in front of TV sets cheered as well, and many paused to offer prayers of thanksgiving that the child had been rescued from such a fate.

As we have learned tonight, we face a tragedy just as real and as pressing as the plight of that little girl in the well. Our children and our society are in danger, very grave danger. Perhaps it hasn't been publicized as well; perhaps it lacks the appeal of a helpless child in immediate peril; perhaps the rescuers are waiting for others to volunteer because the danger somehow doesn't seem as real.

Yet the danger is just as real, threatening, and urgent as it was to that child. We have seen tonight how drug and alcohol abuse pose incredible dangers that must be addressed here and now. Like the little girl in the well, time is running out, and our children must be rescued before they face an ultimate peril.

And the questions remain. What can be done, and what can I, personally, do to enact change. It it were a little girl stuck in an old well, the world would rush to her assistance. Our children are in a similar situation. Who will rush to their aid? Who will pray; who will comfort; who will work ceaselessly through the night?

These are questions we must each answer within our own hearts. Thanks to tonight's program, we have heard the call; we have been given the particulars; we have been shown where to dig.

What can I, personally, do, starting this evening.

It is something to think about.

Thank you for coming. Good night.

Special Data: *Time of closing: about two minutes. This type of closing has sometimes been called the "challenge" close. It is one in which the audience is "challenged" to do something about what they have heard or learned throughout the program. Understand, you are not looking for volunteers, but are giving the audience an incentive to go out and do something. It is inspirational in nature, and as such is a very effective type of closing speech you might wish to try.*

50

TOPIC: Closing for a program on AIDS.

AUDIENCE: Suitable for an adult audience.

Sitting on a fence is no easy task. One tends to get splinters that make one jump to one side or the other. I think this has been borne out by what has transpired here this evening.

One thing is clear; there are no fence-sitters in this audience or on this stage.

This evening we have heard many viewpoints about AIDS, its treatment and prevention, and about AIDS education in our schools. Obviously, there have been represented here a variety of opinions and viewpoints, some of which exist as diametrically opposite to others. Most certainly, there has been disagreement, but I think that there have been areas of agreement as well; areas in which we all share a common ground.

From what I have heard tonight, I believe that each of us agrees that AIDS is a scourge, a plague, a sorrowful disease affecting our society. I think we further agree that it is a clear and present danger to members of our society and a potential danger to our children as well. Moreover, I believe that we agree there is a pressing need for both treatment of the problem and preventive measures.

We do have these facts on which to agree, and if nothing more, they are a starting point. If this is encouraging, then it is also encouraging that we come out to programs such as this one and air our concerns and discuss our areas of dissension. Of course there will be disagreement; of course there will be conflict; of course we clash in our approaches, our beliefs, our moral standards, and in any one of a dozen areas; but without this conflict there can be no growth, and without conflict there can be no victory.

Yes, a victory. A victory for which side? Why, a victory for our children, of course; a victory for them and for their future. You see, that is one final area in which I know we tread a common ground.

We are about to leave and go to our individual homes. As we do so, let us take with us what we have heard and learned this evening. We don't have to agree, but let us consider; we don't have to approve, but let us understand; we don't have to accept a belief that goes against our own, but let us realize that it is in working together that we will find solutions.

Finally, let us realize that it will be our children who will face the challenges of the future, and that our willingness to understand and work together today will provide the foundation for their tomorrow.

Let us all hold to that goal.

Thank you, and good night.

Special Data: *Time of closing speech: two and a half minutes. As we stated in the data on the opening speech for this topic, this is a sample for handling a "controversial" topic. Notice that no attempt is made to claim that everything has turned rosy because of one pro-*

gram. There is still, even in the closing, the acknowledgment that differences and controversies still exist. If there have been any areas of agreement during the evening, then these should be stressed in the speech. Finally, if you can end on any sort of common ground, as this speech does, then so much the better. Your audience for something controversial such as this should go away thinking that you, at least, were fair and impartial and sought to present all sides in an equitable manner. If you can achieve this, you did well!

51

TOPIC: **Closing speech for a program on the middle school.**

AUDIENCE: **Suitable for an adult audience; mainly parents.**

Ladies and gentlemen, we are at a point where we face a beginning, a middle, and an end.

We are at the end of this evening's program; we are in the middle of your child's education; and, we stand at the beginning of a new educational system for our community.

This evening's program has certainly been one filled with information. Your questions have certainly been reflective of an understanding not only of the general concept of the middle school but of the finer points of child-centered education as well. I believe that our panelists have done an outstanding job of clearly and succinctly presenting the mulitfaceted concept of middle school education, and I congratulate them and thank them for us all.

If one thing has become clear this evening, it is the fact that the middle school setup is better able to meet the needs of the developing preadolescent than any previous system. I know that as a parent, I find that very encouraging, and I feel certain that many of you join me in that enthusiasm. I think that the more we can look at the total, developing child rather than an "entity" to be fed a certain amount of knowledge, the better and stronger we will become as a school, and the better that will be for the total educational and personal development of our children. At this age level, we stand in the middle of our children's education, and the middle school concept I am certain, will help to make their future education that much more productive and bright.

Finally, this evening has made me look forward with happy anticipation to a new beginning as we inculcate the middle school philosophy in September. Of course we will face the challenges you have heard about this evening, but these challenges promise great rewards for those who face them and overcome them. I have no doubt that we shall not only overcome, but that we will build a middle school system that will hold bright promise to all the children of our community.

Finally, I hope that you are glad that you have come this evening; I am happy to have hosted this vital program. I hope that you had as good a time listening and asking questions as our panel had in presenting the material and answering your inquiries. I hope that your curiosity has been satisfied; your minds enriched; and, your concerns addressed.

I hope, also, that you leave now with a sense of anticipation for the start of the middle school in our community; with a knowledge that it is something well-thought-out; and with the certainty that the middle school will well serve the needs of your sons and daughters both throughout the coming academic year and throughout their entire educational careers as well.

Thank you so much for coming; have a safe trip home; and good night. . . .

Special Data: *Time of closing speech: a little over two minutes. This audience, unlike the one for the previous closing, is a receptive one. It has been our experience that parents of pre- and early adolescents really like the middle school concept once they have gotten to know it, which is why programs such as the one described here are held. Consequently, this friendly, relaxed, almost "informal" ending bespeaks a parting between people who like each other. If you are going to compose your own closing, this is an excellent concept to keep in mind. If you like your audience, they will most certainly like you.*

$$\boxed{52}$$

TOPIC: Closing for a program on Special Education.

AUDIENCE: Parents of special education students; teachers; community members.

Ladies and gentlemen, we are at the end of this evening's program and activities, but we all realize that we are nowhere near the end of the education of your very special children; that continues.

It is programs such as these that provide us with the encouragement that we all need from time to time. It is programs such as these that give us the knowledge we need in order to cope with today's ever-changing educational scene. Programs such as these let us know that our children are being educated, and are finding the enrichment and learning they need.

Therefore, I would like to thank the participants in this evening's program for their time, the thoroughness of their presentations, the obvious research and work that went into them, and, most importantly, I would like to thank them for the care, concern, and love that they give to our special children each and every day.

Mrs. Miller, thank you for your encouraging report on the status of special education in our school. We were all heartened by your remarks, and I think we were all enlightened and encouraged by your report on your former student, Jody, and the fine progress he is making. We deeply appreciate your concern for us and for all your students.

Dr. Thompson, your explanation of economic aid to parents of special education children was both informative and most welcome. We are encouraged, as you are, by the attention our legislators are beginning to pay to the area of special education. Thank you for the uplift.

Miss Greene, we thank you for that marvelous report on the mainstreaming of special education students in our school. How wonderful it was to hear of the very positive response to the process from your students. Not only that, but your report on the overwhelming acceptance of these mainstreamed youngsters by other students and the regular faculty just lifted our spirits to the skies. We are overjoyed, as you are, with the success of this program and with the positive and worthwhile feelings it has sponsored in our special students. Thank you for this very good news.

Mr. Schallert, your look into the future of special education which you were kind enough to share with us was inspiring. What hope it has given us for the future of our special children! Thank you so much for joining us tonight.

Finally, ladies and gentlemen, I would like to thank you, the audience, for coming. Your love was abundant; your interest unflagging; your concern most apparent.

Thank you for your attendance; thank you for your attentiveness and your insightful questions; thank you for your care and concern.

Our special students are very fortunate to have such special parents.

Thank you for coming; good night. . . .

Special Data: *Time of closing speech: three or four minutes or longer, depending upon the number of panelists to be thanked. We have used this closing speech as an example of how to thank each participant in the program. If it had been a controversial program or one filled with dissension, it would be much better to end the program (as we did with the closing for the AIDS program) rather than to attempt a thank-you session. When the program has been pleasant or productive, however, you may, indeed, wish to thank the participants. This speech gives you a good model for doing just that. Notice that each person is mentioned individually by name, and a little something said about individual presentation. This not only lets the audience know that you've been listening, but it refreshes the audience's memory, stirring up what it has assimilated during the evening. Finally, thanking the audience and complimenting them as a good audience is a fine tactic* if you really mean it. *If you say that merely to be ingratiating, they will know it, and it will have the opposite effect. If, however, you can say it and mean it, it will go over well, and it's a pleasant way to end the program for that evening.*

$$\boxed{53}$$

TOPIC: Closing speech for a professional in-service.

AUDIENCE: Teachers; administrators; the building staff.

I remember as a very young teacher the first in-service I ever went to. There was this older, obviously more experienced teacher in our building, and the day before the in-service I asked him, "What's the best thing about an in-service?"

He fixed me with a weary eye and answered, "The best thing about an in-service is that it is eventually over!"

It may surprise you to know that I subscribe to that very same philosophy.

You see, it seems to me that I have spent a lifetime going to meetings like this. Whether as a teacher myself or as an administrator, year after year I have attended in-service meetings and others aimed at improving the educational process. I have heard speaker after speaker, teacher after teacher, authority after authority inform me about creative and sometimes not-so-creative approaches to classroom discipline and control, innovative curriculum development, and how to bring vibrancy and liveliness to the study of possessive pronouns.

My reaction to all this has been, to state it euphemistically, somewhat mixed. There have been times when I would have welcomed a minor earthquake or an invasion from the planet Mongo—anything to have gotten me out of the torture that I was undergoing. At those times, my mind felt as numb as the seat of my pants. Although thousands of words had filled the air; although several trees had given their all to provide the paper for the handouts I had received; although chalkboards had been covered with what seemed acres of chalk, none of it—*none of it*—had penetrated my wall of personal indifference and taken up residence in my mind.

In short, the day had been a complete waste, and I had learned nothing except to view days like that with consternation. I rejoiced when the day was over.

Yet, to stop there would be to tell but half the story; to leave the picture incomplete.

For, in those years of in-service exposure, I have also been privileged to sit in on sessions that have nourished my mind and stirred my very spirit. I have been privileged to listen while gifted and innovative educators have shared their insights, their knowledge and their techniques selflessly. I have been privileged to participate in an exchange of ideas which I knew, deep within myself, I would incorporate into my own teaching; ideas that would enliven my teaching and provide a positive benefit to each and every one of my students. I have been privileged to learn and to grow. I have been privileged to be taught by true teachers who not only knew how to present material, but who kindled fires deep within me that burned and warmed and refused to be either quenched or contained.

On days like that, I couldn't wait for the experience to end. No, not for the reason of the fruitless days; not so I could escape the boredom and nonproductiveness, but for the exact opposite reason.

I couldn't wait for the day to be over so that I could get back to my students and my classroom and begin to inculcate the wonderful, exciting and innovative ideas I had assimilated. I wanted to get started; I wanted to begin; I wanted to bring what I had learned to the front-line of my classroom and my teaching.

That is why I could agree with that teacher from my past. The best thing about it is that it will come to an end.

And the best thing about its coming to an end is that tomorrow will begin, and we can bring what we have learned to the place it belongs—to our classrooms; to our teaching; to our students in order that they may learn and grow and be challenged as we have.

The best thing about the end of today is the promise that tomorrow holds.

I know I speak for each of us when I express my deepest thanks to everyone who participated in today's in-service. From the various committees who have provided us with refreshments, name tags, programs, and the other amenities, to the presenters of the various sessions which, from what I have heard from many of you and witnessed for myself, were outstanding in all ways, everyone involved in today's in-service deserves our thanks for their selfless contribution to the success of today's program.

Thanks to you for your willingness to learn and grow; this day has been presented for you, and without your cooperation nothing would be possible, just as, without your talent, education in our district would not be the fine thing that it is.

Have a safe trip home. Today is over and tomorrow is waiting for all of us.

Thank you, and good afternoon.

Special Data: *Time of closing: about five minutes. This is an example of a more lengthy, "formal" type of closing. Note that the thrust is positive, assuming that the day was successful. There is also an implied challenge to use knowledge that has been gleaned. Finally, everyone is thanked, including the audience, and there is a definite ending to the day. We think this works very well.*

$$\boxed{54}$$

TOPIC: **An all-purpose closing speech.**

AUDIENCE: **Suitable for all places, times, and audiences.**

When I was a child, I remember one relative we used to visit on a regular basis, Aunt Lillian. We always had a good time there as I recall, and even as children, we enjoyed going to Aunt Lily's for the day.

When it would come time to leave, she would enfold us in her ample arms, sigh deeply, and state with resigned reserve, "Well, all good things must come to an end."

I recall that at the time, that statement would sadden us, adding just the right bittersweet touch to the day. As I grew older, I learned to recognize that statement as one of life's truisms, applicable to all times and all situations. Most certainly, all good things must come to an end, because *all things* must come to an end.

And that includes tonight's program as well. . . .

Please allow me to express my deep thanks to everyone who participated and made this evening possible. Please know that your hard work is both acknowledged and appreciated.

And thanks to you, ladies and gentlemen, for your attention, understanding, and cooperation. In a very real sense, it is you who have made this evening worthwhile.

Well, Aunt Lillian, I guess you were right; all good things must come to an end.

Tonight has been very, very good, indeed.

Have a safe trip home, thank you so much for coming.

Good night!

Special Data: *Time of closing: less than two minutes. If you wish, you might want to thank each of the participants individually, along the guidelines established in speech number 52. As it stands, however, this is a safe speech for ending almost any program that you have had to host. It revolves around an anecdote with which the audience can identify, it thanks everyone in the program, albeit not specifically. It thanks the audience for their attentiveness. It is also short—it should be remembered that at the end of a long evening, this is a quality appreciated deeply by virtually all audiences.*

Afterthoughts

We are certain that you appreciate that to stand up at the conclusion of any program and say something like, "Well, folks, that's it! G'night!" is not only highly inappropriate, but will leave the entire audience feeling let down. Whatever has gone on during the evening, the audience expects you, as the host/moderator, to say something "appropriate" in order to close the evening. Therefore, it will be up to you to sum up what has been said, make a meaningful comment about the program, give direction for the next step suggested in the program, challenge the audience to act on what it has learned, give the participants a meaningful reason for attendance, express thanks, compliment the audience on its intelligence or participation, and/or all of the above. It is hardly an effortless job, but if you can be enthusiastic about what has taken place and truly see the audience as benefitting from the experience, then you will do just fine.

You will be the last person they will see or hear from. Be certain that they remember you!

NEW SPEECHES BY ADMINISTRATORS FOR THE LAY AUDIENCE

If all the public speaking that the school administrator ever did was before groups of *other* school administrators, perhaps this book and its predecessor would never have been written.

Certainly, when you get together with people who basically do the same thing you do, there is a wide and fertile "common ground" on which to meet. You are together for only moments, or so it seems, before you are swapping "war stories" or commiserating on the particular difficulty of a certain task or telling each other of ways you have found to make the job easier or get something done more efficiently. The talk is easy, because you share the same experiences, and you speak the same language.

However, not all the public speaking an administrator does falls into that particular set of fortunate circumstances. As likely as you will be, due to the nature of your position, to speak before administrators and other educators, you will just as likely be asked to speak before groups of parents or senior citizens or concerned community members. These are people who, while they are certainly concerned about education, may have a knowledge of the subject based on the fact that they went to school and/or have seen their own children through the process. In cases such as these, you cannot make the same approach you would to fellow educators.

With the lay audience, your job is as much "teacher" as it is "speaker." Perhaps you are addressing parents about their contact with school or how to help with homework; perhaps the community is curious about that new "middle" school; perhaps they want to know about the responsibility of the school as opposed to their responsibility. All of this is certainly within your purview, and all of it requires that you use your best *teaching* skills.

In terms of vocabulary, approach to the subject, assumption of prior knowledge, and even attitude toward the audience, your approach must incorporate the best teaching techniques possible. You must present a subject with which you may be intimately familiar as if it were brand new and being discussed for the first time.

The following speeches and the "SPECIAL DATA" sections that follow each speech investigate some very common and useful topics as well as effective, workable approaches toward delivering a winning speech to a lay audience.

$$\boxed{55}$$

TOPIC: Becoming Involved with Your Child's School

AUDIENCE: Parents, such as might attend a PTA meeting or "School Information Night."

Over the years, I have been asked many questions by parents about our school. These have ranged from questions about procedures for reporting an absence, to serious concerns about a child's promotion to the next grade. If I had to select the one question asked most frequently by parents, however, I think it would be this: "How can I best help my child do well in school?"

That question seems to say it all. Every parent wants his or her child to "do well" in school. Virtually every parent realizes the importance of proper schooling for children in today's society. Every concerned parent is anxious to help the child achieve to the best of his or her ability. Therefore, this question is a serious one that bespeaks a deep concern for positive involvement in the educational process.

How can I best help my child do well in school? My answer has always been the same—to help your child do well in school, become involved with the school. In my experience as a teacher and an administrator, I have found that where the home and the school are allies, the child's education flourishes.

Children often play what has been called the "Mama/Daddy Game." In this game, the child approaches father in the living room and states, "Daddy, can I go over to Billy's house tonight? Mama says it's OK with her if it's all right with you." Moments later, the child has moved to the kitchen, where he confronts mother and pleads, "Mama, can I go over to Billy's house later? Daddy says it's all right with him if it's OK with you." Another name for this game has been called, "Divide and Conquer."

I will tell you from personal experience that kids play this game with you and their teachers as well; at home and at school. You see, as long as they can keep the home and school separated, they are free to do virtually as they please. When neither the home nor the school knows what's going on with the other; as long as there is no communication; as long as the school does its thing and the home does its thing then nobody knows "*any*-thing" about "*no*-thing"; the child's grades and relationship to school plummet in a downward spiral that becomes harder and harder to correct.

Given a positive relationship between the home and the school, however, time and again we have seen failing grades pick up; unfinished homework completed and turned in; and potentially wasted academic careers made into something fruitful.

Someone once said that he was in favor of educating every child who was willing and anxious to learn, to which someone else answered that if that were the case, we might as well close down all the schools tomorrow. The truth is that education of any child is a struggle. Children lack the perception and appreciation that we have gained by years of experience, both pleasant and not-so-pleasant. Left to their own devices, children will take that fabled "path of least resistance," and if that includes not doing homework or watching TV instead of studying for a test, then that is what will happen.

It will happen, that is, unless the home and school are working together for the good of the child; unless a positive relationship has been forged between the home and the school.

You see, it is rather hard for a kid to tell Mom and Dad that he doesn't have any homework or that he need not study when Mom and Dad have just spoken to the teacher and know about a unit test that's coming up the next day.

This only happens, however, when the home and the school are united in a quest for the best education possible for the child.

Tonight, I'm going to offer you 10 steps for building a relationship between the home and school that will help parents and teachers make certain that each student is getting the best education possible. The steps are not long or drawn out; rather, they are highly efficient tools that have been proven effective in bringing the home and the school together in the best possible manner.

Let's start with something you're already doing—right now. One of the most effective tools for home/school unity is to attend school programs such the one you are attending tonight. Whether an informational meeting or an open house, or an exhibit of work done in school, each time you attend, you will learn something new, and not only will you get to know the people involved, but they will get to know you, and communication between friends is always appreciated.

Next, you would do well to take an active role in your school's Parent-Teacher Organization. PTAs and PTOs have traditionally been supportive of everything that goes on in a school, and as an active member, you truly become involved in your child's education intimately.

Get to know your child's teacher. This doesn't mean that you have to become personal friends or hold dinner parties for the teacher, but I know that when I taught, I always appreciated matching a face to a name. If I knew the parent, I was able to explain on a personal basis just what I was doing in class, my expectations, what I required of a son or daughter, and I did not hesitate to contact the parent when something was going amiss with their child's learning.

Toward that end, it is essential that you, as parents, work to establish a line of open communication between the school and the home. Make certain that the teacher has your phone number; tell her or him where you can be reached at all times. Let the teacher, the guidance office, and the administrative offices know that you want to be notified whenever appropriate. Contact the teacher when you have a question; encourage the teacher to contact you. Keep those lines of communication open, and they will be used.

Essential in this open communications process is the fact that you should try to attend all parent/teacher conferences. Not only will that help you to know your child's teacher, but it will help your child's teacher to know you. It also keeps you current on what is going on in class, how well your child is doing, and what needs to be done to remedy the situation or to "keep up the good work." In short, you'll be informed and able to give your child informed help for his or her schoolwork.

Tied to this is your support of the school and school projects. If it is at all possible, attend the school functions in which your child is involved. Certainly, we are all aware of the interference of work schedules precluding attendance at times, but you should try to come when you can—make a real effort to be there. That is one of the strongest actions you can take in giving your child a positive attitude toward the school and toward learning. Don't send your child to a basketball game—if possible, go with him.

You should know that teachers are constantly on the lookout for parents who want to help out with field days or class trips. These are acknowledged parts of your child's education, and your presence not only helps the organizers of the day, but makes a real impression on your child as well. Understand that your child may tell you that he or she will die of embarrassment if you show up on the trip to the power plant, but I will tell you frankly that not only will your child *not* die from advanced embarrassment, but a connection will be planted in his or her brain forever; the idea that you are really and truly concerned about the learning that is taking place, that you are taking part in that learning, and that school is really important—important enough for you to be there.

Just as you can take part in class trips, you can also take part in classroom activities. Especially as members of the PTA or PTO, you can visit the classroom often. You can help out on classroom projects; you can volunteer to be an aide or to tutor; you can tell stories, give lectures, show slides, and participate in a myriad of other activities that will enrich the classroom experience of your child and his or her peer group.

And, let me break off here for a moment to say that very few people in this world are independently wealthy. Indeed, everyone I know has to work for a living, and that means, for most of us, being at a job between certain hours. No one is suggesting that you quit that job in order to go on field trips to the beach to study sea shells. The key thought, I believe, is this: Try to be available whenever you can be available. Children understand why you can't be there every time someone uses a pass to the lavatory, but they have difficulty, I believe, when a parent shows a disregard for any activity, and won't even try.

Two more aspects of building that positive home/school relationship remain, and they are extremely important.

I'll state the first very succinctly—*help your child with homework.* Please notice that I did not say "Do your child's homework," but that you should help your child whenever assistance is appropriate. This would include providing an environment for your child to do the work, a suggestion or two along the way if your child gets stuck, and, *most importantly,* seeing to it that your child completes *all* homework. Nothing affects grades like poorly done, half-done, or not-at-all-done homework. If you have opened those lines of communication, you will be able to see to it that the homework is done and done properly. Invariably, if *you* are convinced that homework is important, eventually, your child will as well, to his or her ultimate benefit.

Finally, when a problem arises (and none of us is naive enough to believe that there will never be a problem), deal with it quickly and appropriately. If it is a question of policy or procedure, call the school; if it involves the classroom, call the teacher; if it regards a conflict with another child, call everybody. Problems with our children, both academic and personal, can be handled efficiently if caught early. If you have established the type of positive involvement of which we have been speaking tonight, then help is a phone call away. Once the problem is noted and recognized, then the home and school will begin to work together as partners, and it will be your child who will reap the benefit.

You know, my grandmother used to say, "When I die, I don't want any flowers at the wake." When we would ask her why, she would reply, "If they didn't care enough about me to send me flowers while I was alive, they can keep their flowers when I'm dead!"

Don't wait until the situation is "near death" before you seek out the school. Become a positive and active participant in your school *now*, today. Actively strive to build a positive relationship between yourself, the home, and we, the school, in order that there will be no "us" and "them," but just "us," the home and the school, working together for the sake of the most important person there is—your child.

If you develop a positive relationship with the school, your child will become aware of the importance of school, and it is a fact of human nature that we all work at that which we consider important, kids included. If *you* set the best possible example of caring about school, learning, homework, about what the teacher is doing, the class project, field trip, school play, the basketball team, that upcoming pep rally, about the thousand aspects of learning and socializing and personal growth that are a part of your child's total school picture—if you set an example in all of this for your child, I can all but guarantee that your child will follow.

The "Mamma/Daddy Game" I mentioned at the outset, that game of divide and conquer that children have played for ages, will cease to exist, because it will no longer be possible for it to exist. With the positive relationship of home and school established; with the unity of friends working together for a common goal; with the knowledge that any problem is a common problem that will be solved mutually, the home and the school will have forged an unbeatable alliance engaged in the common effort towards your child's success in school.

That's an attainable goal; that's a struggle *everybody* can win. . . . Especially your child!

It's something to consider.

Special Data: *Time of speech: approximately twenty minutes. This speech is much longer than those you have read up to now, but the length of any speech must be geared to the purpose and situation of the speech itself. This speech is ideal for a PTA/PTO meeting, a "Back-To-School Night," an American Education Week activity* *and the like. Indeed, it was presented originally at a "Parent Information Night" function for the parents of incoming students. Of course, some of the procedures mentioned in the speech may differ in your setup, but these can be adapted easily. We think that you will agree that the basic philosophy of the speech is very sound and, if inculcated by parents, would prove a blessing for any school. Since addressing parents is an essential part of the administrator's responsibilities, we think you will find this speech useful. Parental response to it can be most positive and gratifying.*

$$\boxed{56}$$

TOPIC: Helping With Homework.

AUDIENCE: **Written originally for parents. With adaptation, it might be delivered to groups of students.**

How many folks here tonight can ride a bicycle? Let's see your hands. That many? I'm going to add my hand to that as well. Thank you, please put your hands down.

How did you learn to ride that bicycle? You don't have to answer, because I'll tell you—somebody taught you how to do it. Perhaps it was your older brother or sister; perhaps it was Mom or Dad; perhaps it was a friend—somebody showed you how, and that's not all.

You didn't learn just by being shown. You tried; you fell; you tried again; you fell again; you tried, and you got it! That first ride was precarious to say the least, filled with near falls and wavering wheels, but you got it! The next time you tried it was a little bit better. The time after that was better still. Within a week, you were zipping down the block, controlling that bike as if it were an extension of your body, and marvelling at the fact that there might be people in the world who didn't know how to ride.

What I've just described is an educational process, exactly like what every student in this school should go through each day. In class, the student is taught a concept, just as you were shown how to ride the bike. That concept is reinforced in class, but for it to be retained, to become a functional part of the student's learning, it needs to be practiced.

That's where homework comes in. Reinforcement of learning is one of the biggest reasons why homework is given, and if that homework is not done, or if it is slighted or half-done, then it certainly isn't the teacher that suffers, it's the student; for that concept goes unlearned, quickly slipping from the short-term memory. Since our learning is basically sequential (that is, tomorrow's work is based on the knowledge that got learned today), I think you can see how unfinished or unattempted homework could fairly quickly lead to serious academic problems for the student.

Teachers give homework for a variety of other reasons as well. The experience of having and doing homework provides a discipline that, if taken seriously by the home and the student, helps to prepare the child for study on his or her own—a very useful tool in life as well as in school. Moreover, homework can supplement the activities of the class, helping a student to learn more about topics that were perhaps only touched on lightly due to lack of time. Homework can also be used to ensure that what is being taught by the teacher is, indeed, what is being learned by the student. Whatever the reason, homework is given regularly by all teachers. In this school, we do not give homework for the sake of giving homework, but it is given as an integral and essential part of the learning process.

One of the questions that parents ask of the school most frequently relates to the homework process. They want to know, "What can I do to help my child with homework?" That is an extremely legitimate question, and one in which I always take delight, because it shows me a parent who is not only interested in his or her child's education, but one who is deeply involved in the process as well.

There is a great deal that every parent can do concerning their child and homework. The absolute first rule is this: Help your child with the homework; don't *do* the homework. Your task is to help your son or daughter do the homework. If they get stuck on a certain problem, give them hints on how to solve it; point out the section of the book that contains the answer; lead them to the page in the dictionary or the volume of the encyclopedia—then, allow them to find the answer. If the answer comes out wrong, tell them so and even show them where they went wrong, but don't give them the right answer. Remember, you are not going to school, they are; you don't have to learn this material, they do; if you give them the answers, you are getting the benefit of the work,

they aren't—and, they aren't learning either. So, that's the first rule—
help your children to do their homework, but *DON'T DO IT FOR
THEM!*

This next step in helping with homework is not going to be popular,
but, believe me, I have seen it work time and time again.

Take a large sledgehammer and pound your TV set into dust! All
right, all right, perhaps I am a bit extreme, but I think you get the idea.
You don't have to destroy your TV set, but learn to *TURN IT OFF!*
Keep TV viewing limited to *after* all homework and schoolwork is finished. Homework cannot be done with the TV on, and sending a child to
do homework in his room where he has his personal TV is like sending a
rabbit to guard the carrots! Indeed, many families have instituted a
"quiet hour" where, for one hour a night, there is to be *no* radio, *no* stereo, *no* television, and *no telephone.*

If you try to institute that last suggestion, you will meet with almost armed resistance from your children. If you carry through with it,
you will have a week or two of long faces and sour looks. If you keep it
up, you will produce a family that is closer, containing people who have
rediscovered the joy of reading, and children whose completed homework is contributing to better grades.

Try it; you just might like it.

In helping with homework, you should also provide a good work
area for your child. What does that mean? Well, it means a place where
there is plenty of good light, a flat surface to work on, the right tools
such as pens, pencils, paper, perhaps a dictionary or other reference
source, and most importantly, *no distractions.*

Remember, sending your child to his room to do his homework is
fine, if it gets done and gets done well. However, when a child's room
contains a TV, TV games, a stereo, and records and (most devastating
of all) a telephone, it is an open invitation to put the homework on the
back burner and take care of important things like shooting down invad-
ers from outer space on the TV set. The moment—the *moment*—the
word comes to you that homework is not being done under circumstances such as these, take your child out of his room and have him do
his homework on the kitchen table while *you* can observe. Actually,
peace and quiet is more important than all the references, typewriters,
or computers you might otherwise supply. Give your child a good place
to work in an environment that is free of distractions, and you have
given him a step up on learning.

It is also important that you establish "homework time" for your child. This is a regularly scheduled time each day for homework to be done and *only* for homework to be done. Of course, this time will suit the schedule in your home. There may be circumstances from time to time where that particular period will have to be changed or even dispensed with for a day. However, for the majority of the time for the day-to-day operations of the home, this time should be held sacred.

Children desperately seek structure. Oh, they may react against it, but for every child the structure of routine is both comforting and reassuring. Establish that "homework time" and stick to it, and soon your child will fall into the "routine" of doing homework in the same time and same place each day. When homework becomes a habit, success in school follows.

Finally, I'd like to tell you about a boy I had when I was a teacher. This young man often handed in sloppy, partially done homework or none at all. His grades suffered for it, and try as we might, none of his teachers could get him to do the work steadily, consistently, or seriously.

Finally, we called in his parents for a conference, We explained the situation to his mother and father and awaited their response. The boy's father answered that he didn't know what to do; he had told his son to do his homework, but the kid just didn't do it. What was he to do?

Then the boy's father remarked, "You know, I was never much at doing homework when I was in school. Everybody told me I should do it, but I never saw much use for it. I got through school anyway, and I think I turned out all right. Are you sure this is really a problem?"

We asked him if he had ever told his son about his attitude regarding homework, and he replied that he often talked to his son about the days he was in school and how he used to act.

Now, I'm not going to press that point, because you don't have to be beaten over the head with a dead fish to see the point in that anecdote. Children have been described as little sponges, absorbing attitudes and actions from people around them, and this includes the people they love with whom they will spend the most time during their formative years—you. Watch your children, ladies and gentlemen, and see if you don't notice little bits of *you* coming out in *them.*

So, the final way in which a parent can help is by keeping a positive attitude about homework. If you talk about homework in a positive manner; if you take the time to check with the teacher when the homework practices are in doubt; if you ask regularly at conferences about your child's homework status; if you take the time to check your child's homework each and every day—if you convey to your child an attitude that homework is important and something that *you* value highly, then your child is sure to assume that same attitude, and doing homework will become as natural in your home as washing hands or brushing teeth.

Yes, your children need your help and support in doing homework; yes, you can help them with their homework and prove to be a vital part of their total education; yes, by caring enough to be strong, you can help to make their academic careers successful and productive.

By the way, you folks are here tonight, and your child is elsewhere. Does your child have his homework done? Do you know? When you get home, will you find out?

It's your child's future that is at stake.

He or she is worth the effort.

Special Data: *Time of speech: about twelve to fifteen minutes. Again, this was presented originally to a group of parents as part of a longer program on how parents can become involved in the education of their children. We can see how this might be adapted to give to a group of older students, stressing that if they wanted to do well, there are certain procedures with homework that have worked well and that they should be trying. Much of this speech is personal opinion gleaned over three decades in education, but we think you will find much here that makes universal statements relevant to students today. We've heard parents describe it as a "tough stand," but they are willing to try it, and it works, much to each student's benefit. You might want to call for questions and answers afterward, but we tend to think that the speech is strong enough as it is and leaves a good and powerful impression, with concepts that are easily remembered.*

57

TOPIC: **Who Will Take the Credit; Who Will Take the Blame.**

AUDIENCE: **Adults; community members; parents; citizens.**

I believe that it was the American patriot Benjamin Franklin who commented that the rightness or wrongness of a revolution was basically a matter of grammar. "Revolution" was right in the first person, as in *our revolution* and wrong in the third person, as in *their revolution.*

I believe that it was the World War II Russian General Marshall Zukhov who wrote that in war, the difference between a hero and a villain most often depends on which of the sides won the war.

Are these cynical statements tinged with sarcasm? Oh, yes, of course. I firmly believe that there are objective standards of right and wrong that easily identify the good from the evil and the hero from the villain.

Like most statements of this nature, however, there is enough in each of them to merit our thoughts. How often is the value of some person or some action determined by the point of view of the people who were involved? History comments on the greatness of President John F. Kennedy, for example, and there is no denying that greatness. Yet as a person with an excellent memory and one who, as a college student, lived through those days, I can tell you that there were many people who had a great deal of criticism for his administration and some who even wanted his impeachment for actions they considered to be wrong. At the time, a great deal depended on one's point of view.

I tend to think that this has a great bearing on the public's perception of American education today. Certainly, we are all aware that critics exist who freely give us a very bleak view of the state of education in the United States. Then, you have people like me, and I can tell you with unabashed purity of purpose that I am an advocate of, apologist for, and fanatic in the cause of American education.

That is not to say that I think that everything is part and parcel of the "best of all possible worlds." Of course we have weak spots; of course we can stand improvement; of course we must keep working constantly to improve our schools. However, I know and want you to understand that we work *not* to save a system that provides only detriment to its students, but that we work to make a good system even better.

Our schools, in general, and particularly our school, have done, are doing, and will continue to do the very best for the education of each child. The vast majority of the time we succeed at making positive changes; sometimes we fail; always, we keep trying.

Let me give you two examples.

John and Bill are not their real names, but they are real people, and I'd like to tell you about their school careers, since both have graduated from this system.

When John was in the third grade, he was having some trouble reading. He was referred to the Child Study Team who determined that John had a perceptual problem. He was given an educational prescription that was implemented in the school. In the seventh grade, a teacher noticed that John was straining to see the blackboard. This teacher saw to it that John's eyes were examined and that he got the glasses he needed. Another teacher stayed after school and came in early in the mornings to give John the extra help he needed when he experienced difficulty in math. In high school, John's talent for dramatics was discovered, and the extracurricular activities the school offered helped to develop that interest. The guidance people were able to suggest courses that would develop his ability. Later, the school was able to find an opportunity for John to compete for a scholarship. His teachers helped prepare him, and he is, today, in spite of the fact that he had a learning disability and in spite of the fact that in John's family money was so tight that he would have gone without had not the school stepped in; John is doing very well in college, majoring in dramatics.

Then there was Bill. In elementary school, an attempt was made to help Bill after the boy hit another child with a window pole. The parents refused to have the boy seen by the school psychologist. Bill's records indicate that he was suspended seven times for violence-related reasons during the ensuing elementary school years. During this time he squeaked by on Cs and Ds, and his parents got him a special tutor. In high school, he was suspended five times for fighting in his freshman year alone. There was a recommendation that he be retained, but it was not implemented due to parental pressure. His record of suspensions continued, as did his parents' steadfast refusal to recognize any problem. In his senior year, Bill quit school. At present, Bill is in the state correctional facility for atrocious assault.

Two boys, both of whom passed through our system; both of whom were faced with the same opportunities; both of whom had the same chances.

Who will take the credit for John; who will take the blame for Bill?

It would be easy to place the blame for Bill on his parents and the way in which they fought the help offered to him; it would be easy to take the credit for John and point out the fine things that the school system did for him. It would be easy, but that would be only half the story.

John succeeded not only because there were teachers who cared and staff members who went out of their way to see to it that he got the help he needed when he needed it, although that is true and plays a significant part in the story, but he also succeeded because he had parents who cared and who trusted the school enough to allow us to help; because he, personally, had a desire to learn and a hunger for education; because, working together, the school, the home, and the student were able to take advantage of the programs and courses and help that the system is geared to offer to our students.

Who will take the credit for John? We all will—the school who did its job, the home who cared above all else for his welfare, and John, himself, who provided the spark and fanned it into a flame.

Bill failed not only because his parents refused, for whatever reason, to recognize that their son needed specialized help ever since the first incidents in elementary school, although that attitude did play a significant role in the final outcome, but he also failed because we, in the school, were not prepared to push for what we knew was best for Bill, in spite of parental pressure to the contrary and threats of lawsuits; because, perhaps, we grew tired of fighting, and it was easier to contain the problem than to fight it; because Bill, himself, refused to see a future and wanted only what he wanted when he wanted it; because we—the home, the school, the student—failed to work together and were unable to get this boy the help he may have needed to allow him to become a normal and functioning member of our society.

Who will take the blame for Bill? We all will—the home who refused to see the problem and refused to allow the school to act, the school who was too tired or too reluctant to fight the system for Bill's ultimate good, and Bill, himself, who gloried in the temporary sense of power that violence provided him.

The school, the home, and the student have always been intricately intertwined with each other. Where one suffers, all suffer. Where all three work together, the result is success after success.

Therefore, when a child who has gone through our school system does well—and let me interrupt myself to say that "doing well" has very little to do with economic status, but rather means that the person has become a functioning and productive member of our society; someone you'd like as a neighbor—when that exstudent "does well," then let us *all* take pleasure in it, for we can *all* take credit for it—the home for doing its part; the school for doing what it is set up to do; and the student who must, inevitably, answer for his own action, whether productive or destructive; whether good or bad.

Just as certainly, however, when a child who has gone through our school system fails in life—and let me reiterate that this has nothing to do with money earned or status symbols acquired, but rather that the person's life and actions have placed a burden on our society so as to drain society's resources or even pose a threat to the fabric of society itself—when that exstudent "fails," let us take no pleasure in that, for we can *all* take the blame as well—the home for not providing the nurturing that it should have; the school for not taking a stand and for not pursuing the welfare of the "outcast" student and the student himself who must, inevitably, answer for his own actions, whether productive or destructive; whether good or bad.

Yet, there is nothing which is wasted in this world, unless we allow it to be wasted. With everything that happens, good or bad, we can learn from it; we can grow.

We can resolve that from the success stories, we can keep on learning what we are doing right and gain the resolve to keep on doing, keep on trying, and keep on caring.

From the failures, we can also learn—learn where we failed; learn where we should have stepped back; learn where we should have pressed forward; learn what can be done for the next student who wants only to pull him- or herself down instead of build him- or herself up. We can learn, and we can gain resolve that this failure shall not happen again; that whatever is within our power to do, we *will do* until every story is a success story, and every student, according to the best of his or her ability, is a vibrant and positive member of our society and our world.

Who will take the credit; who will take the blame?

We will.

And, from it, we shall learn. . . .

Special Data: *Time of speech: fourteen or fifteen minutes. This could be delivered effectively to parents or to the community at large. We are certain that you have noticed that there are several places where it could be expanded should it need to be lengthened. Lay audiences, so we have found, like to hear anecdotes about what happens in school. If you have similar stories to the ones used as illustration in this speech that better bespeak your district, please use them to personalize the speech as you see fit. The ending is powerful, and should be spoken strongly, with resolution in your voice.*

$$\boxed{58}$$

TOPIC: The Role of the Middle School in the Development of the Total Child.

AUDIENCE: Parents; community members; interested citizens.

I do not have to tell you that the children we service in the middle school are a unique, fascinating, and often frustrating group with which to work. The early adolescent, the "preadolescent" if you will, has very special characteristics and some highly specialized needs. One experienced parent once told me that it was easy to understand: When they got to be twelve years old, they went insane, stayed that way for five, six, or seven years, and then returned to sanity; at either end it was a pleasure, and in the middle of it, it was like taking your vacation in Dante's Inferno!

Well, I know that parent had his tongue planted firmly in his cheek, but like all good humor, there is a grain of truth rattling around in there somewhere. The wonderful, cute, cooperative elementary-school student who was such a pleasure and who did so well in his subjects is suddenly caught up in music that makes your head ache, TV games, sports, friends of his own sex, friends of (gasp!) the opposite sex, seeing how loudly he can burp, and talking on the telephone twenty-three hours and fifty-nine minutes per day. School work? He may tell you that he has none; did it in school; or that the teacher forgot to give his class any—this just before you receive notice that his last 123 homework assignments are missing, and he has this weekend to make them up.

At the same time, this child (could they have confused babies in the hospital?) who one minute will try to do a handstand on top of the dining room table, the next moment will make a highly intelligent comment on the world situation or tell you of a character in a book with such enthusiasm and concern that it flames to life for you. This child who, an hour ago, broke down in tears because "everybody hates" him in school, can pick up his little brother, wipe away the tears, and provide unlimited aid and comfort.

Oh, yes, these emerging adolescents are a very special group, and as such they have some very special needs as well.

This is where the middle school comes in. The middle school provides a balanced, tailor-made environment and learning program that helps to meet the preadolescent's needs, provide a superior education, and provide for individual differences within each child.

Often, this is easier said than done. There is quite a distance, for instance, between the highly structured halls of the elementary school and the student freedom of choice and action provided by our high schools. The ground for the transition is the middle school, and that innerdisciplined self-reliance is one of the goals we hope to accomplish. This is done not only in the classroom, although the classroom and how the child performs in it is extremely important, but in terms of positive guidance and counseling as well. The child is provided with a large range of extracurricular activities and is encouraged to participate. Situations are engineered to provide children with opportunities for social development and leadership activities that are appropriate for the age level.

We work toward the goal of having a school that will be sensitive to the needs of its students during this period of dynamic and often drastic change in their lives. Certainly, the middle school must and does furnish an academic program that provides these children with the knowledge and learning they will need in both high school and in life, but we also seek to facilitate the transition from elementary to high school in personal areas within the individual child; we seek every opportunity there may be to develop each child's personal potential.

To accomplish these goals, we have a staff that is committed to the principles and philosophy of the middle school and dedicated to giving that "hand up" to the emerging adolescent. This staff provides a strong academic program, to be sure, and one that provides for a maximum of flexibility and variety in order to accommodate all learning styles. As one teacher put it, "In the middle school, we do whatever it takes to get the child to learn." This might include the planning of interdisciplinary units, conferences in which all of the child's teachers meet with the student and possibly the student's parents as well, and, one of the hallmarks of the middle school, extremely close contact between the home and the school.

Indeed, in the middle school as few places else, we want to witness the development of the total child in order that each individual potential may be realized. It is this focus, this spirit that pervades the entire operation, and it is this philosophy that marks the essential difference between the middle school and other educational structures for the adolescent.

In the middle school, we are asking each student to change. We ask each student to think in terms of what he or she can accomplish. We try in a myriad of ways to show the student what can be done; what he or she is capable of doing; to put aside the child's view and take a longer and more realistic look at the entire educational process, including the role students play in their own education. We try to show them that teachers don't "give" them grades but record the grades the student creates for him-or herself. Within the middle school setup, it is not possible for the child to get lost in the system and keep home and school happily ignorant of each other while he or she spends three years in the building and does nothing. Whether it be homework, behavior in class, social interaction with other students, lack of studying, inattention in class or anything else that affects the child's academic progress, it will not continue for long, because it *will* be noticed; it *will* be addressed by all of the child's teachers as well as the guidance staff; and, if it involves the home, the home *will* be notified and *will* become involved. Yes, that is time-consuming; yes, it takes a great deal of energy; yes, it may be bothersome to you as parents; but, yes, it does work, and yes, it is the child who ultimately benefits from it.

As these children grow academically, every attempt is made to help them develop a positive self-image; the self-concept of persons who, with work and application, can succeed in the tasks before them. Again, if this needs to be accomplished by creative engineering of situations, that is precisely what we are set up to do.

To develop that self-concept, it is essential for the student to grow in self-discipline and social consciousness as well. In elementary school, these children were told when to do everything, from doing assignments during class to learning when it was time for their cookies and milk. In high school, they will be getting a great deal of material, but they will be expected to organize and produce on their own. The research paper is due on the day for which it was assigned—no questions; no excuses; it either is there or it isn't. To go from the one state to the other, to go from external discipline to self-discipline is a journey over many a bumpy road. It is not a change that is achieved overnight; it is not a change that is achieved easily in many cases. The middle school, however, with its ability to be flexible and pay particular attention to each individual child, is in a position to provide opportunities that will foster that development as well as teachers and counselors who are willing to provide the guidance the individual student needs, whatever that may be, in each *individual* case. We want each child to develop as much self-discipline as he or she is capable of attaining, and we do whatever we can to achieve that goal.

Moreover, this self-concept should include a degree of social consciousness as well. The child, the parents, and the home are the center of a child's world, but as he or she grows, that world expands, until the adult realizes that he or she is a member of a much larger society to which he or she may contribute and in which behavior plays a significant part. In the middle school, as the child begins to learn to rely upon him-or herself more and more, this sense of civic duty and social consciousness is also promoted, in order that the child may realize his or her potential as a functioning and contributing member of society in his city, state, nation, and world.

And one thing more. Beyond the academic, beyond the self-awareness, beyond the development of social skills and living skills, the middle school attempts to develop within the child an appreciation for learning and the view of learning as an on-going and life-long experience.

As adults, we are only too aware that our learning did not magically stop when someone handed us a piece of gilt-edged paper and we cleaned out our high school locker for the last time. For many of us, that was far from a conclusion; it was the start of a learning process in which we are still engaged; continually engaged. For many of us, that meant college and possibly graduate school; for some that meant job training; for some it was apprenticeship; for some it was the need to constantly keep up with changing trends and rapidly changing technology; for all of us, it meant going through the lessons that life in general has to offer, including tough realities. Whatever the case, we came to realize that they call high school graduation a "commencement exercise," because it is exactly that—a "commencement;" a start; a beginning of the learning that we will do throughout life.

That is why, during the middle school years, we try to develop in the child that lust for learning; the knowledge that there is always something to learn around the next corner; the ability to look on life as another learning experience that, due to what he or she has learned and is capable of doing, is to be met head-on with enthusiasm and joy.

If the middle school accomplishes that goal alone, we will have served our students very well indeed.

When a child enters the middle school, he is a child, fresh from elementary school; when he or she leaves the middle school, he or she is supposed to be ready to assume the position of a freshman in high school with all that that implies. To effect that transformation is not easy, given the very special needs and diverse characteristics of the emerging adolescent. The middle school, therefore, is arranged in such a manner that its flexibility and its sensitivity allows for a very wide variety of approaches to the academic, social, and personal growth and development of each individual child. Individuality is the watchword, as teachers and guidance people work closely with the individual child and the child's home in order to develop and foster within the changing child that self-discipline, self-worth, social consciousness, love of learning, ability to learn, social and life skills, and the self-reliance that will serve the student in his future years in high school as well as throughout his life.

There would be no point of disagreement whatsoever if I were to tell you that we, in the middle school, want your children to become creative, responsible, and productive members of society, ready and able to meet the challenges of an ever-changing world. That is a goal that we want to accomplish for our students, and that is a goal that every parent wishes to see accomplished. We are of one mind on that subject.

We believe that the philosophy of the middle school as it is implemented will be able to challenge your children, our students, to reach their potential in the most effective means possible. We have seen it happen time and again, and we know that we are up to the challenge, just as we know that we shall work with you as we travel that road together.

The middle school can play a most significant role in the development of the "total" child; an individual emerging gradually from childhood into adolescence and well on the way to adulthood with all the skills necessary for success.

Working together, it is a goal that we can accomplish.

Your children are well worth our effort.

Special Data: *Time of speech: twelve to fifteen minutes. This is a speech that might be given to the parents of incoming students at one of the "parent orientation" nights that are very popular, at least in our area of the country. If necessary, it could be made longer by giving some examples in the form of anecdotes about former students, the difficulties they faced, and how they overcame them (we would not mention failures to a group of new parents). Of course, you would not mention any names and make certain that the audience understood that the names were fictitious. One excel-*

lent way in which to explain something to a group of laypeople is to take the statement of philosophy and explain it line by line in clearly understood language. In that way, you will have covered all the points and the statement will serve as an outline for your speech.

Afterthoughts

The speeches in this section have been relatively long, because they are indicative of speeches that you might give as a main part of an evening's program. While it is always a good rule to keep a speech short and to the point, if you are the featured speaker for an audience of parents, and your entire speech lasts less than three minutes, the audience is going to feel "cheated." What's even worse, it may feel that you don't care about your subject.

And, if you *really* want to alienate these parents to the point where you will be assured that you will meet with nothing but resistance, then here's the secret—talk down to them. Nothing upsets a lay audience more than the feeling that it is being patronized. Look upon your audience as unworthy subjects for a lecture, and you are inviting destruction.

On the other hand, if you see your audience of lay people as social peers with whom you would like to share the good things you are doing or the special knowledge you've gleaned in order that you may work together for a common goal, then your audience—*any* audience—*will* respond. Go about your speech as if you were sharing some news with your best friend, and the audience will return your warmth and feeling.

Believe us, it works.

NEW SPEECHES
FOR EDUCATORS

For an educator to speak to a group of fellow educators *always* involves a challenge. When you are addressing the lay audience, such as a group of parents, you have the advantage that although they may disagree here and there with what you have to say, they are not involved in your day to day work, are really not familiar with the "inside" of the educational scene, and your very position gives you some measure of authority in what you tell them. Fellow educators, on the other hand, are probably knowledgeable on the subject you will speak about, and it has been our experience that many of them hold extremely strong, sometimes diametrically opposing, viewpoints from what you present in your speech.

By no means let this frighten you. If you present an honest, straightforward, lay-it-on-the-line speech, and while so doing, treat the audience as your peer group, then the absolutely worst that can happen is that someone can disagree with your position on something while still respecting you as the speaker. That's not bad.

Again, it has been our experience that most of the "speeches for educators" that you will give will be before teachers. This is so due to the nature of the school administrator's position which requires you to explain Board of Education policy, conduct faculty meetings, explain and elaborate on the curriculum, etc. All involve your speaking to teachers.

But, whether your audience is composed of teachers, fellow administrators, or members of central administration, you will succeed if you can give heartfelt and genuine compliments where they are appropriate, treat your audience as you would wish to be treated were *you* listening to them, and give its members credit for intelligence and perception.

Above all, if you care for your audience, it will care for you. That's true of every audience, including your audience of fellow educators.

$$\boxed{59}$$

TOPIC: The Secret of Teaching That May Not Be Spoken.

AUDIENCE: Educators: almost entirely teachers.

Ladies and Gentlemen, good afternoon.

The man stood at the Heavenly Gates,
His face was lined with care;
He stepped up to the "Man of Fate"
And sought admission there.
"What have you done," St. Peter said,
"that you should enter here?"
"I've been a teacher, Sir," he said,
"For many and many a year ... "
The Pearly Gates swung open wide;
St. Peter rang a bell;
He said, "Come on into Heaven, son;
You've served your time in Hell!"

This afternoon, I'm going to tell you the secret of good teaching, but most of you will not believe me. Most of you will think, "My, he has a way with words, but what he said ... Well, he's being cute; he's being clever. ... "

Nevertheless, I shall tell you, even though you already know it. It is the one—and, from what I can see—the only teaching secret that has applied to every good teacher I have known in my three decades in this profession. Indeed, it is the hallmark of the good teacher, as clear as the evening star, and yet it remains the teaching secret that may not be spoken; that is never voiced among those who know it and live it. That is why I will not be believed; that is why you will think of it as nothing more than "cute."

Over my years, I have known many people whom I have mentally labeled as "good" teachers. These are people with whom I have lived and worked with passion and with pride. Many of them are in this auditorium; some are in other schools, other towns, other states. Some are taking well-deserved rests: and, some are no longer active.

They are male and female. They represent almost every nationality. They are brown and black and yellow and white. They are ardent churchgoers, Christians and Jews; they haven't seen the inside of a church or synagogue in years. They are Democrats and Republicans; conservatives and liberals. They teach in tailored suits and dresses; they teach in sweaters and jeans. They are happily married; they are divorced. They are teetotallers; they like to take a drink. In short, they share not *one* single attribute except this—that they have been and are "good" teachers.

Yet, if there is something within me that has allowed me to call them by that term, then surely there must have been a common thread; something that I recognized in each of these varied and multifaceted individuals.

If you would seek to appreciate something, first know its opposite. We appreciate health only when we are ill. It has been said that life is dearest when we face the danger of death. What is good teaching? Bear with me while we look at what it is not.

I give you Mr. Smith. His class consists of his writing on the board the page numbers the kids are to read that day and the questions at the end of the chapter that they are to answer in writing. While this is being done, Mr. Smith reads the newspaper. Perhaps he perceives that several students are not working. Some are daydreaming; some are throwing spitballs. Well, he thinks, at least they are not bothering him; why say anything and start a commotion? Maybe he can finish this article by the end of the class?

The bell rings, and the students file out, many of them leaving papers on his desk. When the last student has gone, Mr. Smith dumps the papers in the basket. He takes out his mark book and puts a check by everybody's name. It doesn't matter. Come report card time, he'll give everyone a B or B +. That way, nobody ever complains.

There is that kid in the first row—Mr. Smith can't recall his name. In the teacher's lounge, somebody said that he had an IQ of 135 but refuses to work. Well, thinks Mr. Smith, that's his problem, not mine. What could I do anyhow?

As she left the room right now, one of the girls was crying. Well, kid, thinks Smith, I guess that's life.

There's a class coming in. One of the kids is back after being out for her father's funeral. Maybe he should say something? No, as long as she doesn't start crying and disturb me, thinks Smith, it'll be all right.

The class is directed to the assignment on the board, and some begin to work. Mr. Smith returns to his newspaper. With any luck, he'll be able to finish the sports page by the end of the period. If not . . . well, there's always next period. One is very much like the other, just as one day is very much like all the days that have gone before and all those that are yet to come.

There is a loud noise from the back of the room. The article he is reading must be particularly fascinating, because Mr. Smith doesn't even look up.

There is a word for Mr. Smith. Actually, there are several words that we all feel like using right now, because Mr. Smith is an insult to all present here today, so I'll just leave the more vituperative words to you!

Emotion aside, the word for Mr. Smith is this—indifferent. He simply does not care. He has no special problems, because he does not choose to recognize them. He has no involvement with his class, so what they do or do not do means nothing to him. He will never complain, nor will he get angry when supplies don't arrive or the book order is delayed, because to Mr. Smith, firmly and safely encased in his tower of indifference, it simply *does not matter*. When you don't care, there is absolutely no reason to get upset.

And there it was—my first clue to the hidden secret of good teaching, for, unlike Mr. Smith, *all* good teachers that I have known have complained like mad. They have gotten angry and upset when orders didn't materialize, when kids refused to learn, when they thought that administration was overlooking a problem, when a stronger child picked on a weaker one, when a child was hurting and it seemed that no one noticed but them. Yes, they have raved and complained, and then they have done something about it. They have formalized plans and spent midnight hours fretting over ways of getting to the kid that won't learn, turning the bully away from a path disastrous potentially to himself and others. They have bearded the lion in his den and sometimes in the hallway or the parking lot to make certain that they had the materials or cooperation they needed in order to ensure the best possible learning for every child in their class. Indeed, when it seemed that no way was possible, they found a way.

And, through it all, they lied through their teeth to their colleagues and their families and their friends. They have said, "I can't bother with that kid; it would take dynamite to get anything into his skull." Then, they have spent hours and hours both in and out of the classroom giving that kid extra help, explaining over and over until a fire kindled someplace behind the child's eyes. They have said, "He's a bully; somebody should take a good, heavy strap to him." And then, they have worked with that child with gentleness and understanding, searching out the underlying fear and replacing it, bit by painful bit, with the security of moral values, even if it has taken months and months of daily frustration. They have said, "So, the books didn't arrive. So what? They can't hold me responsible if the kids don't learn." And then, they have stayed late and missed lunches in order to run off dittos they have typed with the needed materials. They have gone and gotten the books and transported and lifted and stacked them in order that their classes might get the knowledge they needed.

In short, what they have *said* was that they didn't care, but what they have *done* has belied their words. Indeed, what they have done and continue to do shows that these "good teachers" care very, very much.

And, there it is—the unspoken secret of every good teacher I have ever known.

Long ago, a professor of philosophy asked my college class, "What is the opposite of love?" Twenty voices raised as one answered, "Hate!"

"Think about it," said our professor. "In both love and hate you care vehemently about the object of your passion, albeit in different ways. No, the only time you stop loving is when you cease to care about the object. The opposite of love is not hate—it is indifference!"

If that is true—if the opposite of love is indifference—then the opposite of indifference is love. The opposite of Mr. Smith, the indifferent teacher who does not care—the "bad" teacher—is the good teacher, the teacher who *does* care, and, yes, the teacher who loves.

And now it all makes sense. Of course good teachers rant and rave and complain, for are we not the most upset about that which affects those we love?

Of course good teachers lie—making clever and even sarcastic remarks which they belie in the very next moment by their deeds. If I were to ask you why you love your husband or your wife, it is very likely that I would get an answer such as, "Well, she's better than nothing on a cold night," or "Look, I had to have somebody to take out the garbage." These are wisecrack answers, stored on the tip of the tongue, because the real answer is far too personal to be shared, even with a colleague or a friend. It is a feeling too internal, too real, too firmly entwined with the soul to be spoken aloud. It is looked at in the glow of the chambers of the heart; not the fluorescent glare of the teacher's lounge.

And, finally, of course good teachers get recalcitrant kids to learn and get them to change their lives against all odds and all difficulties. Of course they do. Has not the Old Testament, the New Testament, Ovid, Virgil, Shakespeare, and every poet who has ever looked into the human heart told us over and over that with love, all things are possible; that whatever the problem, love will find a way.

All good teachers I have known have felt this way, whether they have chosen to acknowledge it to themselves or not. They get angry. They care. They find a way, and they do. And although it is too personal—so personal that it may not be spoken—they love.

I have heard one teacher advise another to stay home if she was not feeling well, because, "The class will survive without you." Then, I have seen that same teacher come in despite personal physical pain, because she had promised her class that they would do something special. I have seen a teacher worry about her own home situation but refuse to take the day off because her class was taking a test the next day, and they needed her review. I have seen a teacher spend her own money to purchase medical supplies for a student who was in need. I have seen teachers buy books for kids, supply them with equipment the kid could not afford for sports, and I have seen teachers sacrifice their time, their comfort, their peace of mind, and their very physical health for the good of the children they taught. Children who would, in all likelihood, never realize what was being done for them.

Do not look for these people in a registry of saints, for they would be the first to tell you that they are not. Rather, turn your heads and look about you, for every example I have just mentioned I observed personally in people who are now sitting in this room.

For three decades, I have seen in people like you the secret of good teaching that may not be spoken. I know what you say when we commiserate together, and I know what you *do* in your classes. I know what you give, and I know what you feel.

Some of us would call it dedication; some would call it doing the job; but . . . we wouldn't want to call it love.

Would we?

Special Data: *Time of speech: about sixteen minutes. This is a rather dramatic speech, delivered to a group of teachers originally during an in-service on good teaching. After the poem, there was loud applause and a great deal of good-natured laughter. The speech itself was, we feel, very well received, and there were many positive comments on it, and no dissenters. We think that the speech proclaims a truth about good teachers everywhere, a truth that all educators* *can stand to be reminded of from time to time. If you are aware of some examples of caring behavior among the teachers you address with this speech, please add them and make it personal to your group. This speech had quite a positive effect upon the audience, as you will see if you decide to try it.*

$$\boxed{60}$$

TOPIC: Working with the Budget.

AUDIENCE: Board of Education members: Central Administration members; possibly parents and community members.

It is never easy talking about money. Whether it is college tuition for your child, bills that need to be paid at home, or the millions of dollars that a school budget represents, it is never easy to talk about it, and it is even less easy to live with it.

Given the condition of the economy, not to mention the wishes of already overburdened taxpayers, the first priority of any school budget must be to get the best results for our educational dollars spent. Toward that end, it is our task to try to make less get more, a seeming paradox on the surface, but a goal that must be accomplished if we are to balance the needs of our children with the expectations and desires of their parents, along with the realistic ability of our community to pay for it all.

In this process, we must all understand that above the figures on the page, we all want the same thing. Our goal is the same goal we have always had, to produce young people who are not only educated in a traditional sense, but who are ready to meet the challenges that today's ever-changing world will provide for them.

Indeed, how well we educate our children is an overriding concern as we go about dealing with the issues that budgetary controls have always dealt with, items such as extracurricular programs in our schools, class sizes, student-teacher ratios, enrichment programs, the boundaries of sending districts, and the like. The education of our children is of foremost concern, and must not suffer under any economic scalpel.

Trimming programs will be a painful process at best. No one wants to be the first to suggest a cut; no one wants to be the person who has to tell parents or teachers or, for that matter, the children of this community that funds will no longer be available for some program that has, for years, served them so well. Yet, in any budgetary crisis, there will be belt-tightening and bullet-biting, and it will have to start somewhere. It is only human nature that we agree that the budget must be tightened by doing away with the other fellow's program, but we must put aside that attitude and take a long and very responsible look at the entire process. Yes, there will be cuts, and we will have to make them.

These cuts, if they are to be effective, will mean that we will have to begin to work together in a team effort to deal with all budgetary woes. Every district employee will have to deliberate very carefully before any funds are spent. The question of absolute need will have to be addressed before funds can be allocated.

Make no mistake about it, we are in a difficult situation, and we will get out of it only by a united effort to overcome; a united effort to see this through; a united conviction that, working together, we can come up with solutions—solutions that will work.

It is the sincere hope of everyone on the budget committee that this will be a matter of arithmetic. We hope that sound and careful fiscal management will be added to responsible and circumspect trimming of existing programs and multiplied by a deep and abiding concern for the welfare and education of the children of this community in order to create a new, balanced, and positive budget with which we can all live and flourish.

We will need your help; we will need your commitment; we will need your understanding, but we have every hope that, working together, we will see our mutual goal fully attained.

Special Data: *Time of speech: five or six minutes. From the speech itself you can realize the circumstances under which it would be made. Budget woes seem to be a constant in the educational formula, and all this speech really says is that you must try hard to deal with these problems. This speech would most likely be given by the chairperson of a "budget reform committee." Again, sincerity is your key. You must sincerely believe what you are saying here, or your listeners will be quick to pick up any negative attitude and translate it into opposition. Believe what you say, and it will go well.*

$$\boxed{61}$$

TOPIC: Legality and Supervision.

AUDIENCE: Faculty and Administrative Staff.

We are educators. As such, we not only perform a job, but we offer a service. We serve not only as imparters of knowledge to the students we teach, but we serve as caretakers as well. Few individuals I know went into teaching because they cared about knowledge; rather, they went into education because they cared about kids.

Therefore, when a child is injured or hurt or, in the worst possible scenario, killed during his or her school years, all teachers are affected in some way. When something of this nature happens in school, during school time, during the normal operations of the school, then it is truly a tragedy, and one with which the entire educational body must deal.

Recently, a tragedy occurred in another school district far away from our school, but it affects us as surely as if it had happened right here. I am certain that you all know to what I am referring; a child was killed when a folding wall closed on him. This ten-year-old boy died as his classmates looked on.

Our hearts ache for him. We love children; we love our students. We wouldn't be in this profession if we didn't. As educators, we care deeply about the welfare of each and every one of our kids, because, in a very real sense, they are *our* kids. So it is that our hearts ache within us for this tragedy; our thoughts and prayers go out to the family of that child; we are all but overcome at the wasted potential of a human life, prevented before it had a chance to begin.

Undoubtedly, you have all read in the newspapers or heard on radio or TV the circumstances surrounding the incident. It is neither my right nor my intention to pass judgment here. Inevitably, that will be the task of a judge and jury who will judge the case on its individual merits. Nonetheless, we all know because it has been widely publicized, that the teacher set the folding wall in operation and left the area, leaving his class unattended and unsupervised. We know from experience (we need only look as far as our own gym or cafeteria) that these motorized folding doors and walls are controlled by a single switch with a built in fail-safe feature—the door or wall stops automatically the moment the switch is not held down physically. It is sometimes called a "deadman's"switch, because in order to operate it, you must continually exert downward pressure, and the moment that pressure is removed or stops, the operation stops. We know that the switch also faces the closing wall in order that anyone at the switch must face the closing edge and see any and all obstacles in its path. From uncontested reports, we now know that the teacher in charge had "gerryrigged" a device whereby downward pressure on the switch would be maintained without his physical presence. That is what had been done before he left this group of unsupervised ten-year-olds. One of those ten-year-olds ended up between the wall and the closing door, ending in the tragedy that has shocked us all so deeply.

Certainly, we all know of the legal requirements for supervision that are placed on educators by civil law as well as the board of education directive. It would be no bad thing, however, to look at these laws every once and a while, if only to refresh our minds about them.

The law requires that the school supervise the children who are under its authority. This means that each and every teacher is responsible for supervising his or her class or the children that may be placed under his or her care.

But, it should be made *very* clear that the courts have held that a teacher (and this includes school administrators) should have, *must* have, a higher degree of care than the average citizen.

In the courts, the test for negligence has been the question (and, you must understand that I do not phrase this in legal terms, but am trying to get across a point): Did the people involved exercise reasonable care such as might be expected that a normal, reasonable and responsible adult might exercise under similar circumstances? If the answer is *yes*, then there is no negligence; if the answer is *no*, then there is negligence, and negligence is actionable; that is, the negligent party may be assessed blame and very likely some punishment in the form of fines or monetary judgments. In some cases, the action may even be judged to be criminal negligence with the penalties stricter and more intensive proportionally.

Where teachers and children are involved, however, it is a slightly different story. As educators, the courts have held that we are expected to have a higher standard when it comes to our students than would that normal, reasonable, and responsible adult we spoke of a moment ago. Teachers, it is argued, are trained to work with children, have a better knowledge of children and their behavioral patterns than do the majority of people, and are by the very nature of their profession intimately involved with children's welfare. Consequently, if an average citizen were to enter our school building and observe one of our students running full-tilt down the hallway during change of classes, and were to turn away and say and do nothing, and that running child were to crash into an open locker and seriously injure himself, that "average citizen" is *not* guilty of negligence. After all, a child running is a "normal" sight; it didn't look as if the kid were hurting anyone; besides, it's not this citizen's job to take care of the hallways of the local school. What's more, that person could not be held either negligent or responsible for the boy injuring himself on an open locker.

Now, let's take the same situation and include a teacher.

I think, sometimes, that my index finger must be a lethal weapon. I walk down the corridors of this school, spot a kid running, point at him, and he stops dead in his tracks. In fact, I have been stopping kids from running in the hallways for more than double the time most of them have been alive.

You see, it is my job to anticipate the danger of running in the hall; I must realize what *could* happen with open locker doors and other students and classroom doors that might open quickly; I must try to see to it that the serious injury and the threatening situation never take place by stopping them *before* they happen. All this means that I must supervise wisely, with an eye to what might happen. In short, I am an educator; I know children, for they are my field of study; it is part of my duty to see to their well-being, whether they are grateful for it at the time or not. I see more than the average citizen, I know more about children's behavior than the average citizen, and I must exercise a higher degree of care in these situations than the so-called "average" citizen. I *am* responsible for a higher degree of care.

Therefore, in that situation we mentioned a while ago of the child running in the hall, if I do not stop him or make the attempt to stop him, and he or someone else is injured, then it just may be held that I am negligent.

I am well aware of your intelligence, ladies and gentlemen, and I won't belabor the point, for I am certain that you see the implications of all of this in our day-to-day operation of the school and in all your supervisory duties.

I will give just one example. Let us suppose that a teacher is in class and has to go to the bathroom. Sure, we can snicker at that, because it is so common a problem; I know it has happened to me, and I'm sure the necessity has crept up on several if not all of you as well.

In the outside world, there doesn't seem to be much problem here, for the person gets up from a desk and goes. In school, when you have a roomful of students, the answer is not so simple. Should you merely leave your class for the lavatory, you are leaving them unsupervised, and, should anything happen while you are out of that room and your students are unsupervised, you are the one who could face action from the legal recourse of the parents. Not only you, for I would face action as well, since the principal holds the responsibility for what happens in the building, and the Board of Education could be sued since they, in a sense, are responsible for my actions or lack of them.

This is why we place teachers on "hall duty" during each class period, for if the teacher in need of the lavatory gets the hall duty teacher to provide supervision while he or she is out of the room, then the situation is covered. This is rather difficult to do if the hall duty teacher is not present, which is why I have been adamant about hall duty people being on time for their assignments and staying through the final bell. You see, even if the teacher asks the teacher across the hall to watch the class while he or she is gone, the action is questionable, since a teacher shuttling back and forth between two classes may not be in a position to supply adequate supervision. This is also why I have told you before and reiterate now, that if the need arises, you need only call the office and tell us that you must leave the room, and someone will be there *immediately,* even if I have to take the steps two at a time myself.

If confession is good for the soul, I will confess to you that there were times, fortunately very few of them, when I left a class unsupervised for a few seconds. I thank God that nothing happened during that time, and I realize now what a horrible chance I was taking not only with my career, but with the welfare of my students, which always has and continues to be one of my chief concerns as an educator.

Therefore, I'd like you to do something for me. Over the next day, I'd like for you to make a private review of your classes and your duty assignments. I'm not going to quiz you about them; nobody is. But, I want us all to ask ourselves within the integrity of our own minds what we have been doing to provide that "higher standard" of care that is required of us. Let each of us ask if we have been taking the care we know we should. Am I there on time? Is my supervision active? Do I look beyond the situation to pursue the possibilities? I promise you that

I will be doing the exact same thing and asking myself the exact same questions.

What happened in that other school district was a tragedy. What makes it even worse is that it was a tragedy that might have been avoided. The death of that child affects us deeply. Whatever future action the courts and our legal system may take regarding negligence and culpability cannot bring back that child, erase the scars from the minds of the classmates who watched him perish, nor cool the anguish of his parents. All we can do is search our own hearts and offer our support and prayers as we may see fit.

It is within our power, however, to see to it that that child's death has not gone unnoticed. We can remember, and from that memory can come a new resolve. We can covenant and propose here today that we will take a fresh look at ourselves as educators; we can agree that we should, must, and can take upon ourselves the "higher standard of care" required of us by the law, the ethics of our profession, and our individual integrity.

We can and will resolve that a tragedy like that will *not* happen again while it is within our power to prevent it. We can resolve that each of us will look anew at his or her classroom duties and resolve to supervise to the best of our ability as professional educators. We can resolve that we will make every effort to establish that "higher standard" as a minimum requirement in our professional lives.

We will do it for our personal integrity; we will do it for the growth of our profession; we will do it for the reason we became teachers—we will do it for our kids.

We always have, and, God willing, we always will.

Special Data: *Time of speech: about fifteen to eighteen minutes. This speech was occasioned by a very real tragedy similar to the one described within it. Whenever something of that nature happens, there is a "buzz" about it throughout a school. This would be the sensible time to review the necessity of adequate supervision as well as just what constitutes adequate supervision. Make certain, in a speech of this type, that you manifest genuine concern for the tragedy and not, definitely not just the fact that legal suit will most likely be brought against the school district. Your approach should be that this was a tragedy, and what you are doing is assuring everyone that every attempt is going to be made to see to it that it* *doesn't happen to our kids. Believe us, if you have ever been in-volved in a death of one of your students, you do not forget it quickly, and it does shape your whole outlook from that point on-ward.*

$$\boxed{62}$$

TOPIC: **Where Does the School Go Wrong?**

AUDIENCE: **Educators, possibly School Board members.**

A teacher I know once taught in a very rural school district. He was driving down a country road one afternoon, when he saw a boy whom he had in class sitting on top of an overturned hay wagon looking rather miserable and forlorn. He stopped his car and went up to the sad-faced lad.

"Billy," he asked, "what happened?"

"The darned wagon overturned and dumped about a ton of hay on the road," answered Billy. "I unhitched the team, and I know they'll find their way home, but I reckon it's my responsibility to take care of this mess and clean it up. I've just been sitting here trying to think of the best way to handle the job to get it done."

"Billy," said the teacher, "I'm sorry for your trouble, but I'm very happy to see that you have such a positive attitude about this. I'll tell you, there aren't many children your age who would be willing to take on this kind of responsibility. You're to be congratulated."

"Thank you, Sir," said Billy, blushing slightly, "I figure I gotta do it."

"Well," said the teacher, "at least let me drive you over to your place, and we'll get your father. I know he'll give you a hand cleaning this up."

"That's just it," said Billy. "You see, my Dad was sitting *on top* of that hay when it turned over. He's been under there about forty-five minutes now, so I figure it really is my responsibility to dig him out!"

Now, as that anecdote illustrates, "responsibility" is a peculiar character. For most of us, it seems to be a quality freely given—to other people. It's his job to . . . it's her responsibility to . . . he was supposed to . . . she should have . . . and on and on it goes. Quite often, it is the stuff of TV situation comedies.

When we apply that same philosophy to the schools in our communities, however, it is anything but laughable. A couple of decades ago, there were a number of works published along the lines of "Why Johnny Can't Read." Throughout that time, I am sure we all heard and saw the reports that come along every so often about individuals who were suing this or that school because they were graduated from the system but were unable to read, write, or do simple math. All of these stories tended to "nudge" the general population into asking "Where has the school gone wrong?"

Well, let's begin by affirming a few facts. First of all, instances such as the graduated nonreader are exceptions, not rules. For every one student who goes through the school system and graduates unable to read his diploma, there are millions, yes *millions* who read, and read very well. I saw a bumper sticker once that proclaimed, "If you can read this . . . thank a teacher!"

Of course, perhaps it is natural that the normal, the median, and those that fill up the vast majority of students tend to go unnoticed, while the extremes, albeit on both sides of that infamous bell-shaped curve, tend to capture our imagination and our interest.

So, let us begin by understanding that what we are talking about is an extremely small percentage of the general population that have gone through our schools. Yet, as educators, we are aware that if even one child who has the ability to learn goes through our system without learning, then there is, indeed, something wrong; something we must address.

You see, I believe that we *do* have to take responsibility for seeing to it that every student learns to the best of his ability. I believe that our system works, but, like any system, needs constant overhaul and "maintenance" if it is to continue to operate efficiently.

We are engaged in this process already. We overhaul and revamp our curriculum as a matter of course. We seek out and encourage new methods of teaching and learning that will better reach our students. We realize that we live in a changing world, and our approaches and techniques of handling situations change with the times. Education is a living entity, and all living things change.

In a changing world, we try; sometimes we succeed; sometimes we fail; when we fail, we pick ourselves up and go back to try again. It is a long and tiring process, but it is one which we follow under all circumstances, because our children, the hope for our future, are involved.

These are places where the school is *right*. Let us never forget that. We have gone from one-room schoolhouses to multilevel buildings housing a thousand or more. We have gone from the time when a child in a wheelchair was kept at home and a mentally retarded child locked away somewhere to a day when our schools *must* accommodate the handicapped and programs for special education students *abound,* including their "mainstreaming" into the regular school day.

Of all of these achievements and more, we may be proud. Millions have benefitted from the reforms, improvements, and growth that American education has undergone.

Yet, let me reiterate, if only one child "slips through the cracks," if only one child refuses to learn, then it is one child too many.

We have all known children who have refused to learn. They have sat and occupied space in a classroom, but they have refused to work, refused to cooperate, refused to learn. They have challenged us, and, sad to say, they have won that battle—to their loss.

We are not talking about the child who *can't* learn, but about the child who *won't* learn.

Of course we realize that in the final analysis, we are all responsible for our own lives, and the recalcitrance of the child and/or a home that allows such a child to get away with that behavior must take a major share of the blame, but we, the school, are also involved with that child, because he or she is under our charge while attending our institutions.

Happily, programs such as those implemented in the middle school are beginning to address the personal and psychological growth needs of the child and emerging adolescent as well as that student's purely academic needs. With these child-centered approaches that revolve around the fact that each child is an individual highly visible to a group of teachers who truly care about his total growth, there will, hopefully, never be a case where an individual can get "passed along" without having mastered the skills necessary for growth. Moreover, because of the personal attention provided within such setups, the child who refuses to learn will be on the receiving end of some very specialized therapy and very close home contact, until, (if the student still refuses to cooperate), there will be no doubt in anyone's mind about where the fault lies; for the school will have done everything in its power to help the very person who fights it at every turn.

Finally, I'd like to read you something. This is a short essay that

I've had in my possession for over twenty years. I don't know who wrote it, and I don't know where it came from originally, but I do know that over the years, I have taken it out a number of times and read it through. I would like to share it with you. It's called, "I Taught Them All."

As a teacher, I have taught a thief, a schizophrenic, an evangelist, and a murderer.

The thief was a tall boy who spent a lot of time hiding in the shadows; he was a boy whom the other children avoided. The schizophrenic rarely spoke but gazed at me with tiny eyes filled with terror. The evangelist was class president and surely the most popular boy in school. The murderer sat in a back seat and stared out the window, occasionally letting out a shriek that would shiver the windowglass.

If the thief stands on tiptoe now, he can just make out the roof of the school through the bars of his prison cell. In the state mental hospital, the schizophrenic has to be restrained from beating his head on the floor. The evangelist sleeps in the church yard, victim of a rare disease contracted during his missionary work. The police no longer search for the murderer, since he was killed in a barroom brawl.

And all of them sat in my classroom and looked at me and listened as I taught.

I must have been a great help to them. After all, I taught them the difference between a noun and a verb, and how to diagram a compound sentence. . . .

Let us learn to deal with each child as an individual and to care about that individual in a personal and active manner. There is so much that we, in education, have done that is right and good. Let us rely on that but not rest on it. Let us take every opportunity to work toward a child-centered curriculum that takes each and every individual into account.

Let's start today. Certainly, we must be mindful of the question, "Where has the school gone wrong?" But we must also be quick to point out, "Here's where the school was right!" Moreover, each of us must add our voices and say, " . . . and just look at what we're going to be tomorrow!"

Special Data: *Time of speech: about twelve minutes. The brief essay at the end is an extremely powerful piece to use with educators. Unlike the theatre, where you " . . . always leave them laughing," in speeches such as the ones you will give before fellow educators,* *your motto should be to "... always leave them thinking!" As shown in this speech, a little humor at the beginning is always appropriate, especially when the point of the story fits in with what you are about to say, such as this speech did with its anecdote about responsibility. It would be a mistake, we feel, to continue with your speech, get very serious, and then, when they are really into deep thought, end it with some frivolous remark. Rather, if you can send your audience away from a serious speech with something that it can mull over, then that speech will be remembered for some time to come.*

63

TOPIC: The School and Civic Consciousness.

AUDIENCE: Educators; administrators; possibly civic leaders.

Everyone has a goal in life; something worthy for which they work and strive. Perhaps for you that goal is something like financial security, or seeing that your children get the best education they can get, or having a vacation home in the mountains. For a kid, it might mean being the person who can spit the farthest of any kid on the block. Whatever it may be for you, we all need some objective; some goal to give us direction and make our lives worthwhile.

The same is true of education. Every school that I know of issues a statement of philosophy followed by a list, some longer than others, of goals that support its philosophy. If, for example, a school district's philosophy includes the fact that it wishes to prepare its students to take a part in a democratic society, then one of its goals had better be to provide experiences designed to develop attitudes and beliefs necessary for their functioning as part of that democratic society. We need a goal in order to guide us; in order to give us the guidelines within which we can shape the curriculum.

There is nothing mysterious in this, nothing incomprehensible or mystical; nothing that has not been part and parcel of American education for most of the last century.

Yet we who are a part of education today realize that this is only part of the story. At one time in our history, the school may well have been somewhat myopic, shortsighted enough to look upon itself as a separate entity, if not divorced then at least separated from the very community in which it existed. Then, with a view such as this, the only thing the school concerned itself with was its own limited goals. They were to teach Reading, 'Riting, and 'Rithmetic, perhaps some approved history, and, if there were time, perhaps a student got to know where Canada and Mexico were located. If this happened, the school considered that it had done its job, and the school continued doing this job, oblivious to the needs of the community that fed it, which later received its graduates.

But that was long ago, and our world has undergone a number of changes during the intervening years, not all of which have been strictly material. Most certainly, new and better medicines have been developed, new materials and construction techniques allow for safer and better built homes, and new fabrics provide for clothing that our ancestors could not even have dreamed possible. But along with these material changes there have come several changes of the human spirit as well.

There was a time when comedians got belly laughs by telling racial or ethnic jokes; there was a time when some people were relegated to the back of a bus on the basis of their color; there was a time when handicapped people were locked away in bedrooms or even placed in mental institutions in order that the genteel, "normal" people would not be forced to associate with them. Fortunately, these horrors have faded and keep fading, because along with material changes have come changes of the spirit, changes in the essential consciousness of the nation as a whole.

And education has been, is, and will continue to be a part of our nation—a vital part. As the nation has changed in perspective and outlook, so has education. If it is true that our nation as a whole has developed a new consciousness, then so, too, has education.

Today, there is not an educational system that I know of which does not realize that it is a part of the whole; that the community in which it operates is its strength, just as it is, often, the strength of that community; that it could not survive without the support of the hundreds and thousands of people whose taxes and children contribute to it. This is the new *consciousness* of education, if you will; the civic consciousness that realizes that we draw from the community and, consequently, we owe a certain debt to the community that we must pay back.

Certainly, the school continues to educate the children of the community, but, because the needs of the community have changed, the curriculum of the school has changed to meet them. No longer is an education in the basics *only* considered sufficient for a future community member. Courses in computers and computer science abound, as do courses in government, home economics, current events, art, and music—those subjects that, in addition to the basic reading-writing-math formula, will be needed by the student when he leaves school to become a functioning member of the community from which he comes.

Certainly, the school exists within the community, but a civic consciousness demands that the school recognize the community in more than word only. Look at the number of recreational activities from school sports teams to adult intramurals that are sponsored by and even held at the school. Look at the programs for "latch key kids" and the innovative courses that train kids how to be alone after school, all in reaction to the needs of a number of working parents within the community. Look at the new and varied extracurricular activities that allow kids not only to express themselves but to learn to utilize their free time wisely and profitably, a most definite need in today's society. Look at these, and you will see the civic consciousness of the school at work in the community now—today.

Certainly, the school could not exist without the children from the community, and the civic consciousness of today demands that the worth and contributions of all people be recognized. Toward that end, not only does a new curriculum stress the contributions of Americans of all racial and ethnic backgrounds, but equality of opportunity is a part of every school's structure, with antidiscrimination policies established and enforced. For those who may have faced discrimination in other ways, new facilities must offer easy access to all people regardless of physical handicap. Even special education students are mainstreamed in order that every child may realize the special potential that is that child's alone. In terms of people, the civic consciousness of the school means untold opportunities for each and every member of the community.

We are, therefore, back where we started with the establishment of goals. Since the goals must support the philosophy, then if that philosophy inculcates a heightened civic consciousness, the goals of the school will reflect the needs and aspirations of the community it serves. This is a civic consciousness where not only does the school grow and prosper, but each and every member of the community flourishes as well. That's good for the school; that's good for the community; that's good for each and every one of us.

With this increased sense of civic consciousness, the school is perceived as caring about the community, and, consequently, the community cannot help but care about and sponsor its schools. That is a winning situation that cannot be altered by time or adversity.

Everyone wins, and we are all the better for it.

Special Data: *Time of speech: about ten to twelve minutes. This speech tells a great truth about education that anyone who has been involved in it for a few decades realizes very well. This is a good speech for addressing a group of fellow administrators or if there were some sort of gathering where leaders of the community were to be present as well; particularly if those community representatives were part of the local government. This speech could also be made rather patriotic in tone to suit any given holiday. You might want to alter the speech a bit when you get to the paragraphs beginning with the word "certainly." Exchange the name of your school or your school system for the phrase "the school."*

Afterthoughts

The speeches in this section were written for, delivered to, and aimed at educators. Consequently, they may often contain material that, while familiar to teachers and administrators, might be alien to those not involved in the day-to-day operation of the modern school system.

As we have stated before, the successful speaker is one who tailors his or her speeches for the audience expressly, rather than having one speech for all audiences.

Therefore, should you decide to adapt any of these speeches to present to an audience composed of parents or community members or anyone not familiar with the educational scene, then take particular care that all terms and references that might apply only to the teacher or administrator or to someone in daily contact with the school are either changed or explained.

In your speeches to fellow educators, however, these examples will serve you well. Remember that your audience is composed at your colleagues; treat these people with respect; approach them as friends.

You'll have no trouble at all.

ALL-NEW SPEECHES THAT INSPIRE

If you look at the prefix and root of the English word "inspire," you will find that it literally means "to breathe into." Actually, it means more than that, because there are connotations to the root word; a more specific and precise meaning would be "to breathe spirit into; to breathe life into."

We believe that our own experience confirms that meaning. How many people have gone into their chosen professions, achieved success, or taken on impossible odds and overcome them because they had that "spirit" breathed into them by someone. Indeed, many of the greatest people of this world have claimed that the chief reason for their success was the inspiration provided them by a mother or father, teacher, friend, clergyman, or some other valued person. Certainly, that is true for us, and we'd warrent that it's true for the vast majority of the people who read this book.

But, how does one "inspire?" What qualities are necessary if we are, indeed, to "breathe life into" others?

For us, the answer to this great secret came when a person whom we respected highly confided the following: *Become convinced, and you will become convincing.*

If you are truly convinced of the merit of something, then you will want others to share in it. You will be enthusiastic. You will be "fired up" with your enthusiasm, and that fire cannot help but warm those around you. It is therein that the true secret of inspiration lies.

It is sincerity that is key. If you believe in what you are saying, your audience cannot help but "catch" the faith from you. If you not only believe that what you have to say is important, but that it is going to be of great value to the audience, then that attitude cannot help but be conveyed as well. And if you possess these first two qualities, they will produce in you an enthusiasm that will spread like a cold in a kindergarten. Your speech will become the first domino that will tumble to touch another, to touch another, to touch another. . . .

In this section, we have presented a number of speeches, parts of speeches, poems, and the like, all of which are basically inspirational in nature. Naturally, you may use any of them in whatever way you see fit. If, however, you read one of them and become convinced of its merit and its message, and if you can convey that conviction when you present it, then you will be possessed of the enthusiasm needed to deliver a truly inspirational speech.

What's more, you will have become convinced, so you will have no choice but to *be* convincing.

Now, that's inspiration!

$$\boxed{64}$$

TOPIC: **Let's Do It!—A Poem**

AUDIENCE: **Suitable for any audience.**

Now, we have to take risks if we want to advance,
But we must pay the piper once we start to dance,
So we're really afraid that we don't dare to chance—
 We can't do it!

See, achievement is down while frustration is up;
Our detractors are screaming, "Enough is enough!"
Unfettered upheaval's about to erupt—
 We can't do it!

Yet, just look at those people right over there;
They're not screaming or shouting or tearing their hair,
But they're pulling success, so it seems, from thin air—
 Yes, they do it!

And, just what makes the difference; what do they do
That puts them ahead when we cannot break through?
Do they have some great secret reserved for the few—
 How to do it?

Well, it isn't a secret some genius conceived;
It's a quite simple fact that you take or you leave;
It is not that they're magic; they simply believe—
 They can do it!

See, it either gets used or it stays on the shelf;
Call it confidence, guts, or your own spirit's wealth,
But it falls into place once you say to yourself—
 "I can do it!"

Opportunity's there if we don't pass it by;
There's a chance we'll succeed and a chance that we'll die,
But we surely won't know if we don't ever try—
 To go to it!

So don't let people tell you success is too rare;
There's a world filled with wonder that's all yours to share,
Because when you believe, you are already there—
    You *can* do it!

Special Data: *Time of poem: about a minute and a half. Admittedly, this is a rather "all-purpose" poem. There's nothing to argue with in its content since it bespeaks a widely recognized truth. It may be used effectively with educators, parents, community members and even those students who are old enough to appreciate it. It makes a nice, inspirational addition to any speech where you are exhorting people to get out and do!*

$$\boxed{65}$$

TOPIC: Achieving Communication.

AUDIENCE: Primarily educators, but suitable for any audience.

One bright spring day, a man I know was working in his yard when he found that he really needed a hoe to finish up his gardening chores. He remembered that Tom, his neighbor, had purchased a hoe last spring, and he began to walk next door to ask to borrow it.

On his way to this neighbor's, he began to think.

"You know," he thought, "I borrowed Tom's shovel sometime last winter, and I never did return it. I'll just bet that Tom remembers that. In fact, he's probably really angry with me for not returning that shovel. I wouldn't be surprised if he's watching me from his window right now; just waiting for me to come over and ask to borrow that hoe, so he can tell me off about not returning the shovel."

All at once, he had arrived at his neighbor's door. Tom appeared after the first knock.

"Hi there," said neighbor Tom. "How are you this beautiful after-noon?"

"Oh, yeah!" snapped the potential borrower. "Well, if that's the way you feel about it, you just keep your blasted hoe! I wouldn't take it if you gave it to me!"

You know, there are times when I feel that that anecdote isn't merely a story, but something that's happening every day. I remember talking to a teacher who had complained about having "personality" difficulties with his department chairperson. The teacher complained that the department head did nothing but criticize the teacher's ability and efficiency virtually every chance he got.

I sat the distraught teacher down and asked precisely what the department chairperson had said.

"That's the worst part," complained the teacher, "he looks over my reports and my lesson plans, and he doesn't say anything—but I know what he's thinking!"

Let's learn from that incident. I'll tell you what, I'll be the first one to admit that I am definitely *not* a mindreader. In fact, folks, I lost my crystal ball years ago. I can't tell what's on your mind any more than you can tell what I'm thinking. This fact, however, places a responsibility on both of us—on you and on me.

Plainly put, in order for us to have communication, we must communicate with each other. If we sit and stare at each other across a table, the only thing that is accomplished at all is for both of us to end up with a massive headache and two cases of eyestrain.

Therefore, I would like to propose a really revolutionary idea. If there is something you really want me to know, tell me, and if there is something I would like you to know, I promise that I will tell you. Now, that "something" might be good, bad, positive, negative, gratifying, infuriating, happy, or sad. Once it is said, however; once it is out in the open, at least we will both know about it, and we can begin to deal with it honestly and with both our sets of resources. That, I believe, is progress; that's solving problems rather than allowing them to plague us or grow worse; that's giving both of us the knowledge whereby we can act together for what is right and good.

What's more, *that* is communication.

And, here's my promise to you: If we do communicate; if we allow each other to know our concerns honestly and openly; if we don't "keep things inside," but allow them to see the light of day—if this happens, I promise you that the vast majority of any problems that you and I may have will be well on their way to amicable solutions for both of us.

I don't want to keep my blasted hoe! I want to give it to you!

What do you want?

Special Data: *Time of speech: under five minutes. The speech itself is rather light and breezy, but communicates a very fundamental truth about communication itself. This speech could be used alone, or could be incorporated into a longer speech, especially one in which the primary goal was to elicit cooperation and good will, such as when you may have been appointed head of some committee and are meeting the members for the first time.*

66

TOPIC: Succeeding and Meeting Challenges—A Poem.

AUDIENCE: Suitable for all audiences.

There isn't any secret to
    Succeeding in this life;
The only thing you have to do
    Is overcome the strife.

It's easier to say it than
    To do it, that is true;
At times it seems our lives are lived
    In cages in a zoo.

We're all hemmed in; we cannot breathe;
    We live our lives somewhere
Precariously balanced on
    The edges of despair.

Yet, deep inside there lives a force
    That's nurtured by the soul;
That rips apart the walls of doubt
    And makes the shattered whole.

You know it's there; you've seen it turn
    The gray skies into blue,
So call it "Hope" or call it "Faith,"
    But know it's something true.

Just take it out and shine it up
   And let it be your guide,
And every day's a new day filled
   With wonder and surprise.

Believe you'll meet those challenges,
   Then watch them disappear
Like nightmares melting with the sun
   Into the morning's air.

Special Data: *Time of poem: slightly over one minute. This poem could be used for almost any audience from educators to parents to an assembly program for students. You can use this poem and others like it in your speech on almost any position, although it does make for an inspirational closing, we feel. You might also want to place this poem at the front or the end of any manual, or for some other communication for students and/or their parents. Poems have the added advantage that they can be memorized, and if someone really likes it, it will be repeated. Be sure to suit it to your specific needs.*

$$\boxed{67}$$

TOPIC: What Is a Winner?

AUDIENCE: Adults and students; parents; educators.

NOTE: Admittedly, this speech is intended for a sports-related event, such as a sport's night dinner. It can, however, be easily adapted for any group. See the Special Data section for suggestions.

Without a doubt, almost everyone here tonight has heard the old adage, "It doesn't matter whether you win or lose; it's how you play the game (that counts)."

I know that I have often heard that expression, and it has often set me to thinking, because my own experience, as well as the experience of many whom I know, seems to contradict its wisdom.

If you ask any athlete, any person who engages in competitive sports, anyone who has ever entered a competition of any kind, or anyone who plays bridge or checkers—that person will tell you that winning and losing *do* matter. As a matter of fact, they matter a great deal.

Winning is better, far better, than losing. It feels better to win emotionally. The rewards, either of money or prestige, go to the winner. The winner receives the accolades. It is *better* to win than lose.

However, "how you play the game" is also important. As a nation, America and Americans have always been on the side of the underdog. We like to root for the little guy; for the smaller opponent; for the team that's behind, and when that team comes from behind to win, there is general rejoicing. This is not a "win-at-any-price" situation, however, for we enjoy seeing the result of determination, skill and dedication, and we despise victories that are achieved through underhanded or illegal methods.

Therefore, perhaps that adage should be rewritten to state that, "Winning is better than losing, but it is very important how you play the game in either case."

Now, let us take this idea one step further. If it is good to win, then it is good to be a winner. If it is important that we play the game in a good and fair manner, then perhaps the way in which we play will help to determine whether we are winners or losers.

I speak here, of course, of the athletic field of competition, but this extends into other fields as well. There is victory on the basketball court, the football field, and the baseball diamond, of course, but we all know that there are winners and losers in life as well, and that is, perhaps, the biggest game of all.

What is a winner? Certainly, we've met them. They are not only those who have won contests of skill, endurance and determination on a field, whether singly or with a team, but also people in our community whom we know stand out from the rest of us. They are people to whom others go for advice, for counsel, for guidance; people who have achieved something worthwhile and inspire others to do the same. I think that it is safe to say that we have all met winners.

What are the traits that distinguish one person from another in this area? What makes one person a winner and another a loser? I honestly believe that the big difference lies in how the person thinks; the attitude that governs his or her actions, whether on the field of athletic competition or in the competition of life itself.

For example, how many times in life does something come up that is new; that we must face for the first time; that involves challenges never before met against odds never before encountered? This might mean starting a new job, facing a team with an unbeaten record, beginning a new business of your own. Whatever it is, the loser will see the work ahead and become convinced that the challenge is impossible. The loser will quit then and there. The winner will see it as a challenge. Certainly, the winner will have doubts, but he or she will refuse to quit until it is proven that he or she cannot do it. In short, a winner is always ready to tackle something new, while a loser is prone to believe that it simply cannot be done.

I really think that this is because a winner is challenged by a new problem, while a loser just doesn't want to face it. Both individuals see the problem, but the winner starts to think of ways to solve the problem even as he views it. The loser sees only the problem, large and looming, and it is so overwhelming that retreat is his or her only answer. A winner welcomes the opportunity to use his or her mind and his skills. Maybe he or she won't win, but will give it the best effort possible. The loser . . . well, he or she won't even try.

You see, a winner isn't afraid of competition. Of course, as in all competition, there is a chance of loss. The winner, however, is willing to take that chance. A winner will pit him- or herself against the others; will play fairly; will give it his or her all. If he or she wins, great! But, if he or she loses, there will be no excuses needed or given, for the individual will know that he or she has done the best possible job. Just as inevitably, the loser excuses him- or herself with the idea that the competition is just too stiff.

Of course winners make mistakes. But, a winner is wiling to admit to mistakes. When he or she doesn't win, a winner looks at the actions taken as objectively as possible, finding out where he or she went wrong or what transpired that prevented him or her from winning. The winner learns from these mistakes, and then does everything possible to correct that mistake so that it won't be a drawback next time. The winner does this freely and without reservation while the loser sits somewhere finding someone else to blame for his or her failure.

A key factor in all of this is the fact that a winner is decisive. Winners make commitments. They analyze a problem, decide on a course of action, and make a decision on which they act with a total commitment.

The loser frustrates himself, and usually everyone around him, with indecision. Maybe it won't work out . . . what if I fail . . . what will others think? Winners consciously decide to accept the challenge.

The greatest difference, however, between a winner and a loser lies not in the doing as much as in the approach. You see, I have never met a winner who wasn't positive; I have never met a loser who wasn't negative. A winner thinks positively, acts positively, and lives positively. A loser usually has a negative attitude and a negative approach to everything whether it be succeeding in life or buying a local newspaper.

You meet a person on the street, and you ask him how things are going. He responds that the world is lousy; people are rotten; each person is just out to get what he can for himself and to the devil with anyone else. No, he isn't doing too well, but that is only because his boss was jealous of him, and he just got fired. Some day he'll show them all and open his own store, but he thinks he'd better wait, because the other stores in town would probably gang up on him and force him out of business. Who have you met, a winner or a loser? I think you know the answer as well as I do.

You meet another person, and you ask her the same question. She tells you that she is really excited. Her job is filled with challenges, but she likes that, and each challenge renews her vigor and determination. Oh, yes, in a few months she'll be opening her own office. It's going to be touch and go for a while, she is certain, but she really believes that with hard work, she'll be able to make a go of it. She is looking forward to it. She has to go now, because she has a meeting with a group that is interested in trying to help the city's youth, and she's volunteered to help out. Is this a winner or a loser? I am certain that you know the answer here as well.

If you want to be a winner, you must assume the characteristics of a winner. You must be ready to try new things and new projects; you must face each new problem as a challenge to be overcome; you must welcome competition with a healthy respect rather than fear; if you make mistakes, you must admit them and use them as foundation stones on which to build success; you must be decisive, and your decisions must be backed by your personal commitment; and, finally, you must be positive at all times, especially when the going gets rough. You must think positively, act positively, and live positively.

Do you want to be a winner?

You do? Fine . . . then be one. Think like a winner and act like a winner, and sooner than you think, you *will be* a winner. *Being a winner is something that no one can ever take away from you,* whether on the grass of the playing field or throughout your entire life.

As with most things in life, the choice is up to you.

A winner or a loser—which will you be?

Special Data: *Time of speech: a little over ten minutes. This speech was written originally for a sport's night dinner. It does, we feel, apply the philosophy of winning to life aptly. It could be presented at motivational assemblies, student-parent get togethers, etc. If you wish to play down the sports theme, you could start with the ninth paragraph. You might also revise the speech by saying that you are a sports fan, that you have noticed certain characteristics about winners in sports, and that you would like to share them with your audience. Or, you can just present it as it is. Any way you choose, we feel that it will be effective for your audience.*

$$\boxed{68}$$

TOPIC: What Makes a Champion?

AUDIENCE: Good for students, and suitable for most audiences.

In my career as a teacher, I have taken charge of literally thousands of young people. They have sat in my class and completed the work I assigned, and we lived together and talked and laughed and sometimes cried over the ten months of the school year. All of them had dreams; all of them expected something out of life; all of them looked to the future in one way or another. However, not all of them, in my opinion, could fulfill their dreams; would get what they expected from life; would find the future the happy and successful place they envisioned. This would be for the kids whom I had come to see as the champions.

What makes a champion? What qualities set one student apart from the others; what proclaims a "champion"?

As I have observed over the years, there are three ingredients that I feel are necessary for an individual to become a true champion. I believe that these three elements are desire, character, and cohesiveness.

When these elements "meld" in an individual, I have little doubt but that a "champion" student can emerge to grow and develop into a "champion" adult.

Let's talk about desire first. I believe that every champion has to have the inner desire to be a winner. That student should look forward to learning new material and enjoy facing the challenges that are ahead. This champion student will set goals and objectives, and then work to reach them. The true champion will always know where he or she is going, and, specifically, how he or she is going to get there. Not that the champion is complacent in any way—rather, this person will make an effort to improve poor areas of performance and will constantly readjust goals for continued improvement. This is all part of desire; the student allows the mind to say "I can," and his or her heart responds with "I will!"

Equally important is character, and that is something I look for in every person I meet. Basically, character is the *real* you. It is what you are at the base of all your dealings and doings. I have never met a "champion" who did not possess an essentially good, positive character. That is extremely important.

Consider, if you will, that every person either is or will be a role model for someone else. Perhaps, for a student, it will be for a younger brother or sister; for an adult, a son or daughter; for all of us, friends and relatives—everyone is a role model for someone. Now consider that if the individual does something that contributes to society in a positive way; there will be people waiting to emulate and follow this example. On the other hand, if a role model does something contrary to the laws of society, there are people waiting to stumble into this pitfall as well. Therefore, the true champion has a good, positive character that allows him or her to be a positive role model for others. Character is like the foundation of a house; it is below the surface, but everything rests on it. A good foundation will stand up to all onslaughts, while a poor foundation will crumble under assault. Having good character is an essential element of the true champion.

Finally, I believe that the true champion must possess cohesiveness; a quality that pulls together the personality in order to pull together with others for a common goal. Certainly, we all hear stories of the "maverick," the "loner," and the "rebel" who go on to achieve greatness, but my experience has taught me that the true champion can work with others. Perhaps he or she leads today and follows tomorrow, but he or she *will* work together with like-minded individuals, whether that may be in a school, a business, or a community. The champion pulls together in order to pull forward.

Desire, character, cohesiveness—these are the ingredients that make a true champion. Do you have the desire to be a winner along with the willingness to work for it? Do you have the foundation of good character that will allow you to overcome the obstacles rather than crumble under the stress? Can you achieve the cohesiveness necessary to be an effective member of a team—one who will work for the group's victory rather than for individual glory?

These are questions that each of us must answer separately and alone. But, if your answer is yes; if you feel that you have within you these traits and characteristics, or even that you have the potential to develop them, then you stand the best chance of all of being a true champion; a person who is a winner now and will continue to be a winner throughout his or her entire life.

Be a champion!

Special Data: *Time of speech: about five minutes. This is the type of speech that might do well for older students who could understand it. It might also be used at the start of a project where many different people will have to work together for a common goal. It could also be used to express your views to parents, the board of education, etc. To lengthen this, you might want to add examples of people you know who embody these characteristics and have been true "champions."*

TOPIC: Education and American Society.

AUDIENCE: Adult audience; possibly community members.

I don't think that I'm making any startling or earth-shaking statement when I say that American society has come a long way from the time of the first colonists. Indeed, I sometimes like to fantasize about what would happen if we had some sort of time machine where we could bring one of those colonists into our day and age. After the initial shock of airplanes and automobiles and fast food restaurants and buildings rising into the clouds had worn off, and the time-traveling colonist had gotten a chance to study our society a bit deeper; had seen the social programs at work; had seen the benefits of modern science and medicine—after he had gone through all of that, what, I wonder, would he have to say?

Nuclear weaponry and Middle-East wars aside for the moment, might he not marvel at the advances that we, today, take for granted in our society? I wonder if he might not fall upon his knees and thank the Almighty for those marvels about which he had barely dared to dream? Might he not, also, ask how all of this came about in the scant 200-plus years since he had walked this virgin land?

I think we could do a good job of telling him. We could tell him of a nation that worked for its dreams. We could tell him of people who had visions of what might be and worked to make them a reality. We would tell him how one upon one, people and ideas coalesced, and through effort and hard work, we all found a place in this nation. We would tell him how we grew together into a people of competition and cooperation, speculation and security, humility and pride. In short, we would tell him the story of the education of America.

For there should be very little doubt in your mind that the history of American progress and growth and the history of American education are truly one and the same.

The role of education in the overall development of our society has been and, in truth, continues to be like the "bedrock" of a great city. Education is the foundation upon which the towers of American society have been built. And, do not be misled—it is a good foundation; a firm foundation; a foundation that has not crumbled nor shifted under the onslaught of years.

It has been, is, and will be American education that produces tomorrow's citizens for tomorrow's jobs, ideas for new and vibrant social change, advances in personal productivity, leadership on all levels, and the wherewithal to allow for culture and the arts to grow and flourish and enrich each and every one of us.

We would tell our transplanted colonist that education is truly the lifeblood of our society, not only in terms of producing educated citizens who will be able to cope with and meet the challenges of a changing world, but in being the spur, the breeding ground for ideas, that has prodded our society on to greater and greater achievements and advances; the catalytic agent that produces change, and from change, growth; and from growth, achievement; and from achievement, a measure of greatness for everyone who is part of our family, the family of the American society.

Do you know what? I think that our time-traveling colonist would smile and agree, and I am sure that he would try to speak for all the people of his era and their dreams and hopes for the future of their children, when he would look at us and say, "Well done. Well done, indeed!"

Special Data: *Time of speech: between three and four minutes. Though this is a short speech that would go over well in an educational setting, we wager that it might be equally well-received at a political function, a dinner for some community/school activity, or even at a patriotic function such as a Fourth of July picnic. The major device, that of the colonist being transported into our time, works well, we feel, in allowing the audience to gain a perspective of exactly how great a role education has played in the development of our society. Of course, practical examples could be added to lengthen the speech if desired.*

70

TOPIC: How to Come out a Winner in Education.

AUDIENCE: Adults; educators and fellow administrators.

Who likes to lose? I don't. You don't. It doesn't matter if it is a major confrontation with the board of education or a friendly game of tennis—the fact is that given a choice between winning and losing, people most naturally prefer to win.

Whether you know it or not, you, as an educator, are engaged in a competition, and whether you win or lose will depend largely on how you play the game.

Throughout this afternoon, we have shared with you the secrets we have learned over the years—secrets that may add to the teaching effectiveness for which we all strive. Perhaps some of them sounded simple. If so, that's because some of them are simple, if deceptively so. Yet we caution you not to disregard them because of that. A smile is a simple thing, to be sure, but neglect it during your speaking to students, parents, and the community, and those to whom you speak will start to grow uneasy, and they won't even know why they feel that way. That doesn't mean that you have to talk through clenched teeth and offer a model's smile, but a truly *genuine* smile every so often works wonders in interpersonal relations. Sound simple? Yes, but this is powerful beyond measure.

Therefore, we implore you *not* to disregard something we've shared with you because it's so simple that you feel it couldn't possibly matter. Try it first, and then judge the results. We bet you will find a use for it.

Now, some of the "secrets" we've shared with you might be classified as philosophical. Never disregard this type of approach. Suppose you came upon two bricklayers doing their job. You ask the first what he's doing, and he replies, "I'm putting one brick on top of another in order to get paid, because they won't give me money for doing nothing!" You ask the other bricklayer what he's doing, and he says, "I am participating in a great project. I am helping to build a great cathedral that will stand as a monument to God."

The difference is a matter of *philosophical approach.* Which man will do the better job do you suppose? If you were in charge of construction, which one would you hire?

Therefore, take to heart what we have shared with you. Expect to love your audience, whether it is a class or a group of parents at a PTA meeting, and expect that they will love you, and *it will happen.* We love people who love us. That is a fact of human nature, supported by all psychological evidence, and witnessed in your heart if you would care to look for it. Remember the poem we shared with you, and the line: ". . . when you believe, you are already there." Friend, it's true. Assume the proper philosophical approach, and you'll be successful every single time. We know that to be true from our own experience. If you believe that it will work for you, then it will!

This brings us to the final secret of good communication. We've instructed many people in the techniques of speaking before groups, whether it be for use in the lecture hall or in the school auditorium or parents' night, and, sad to say, this is the one secret they seem to find hardest to accept. Those that do accept it go on to become good speakers, admired and in demand. Those that don't, get mixed reviews. For what it's worth, here it is: *When you get up to speak, leave your pride behind you.* Perhaps these are only a few, short words, but they will allow you to come out a winner in your public speaking and in all verbal communication.

You see, if you do leave that false pride behind, then every audience to whom you speak will become *the most important audience in the world.* It won't matter if it's one of the classes that you see every day or the Commissioner of Education for the state. You will treat them the same, in that you will look upon your speaking to them as important; you will take time and effort to prepare the best possible speech of which you are capable; you will love these people and expect them to love you, and you will make every effort to get this through to them. Never will you "condescend" to talk to anyone. Every audience will deserve your best, and you will give your best to every audience.

The power in that is indescribable. The same way the audience faced by the negative speaker never realizes why it feels uncomfortable, so your audience will never truly know why it likes you, but it will. Word will get around about you. You'll be "in demand." Soon, every audience you face will glow with a warmth that you will return.

Now, we cannot, nor should we, want to force our philosophies on you, but to those of you who can appreciate this ultimate secret, we say welcome. There are no limits! You can become a powerful communicator.

In public speaking, teaching, and in life, we are, in the final analysis, what we make of ourselves. What we make of ourselves so often depends on the concept that we have of ourselves in relationship to the rest of the world. You see, losers make excuses and complain. Winners don't always win, but they are always winners.

Be a winner!

Special Data: *Time of speech: about six minutes. This was the conclusion to a lecture we gave on communication in teaching and in school public relations. We include it here as an example of an inspirational closing to a speech or activity. The content of it is the philosophy that has guided our speaking in the classroom and lecture hall. It does work, and we were truly "fired up" when we got to this point. As we mention time and again, it is that enthusiasm, coupled with the philosophy expressed in this closing, that has served us well and is, we feel, the essence of inspiration.*

$$\boxed{71}$$

TOPIC: Inspirational Opening Speech.

AUDIENCE: Suitable for all audiences.

Good evening, ladies and gentlemen.

Let's begin by remembering that success is a journey, not a destination. In reality, none of us can sit back and tell the world, "Yes, I have succeeded. I have met all challenges; I have won all battles; there are no more worlds for me to conquer!" Indeed, our lives are constant challenges. From the moment we set our feet upon the floor in the morning until we finally lay our heads to rest, life provides all of us with a parade of challenges, some requiring our attention here and now, and some that will test our resolve for days, weeks, or years to come.

We also know from experience that success requires more backbone than wishbone. I doubt there is one of us who has not wished for some "magic wand" that could make all our problems disappear, but we all realize that wishing alone will not make it so. To succeed; to accomplish our goals, we need to work at them day in and day out.

Sometimes, if we will admit to it, we all get discouraged, but most of us stick at it, and, armed with the right tools, we chip away at our problems until they change and lie in dust at our feet.

What are these tools that help us overcome our problems? You probably know them already, but it can be advantageous for all of us to take them out from time to time and look at them in the light of day.

One of our greatest tools is *determination,* often the determiner of both victory and defeat. The poets and great thinkers of all ages have reflected on the person who "keeps at it" after most would abandon their course. Works reflect the fact that the person who is determined to find a solution is, inevitably, the person who *does* find a solution. The determination to overcome is one of the surest factors in overcoming great odds.

And the other tool, perhaps the most important tool of all, is *knowledge.* It has been said that knowledge is power. If so, then the knowledge of the nature of the problem, solutions to the problem, and the matter of the proper approach to the problem we face is what comprises our power to meet the challenge and come out the victor.

Of course you may disagree with this appraisal of success, determination, and power, but you should know that you are also disagreeing with the Bible, Socrates, Aristotle, Shakespeare, Kipling, and a host of others who have looked into the human soul and sung about the experience.

In fact, that's the very reason that you are here tonight. You all have the determination to learn and to grow; to examine new topics; to share new ideas. From that sharing and learning and examining, comes a new appreciation of what faces us and a certainty, born of knowledge, that we have it within us to succeed if we only have the ability to use that knowledge and determination to keep at it until that goal to be accomplished becomes the goal obtained, and the next challenge looms on the horizon.

We are about to have the opportunity to learn. As tonight's program unfolds, we will all begin to see the challenges that face us. We will also see the innovative ways in which these challenges can be met; will be met; will be handled.

Determination and an exploration of the knowledge needed to succeed—you have a fascinating evening before you.

Let's begin.

Special Data: *Time of speech: between four and five minutes. This is a short speech, but it is meant as an introduction to an evening of speeches or some sort of lecture on a given topic. This is the type of opening that might be effective in a situation where the school were facing some sort of crisis (minor or major), such as a budget crunch, possible termination of programs, or the like. The program for a meeting about these problems would of course seek out solutions, so a beginning speech of this nature might be appropriate. Actually, any type of program where the audience is going to learn something would be suitable for this opening speech.*

$$\boxed{72}$$

TOPIC: Inspirational Closing Speech.

AUDIENCE: Suitable for any audience.

This has been a very special night. We have experienced much; we have shared much; we have learned much which we will carry with us beyond this hall.

We have learned, for instance, that there are no quick answers or pat solutions. Perhaps we have learned that "easy street" is often a road to disaster. We have learned to be circumspect about solutions that come with an ease that belie the problems.

We have learned that finding solutions is going to take some hard work on everyone's part. Nothing that is beneficial, stable, or worthwhile seems to come without hard work, does it? To our benefit, we have learned that the people here tonight, whether on this stage or in this audience, are no strangers to that hard work, and have no fear of it at all.

And, we have learned that not only is there a solution, but that it is a solution that is within our grasp. We have learned that, working together with the determination and knowledge born of experience, we can meet the challenges and make them our stepping stones to the place which we all know can exist, and, with our cooperation and our eyes always to the future, that will exist!

In short, if it comes easy, we will question it; if it comes hard, we will work for it; and when it comes, we will enjoy it, for it will, indeed, be ours.

Certainly, upon the start of any venture, it is a part of our culture to wish each other the best of "luck." But, luck is a variant of chance, and if we proceed on a basis of knowledge tied to determination and a willingness to put in the hard work necessary to accomplish the goals that have been outlined tonight, then there will be no "luck" about it. We will succeed not because of the vagaries of chance, but because we have prepared ourselves to meet the challenges.

"Luck" is what happens when preparation meets opportunity. This is true of a football team that has practiced and trained and goes out to play another team, and will be true of us as well, as we set about utilizing the knowledge we have gleaned and take advantage of every opportunity. Preparation plus opportunity, guided by knowledge and spurred on by determination, cannot help but create for all of us the result we all know is attainable and real.

We are about to end this evening. We are about to go our separate ways to our individual homes and sleep for a number of hours to rest our bodies and our minds. Yet we all realize that tomorrow there will come a dawn; tomorrow a new day will start.

Based on what we have shared tonight, we have every confidence that the new day will also be a new start, the beginning of our efforts to work together toward the solution of our common goals. We have every confidence that we are prepared; we are ready; we are willing; and we are able to meet whatever challenges arise.

Without "luck," but with determination, knowledge, and a spirit that will not acknowledge anything less than success, I bid you a *good night*—a very good night, indeed.

Special Data: *Time of speech: a little over four minutes. Again, this is a highly inspirational, even "rah! rah!" type of speech that is meant for the closing of a program where problems and their solutions, perhaps within your school or school system, have been assessed. It also bespeaks the fact that the audience will be working right along with you as you go about solving these problems. If this particular speech doesn't fit in with your circumstances exactly, you can either adapt the speech or use only those paragraphs or sections of it that suit your needs.*

$$\boxed{73}$$

TOPIC: Why Can't Everybody Win—A Poem.

AUDIENCE: Suitable for any audience.

So many people feeling "down";
Their faces hard and etched with frowns;
And feeling just like giving in—
    So, why can't everybody win?

You do your job; I do mine;
We work together, and we'll find
In half the time the work is done,
And what is more, the work's been fun!

We share ideas; let in the light
And find the dawn to end the night;
Just help someone, and in a while
You'll find you can't surpress a smile.

And if you're helped, then pay it back
By helping someone get "on track";
What a chain reaction there might be
Of selfless generosity.

Be quick to see in everyone
The persons that they can become;
Accept a task and set about
To bring the best that's in them out.

What will you have when you are done?
A landscape painted by the sun,
Where troubles end and dreams begin—
A place where *everybody* wins.

Special Data: *Time of poem: about one minute. This is a short poem, but it has a very good inspirational punch to it. We all realize that some people keep raising the rope until everyone is eliminated, while others drop the rope until everybody can take part. That's the message of this poem. You don't have to lower your standards in order to include everyone, but making a conscious effort to help others do effective work along with a willingness to work together, produces a highly efficient and a very productive establishment—a place where everybody wins. Not a bad goal for any school, is it?*

Afterthoughts

We could not leave this section without reiterating a truth that you have seen us express in many ways throughout this section. We do this because it is the one essential element that we have found in the inspirational process.

If *you* believe, your *audience* will believe; if you are enthused about what you are going to say, then your audience will be enthused; if you, personally, are inspired by the content or cause of what you are telling them, then it will be inspired as well. It really works that way.

Keep that goal before you; keep that gleam in your eye and that spark in your voice; keep believing what you are communicating to your audience, and when your audience leaves, they will leave inspired!

NEW SPEECHES
FOR RETIREMENTS
AND TESTIMONIALS

Let's face it friend, we are all growing older. Even as we read this paragraph, we are growing closer to that magic time that we will all face some day—retirement.

Wasn't it only yesterday that we faced our first class, young and nervous and trying desperately not to convey that nervousness to that class? Now here it is years later and all those people we've known and worked with for so many of those years are getting grayer, putting on weight, and talking about what they're going to do once the daily routine of school is no longer a part of their day-to-day existence.

Well, while all this, like it or not, is a part of life, so the retirement of colleagues is a part of the life of every educator. As a school administrator, you become a real part of these people's career lives, and it is only natural, that you would be invited to speak at those affairs that are held for educators who retire after a lifetime in education. Surely, your own experience confirms how many of these functions you have attended over the years.

Less frequent, but certainly as important, are those testimonial affairs that are held from time to time to honor various members of our profession, ranging from a dinner to honor an educator named "Teacher of the Year" to an "Appreciation Banquet" for a Superintendent of Schools.

Your position requires that you offer "a few words" at these affairs. Faced with that task, you will seek to deliver a speech that honors the subject and touches the audience. Since you undoubtedly will be one of a number of people speaking, you will want to keep your speech relatively short and to the point. You will want to be genuine in your praise and heartfelt in your good wishes.

In this section, we have included a number of speeches for retirements and testimonials for a wide range of possible subjects across the educational field, from school secretary to superintendent. In the testimonial section, we have also included two examples of "roasts" that seem to be very popular right now. It should be clear, however, that these are only for those occasions where the avowed purpose of the evening is to have fun.

Adapt these speeches to your subject. Mean what you say and say it from your heart, and you will have a retirement or testimonial speech that will be both appreciated and remembered.

74

TOPIC: **Retirement of a Friend and Colleague.**

AUDIENCE: **Family; friends; colleagues; dignitaries; guests.**

I suppose it is inevitable upon an occasion honoring the retirement of a man like John Martin that people will speak of the "Golden Years" that lie ahead of him. While I am certain that there is not a person here this evening who does not wish him an abundance of "gold" in the years to come, I would prefer, for a moment, to tell you of the golden years he will be leaving behind as a sparkling memorial when he leaves our schools. He has served us so well for so many years.

I have known John Martin for well over twenty of those years, from the day he first came to work here in our township. Over the years our relationship has grown beyond the strict confines of the day-to-day business of education, and I am proud to consider John a good friend as well as a colleague. Yes, I know this man well, and because I do, I am about to tell you some things this evening that John, himself, would most certainly never volunteer to tell you.

I will tell you, for instance, that he has been instrumental in shaping educational policies and curriculum within our school system that have led to tremendous successes in terms of students' achievement and learning and, consequently, the success of their future lives as well. John, you see, recognizes the potential in everyone he meets—whether this be administrator, teacher, or student—and he has always been willing and anxious to work with all people to bring out their full potentials. The number of people both from our school system as well as those former students who have had the good fortune to cross John's path and now stand as valued members of our community present here tonight, provide ample testimony to the care and concern he has manifested toward others consistently over the years.

And I will tell you his secret. John, very simply, loves everyone he meets, and everyone who meets John cannot help but realize that fact and return that love in kind. Ask anyone who knows him, and they will tell you just as simply, but with all the eloquence that the term is meant to imply, that John Martin is a good man.

Of course, I could tell you stories of his dedication to the ideals of education; of the times I have left well after everyone else has gone home only to see him still at his desk, thinking through some problem, working well after all others were safely home. I could tell you how he has fought tirelessly for the best possible education for the students of this township; I could tell you of the changes he inculcated to the benefit of student and educator alike; I could tell you of the contributions of time and personal energy he has made to both school and community projects. Yes, I could tell you all of this and more, but John would not be pleased. You see, I have come to know him very well over these years, and in that time I have come to realize that he is a person who gives in secret and whose joy lies not in the public recognition of the giving, but in the very joy of the giving itself.

John works for the work; gives for the giving; and, he lives for the joy of life.

Consequently, he now leaves behind those golden memories of golden years as an everlasting memory to his spirit—a spirit that will, hopefully, continue to inspire those of us he leaves behind; those who have been privileged to bask in his true warmth.

When John Martin leaves our school system, he will take with him his personal files, the photos and bric-a-brac from this desk, his infamous coffee mug, and an extremely large piece of our hearts as well.

For John Martin and his lovely and charming wife, Ann, we send our wishes and prayers for all the happiness possible in the coming years; the type of happiness that he has so generously given to us during the years he has served with us. If half of those wishes come true, then he will be happy beyond measure, and our own hearts will rejoice that we have had the privilege of knowing a man of honor, a man of integrity, a man of competence, and a man whose love has made our lives all the more richer and full for having shared some space with him on this earth.

Thank you, John, for the golden years. May happiness and love continue to light your path, dear friend, throughout all the golden years yet to come.

Special Data: *Time of speech: about five minutes. Certainly, this is a speech that would not be given for just anyone. Indeed, it is a special speech to be reserved for a very special retiree about whom you* *can say these words and really, really mean them. Sincerity is the key to any "personalized" speech. Say what you mean and mean what you say, and no one will ever be able to fault you for lack of sincerity. Save this type of speech for those rare individuals who have really made an impression in your life. When you do use it, adapt it as necessary to make it specific to each honoree.*

$$\boxed{75}$$

TOPIC: **Retirement of a Person Whose Position You Will Fill.**

AUDIENCE: **Family; friends; colleagues; community members.**

Somebody once said that the meaning of the sentiment of having "mixed emotions" was the feeling that you got when you saw your mother-in-law drive over a cliff . . . in your brand new Cadillac!

Well, I'm not so certain about that, and I'm positive that mothers-in-law have taken unwarranted heat for decades, but I most certainly know what "mixed emotions" means to me. To me, it means being here tonight at the retirement of Martha Stanley.

By that, I mean that inside of me this evening there is a small but furious war going on in which joy and expectation are in hand-to-hand combat with sadness and fear.

Above all, there is joy. There is joy for Martha that after these years of dedication and hard work that have distinguished her career, earning her the respect and admiration of all of us in the educational system, she will finally be getting the time for herself that she deserves. She has told me that she plans to do a great deal of travelling and looks forward to being able to spend some time with her grandchildren. I know she is happy about this and faces it with anticipation, and that thought fills me with joy for her. I know that it is all but a cliché to wish someone the happiness he or she deserves, but if Martha attains one-half of what we who know her believe she has earned over the years, her joy shall, indeed, be qualified.

Along with my joy for her this evening, I also find sorrow. Please don't mistake me; it is not sorrow for her, but sorrow for myself and the other members of our school system who are used to finding warmth in her sunny disposition each day; those of us who are used to coming to her with a problem and finding the knowledge, wit, and willingness of Martha to give of herself that helped us through many a day; those of us who have had ample reason to stand and marvel at her competence, her steadiness, and her we'll-get-it-done-together attitude that has saved many a day. For we who have known this, there is a very real void beginning to form in our professional lives, because she will no longer be there to help see us through.

Which brings us to the emotion of fear. As many of you know, the person chosen to fill Martha's position is . . . me. It is my understanding that Martha was instrumental in that appointment, and right now, I don't know whether to rush over and kiss her or to cry on her shoulder. Martha, knowing the kind person you are, I know that you have no idea of the size of the vacancy that you've asked me to try to fill. That's why fear is one of my mixed emotions this evening.

You see, Martha Stanley is truly a one-of-a-kind person. The contributions she has made to this school system along with the reputation she has so rightly achieved for brilliance, tact, and polish have elevated her in our eyes to a position that no twenty people could adequately fill, let alone one of us.

Yet, I would not have you think that this is a bleak picture, Martha, because I also hold only the finest of expectations for this new post. Why shouldn't I, Martha? After all, for many years now I have been privileged to have the finest teacher available to work with me, offer gentle guidance, encourage me when times got rough, to be there with praise when something good happened, and, of course, to tell me that I was being a "stubborn idiot" when, indeed, I was. With a teacher like that—with a teacher like you, Martha—there is no world that cannot be conquered, because, in fact, there is nothing that has ever conquered you.

So, with hope for the future, because in the past there was a rare and wonderful person such as yourself, and with the love in my own heart for you that is but a drop in the ocean of love we have seen poured out for you this evening, I wish you the happiest of retirements.

Martha Stanley, yours is a life filled with accomplishment. There is accomplishment in the business of education to be sure, but there is also accomplishment in the human terms of education that cannot be measured by charts and accounts and report cards. Yours is an accomplishment written on the heart and measured in the depth of the feeling that this audience and I pour out before you this evening.

Simply put, Martha, not only are you respected by us—but we love you.

May your path from this moment forward be a golden pavement—the same type of path you forged each and every day that it was our honor and privilege to know you.

Thank you, Martha.

Special Data: *Time of speech: a little over five minutes. Note that this speech establishes a strong bond of identification between the speaker and the retiree, tells the audience that the speaker cares as much as it does, and points out that filling her position does not imply "filling her shoes." The warmth and obvious respect shown here can only help the speaker when he or she assumes the new position within the school system. Of course, even if you are not going to fill the position, there are entire sections of this speech, particularly toward the end, that would make a fitting tribute to any retiree. Adapt it to your needs; that's what it's here for. Any way you see fit to use it, it can be a lovely tribute.*

$$\boxed{76}$$

TOPIC: Retirement of a School Secretary.

AUDIENCE: Family and friends; school staff; many educators.

Betty Sumpter, I have one question for you now that you are about to retire. The question is simple, and the question is this—How am I going to survive without you?

This is not a facetious question, ladies and gentlemen. For almost fifteen years, Betty Sumpter has served as our school secretary. Anyone who is involved with the school in any way recognizes that the school secretary plays a tremendously valuable role in the organization of the school building. Indeed, no school would run as effectively as it does without the services of that often unheralded, often underappreciated, always needed school secretary.

And Betty Sumpter has been the best of the best. Perhaps a casual observer might suggest that the secretary's job consists mainly of greeting visitors and answering the phone, but those of us who are deeply involved with the school realize just how much more there is to it.

Over the years, Betty has dealt courteously and courageously with the public, with students, and with school personnel. She has typed hundreds, perhaps thousands, of letters and reports. She has maintained the records of students and teachers; registered all new students; helped in the ordering of school supplies and school budget preparation; handled the increasing volume of school mail; and been responsible for the preparation of payroll information.

All of this she has done with quiet strength and efficiency. All of this she has done, and has done more besides. How many times have I seen her talking to distraught students and calming them in the process? How many times have I seen her handling minor first aid problems when the school nurse was unavailable? How many times have I seen her laugh and cry with teachers and staff and share the day-to-day life of the school? How many times have I seen her *be* the life of the school?

Perhaps most importantly for me, she has been an excellent listener, an invaluable contributor of practical advice, and a friend who was never hesitant about telling me when she thought something was amiss and who made decisions as the need arose that were always geared toward the smooth functioning of the school and the comfort and growth of everyone around her—the kids, the teachers . . . and me.

Now, she is about to retire, and of course we wish her a joyous and wonderful time filled only with the joy and laughter with which she has enriched our lives—but there is something else which we wish her to know.

We haven't told you enough over the years, but we are deeply grateful to you for all the diligent work you have put in for our benefit. Truly, you are one of the most valuable people in our school.

We know you well, Betty Sumpter; we respect you highly; and we love you deeply. Long after tonight, we will remember and be thankful that we had the opportunity to know and work with someone as wonderful as you.

May God bless you richly, Betty, and may your retirement be a time when you find abundant cause for joyous laughter each and every day.

Special Data: *Time of speech: between four or five minutes. Every one of us realizes how invaluable a good school secretary can be to the proper functioning of the modern school. Therefore, a person such as the woman described in this speech is, indeed, worthy of honor. If you wish to make this speech longer, you might want to include a personal anecdote, either a humorous or serious one would do, to show the relationship you have had over the years or how the secretary has contributed to the good of the school. Never choose an anecdote that puts the retiree in a bad light or makes him or her appear silly.*

$$\boxed{77}$$

TOPIC: **Retirement of a Coach/ Athletic Director.**

AUDIENCE: **Family; friends; sports figures; educators; community.**

I would like to set a rumor to rest this evening. Yes, Bill Howard and I go back a long time, but there is absolutely no truth to the story that Bill used to paint dinosaur eggs brown and use them for footballs.

Actually, I've known Bill for over twenty-five years, and in that span of years, you get to know a fellow pretty well. Tonight I am going to take a chance at ending that friendship by telling you some of Bill's secrets; some of the things he has never told anyone before. Bill wouldn't want me to be telling you some of these things but a retirement is a very special occasion, and I believe you have the right to know what kind of a man we are honoring tonight.

What kind of a man is Bill Howard? If a kid had the desire, Bill had the time for him. I've known Bill to stay hours after the rest of us went home to work with a player who had a problem. I've known him to give up his evening, his Sundays, and his vacation time to help a kid who needed help. He never told anyone about this.

What kind of a man is Bill Howard? I have known kids—too many to count—who had personal problems at home; who were flirting with drugs and danger; who were close to dropping out of school and life; who had real problems with parents, teachers, girlfriends, and life in general. I have seen these kids literally turned around in their lives by Bill's counseling. Never in public, but alone, where no one could see, Bill would talk, cajole, threaten, plead if he had to, but he would show them a better way to handle their difficulties; and he stood behind them every minute as they began to take positive charge of their lives. I know of kids who would have ended up in the worst possible condition and who are, today, responsible workers, parents, and citizens, all because Bill Howard took the time to care. Bill never told anybody about this.

What kind of a man is Bill Howard? I have seen Bill reach into his own pocket to see to it that no kid was left out or went hungry because of lack of money. Bill was rarely repaid in cash, and he never asked for it. When I asked him about that once, Bill told me that he got repaid in other ways. Perhaps you know what he meant. Again, this is something Bill never told anyone.

Certainly, we all know Bill's outstanding record as a coach, but what I've told you are those special actions that no one ever saw except Bill and the kid he was helping at the time. Bill never told anyone about the quiet good that he did. For Bill, it was enough that he had done it.

What kind of a man is Bill Howard? You must judge that for yourself. As far as I am concerned, he is a man who is now retiring after a brilliant and spotless career as an outstanding coach and an outstanding human being. He is a man to whom I wish all the best that can be in the years to come. He is a man who has earned whatever good will come his way during his retirement years.

He is a man we can emulate; a man we can respect; a man we most certainly honor; and, most importantly to me, he is a man whom I am proud to call my friend.

Special Data: *Time of speech: a little under five minutes. Admittedly, this speech is very personal and glowing, but you should realize that the speaker is a personal friend of the retiree, has made that clear to the audience, and is speaking from personal experience. One of the things you should never do in a retirement speech is to become glowingly effusive over someone with whom the audience knows you have only a casual acquaintance. Reserve the "glow" for those truly close people who will appreciate your warmth.*

$$\boxed{78}$$

TOPIC: Retirement of a Teacher.

AUDIENCE: Family; friends; fellow educators.

Well, folks, that's the way it goes. There you are, fresh out of college and ready to set foot into your first classroom and your very own class; you close that door, turn around, and there you are again—but it's forty years later, and you are sitting at your own retirement dinner listening to some absurd man like me talk about your career in education.

While this is an experience everyone in education seems to face, what happens in between that first class and the retirement dinner is quite different for each individual.

Tonight, we gather together to honor Mark Caslock who, in a few weeks, will be retiring after forty years in our system. Mark has told me that he has experienced that quickness of time I just mentioned. Just a week ago, we were talking, and he wondered aloud where all that time had gone. If I may, I'd like to tell him.

No, I'm not going to say that the time has gone into teaching hours and lesson plans and report preparations and budget requests and field trips and PTA meetings, although that is certainly a part of an educator's life and eats up our precious time. Rather, I am going to get to the essence of those forty years as a teacher.

That time has gone into students. That passed time has gone to the kids who needed extra hours of help and guidance; to those kids with problems that broke our hearts; to those who refused to learn; to those who were challenged to go beyond the limits of the classroom. That's where your time has gone, Mark, to your students who have needed the special touch that only you could supply; to the students who have sat and cried out their problems to you, problems which you took on yourself as you set about providing the students with help rather than mere sympathy, and as you went to bat for them in order to help them through each and every crisis; to your students who sought out your guidance, respected your knowledge and integrity, and benefited from your willingness to help; to the countless students who have passed through your classroom and learned not only the subject you were teaching, but the roots of the best of humanity as you lived it before their very eyes.

Mark, if the countless parade of students whom you have helped over the years could speak with one voice, I am certain that they would tell you of their wishes that the time before you now might be as full and rich as the time you so unselfishly shared with them.

If the days ahead of you are filled with half the happiness you have given to all of us during these years, then your retirement will be one of blessed joy.

God bless you, Mark.

Special Data: *Time of speech: about four minutes. While the sentiments expressed in this speech could really apply to any good teacher, they can be adapted easily to any specific teacher by either giving examples from your experience or by telling a personal anecdote concerning the teacher's dedication. This is a retirement speech that would work well for any long-time teacher.*

$$\boxed{79}$$

TOPIC: **All-Purpose Retirement/ Testimonial Poem.**

AUDIENCE: **Suitable for any adult audience.**

> **There's a road** that each one of us travels,
>   And each person walks it alone,
> From the first step we take at the dawning,
>   Till a distant voice bids us come home.
>
> And each step that we take on that journey
>   Shapes the path of the next day to come,
> For we fashion the road that we travel
>   In the darkness or light of the sun.
>
> And only a few understand it;
>   To only a few it is known;

That in smoothing the pathways of others,
We fashion our own stepping stones.

So when we meet someone whose life has
Enriched all the lives it has met,
We point in our pride to that passage,
Too golden to ever forget.

Special Data: *Time of poem: about one minute. This poem may be used for either a retirement speech or a testimonial. For a retirement speech, use it at the end of the speech, indicating that there is a poem that sums up all that has been said about the retiree; give the poem and then remark about how no one present will be able to forget the individual. For a testimonial, one possible way to use it would be to use it at the outset, then give examples of how the individual "smoothed the pathways" of others, and then restate the poem and make a comment about how you will not forget, either. Other uses will suggest themselves to you, we are certain.*

Afterthoughts

"Honesty" is a virtue everywhere, and particularly in a retirement speech. If the retiree was a grouch until she had her morning coffee, it would be a fantastic mistake to tell everyone about her lovely and balanced disposition. Whatever you said after that, even if true, would be discredited.

Seek out the best in the retiree's life, reflect on it, and tell your audience about it. You will have a retirement speech that will suit the occasions well.

Testimonials

$$\boxed{80}$$

TOPIC: **Testimonial for a Former Student.**

AUDIENCE: **Adult audience; friends, family, community.**

It is inevitable, when speaking of someone who has achieved something great in his life, that people will say, "I knew it from the moment in first saw him. I looked at him, and I said to myself, 'That person is headed for greatness!' That's exactly what I said!"

I wish I could say that about our guest of honor tonight, but, in all honesty, the first time I laid eyes on Bob Kensler, he was sitting in a class of twenty-seven kids who looked more or less just like him, and, quite frankly, I didn't even notice him.

I don't remember, quite honestly, what I told that class on that particular afternoon, but I think it was something about having to earn your grades as you would have to earn your respect and your place in the school. Obviously, Bob was paying attention, because he started that very day to earn his grades and his status in the school, and he soon earned my attention and that of the faculty, the administration, his fellow students, the community and the Board of Education as well.

If you ask Bob, he'll tell you that he's "nothing special," because that's the kind of man he is. However, if you ask me and the people in our school who taught and dealt with him, we will tell you quite a different story.

We will tell you of a young man to whom excellence is more than a word—it's a commitment. We will tell you of a person who gives 100 percent of himself at all times. We will tell you of someone with an outstanding academic record, who stood out as a shining star; we will tell you of an individual achiever who also put the welfare of his peers above any individual record he might achieve; we will tell you of the student we knew who was never too tired or too busy to help other students who needed him.

I could, of course, detail Bob Kensler's brilliant record. I could speak of his academic standing as an honor student. I could tell you of his contributions to charitable work in our community and elsewhere, most notably through the Big Brother program. I could tell you of the high regard in which he was and still is held by the faculty and administration, by the students who were his classmates, by the members of the athletic teams of which he was a part, and by everyone who has come into contact with him. Yes, I could tell you all of this, but I think that everyone in this audience tonight knows these facts only too well.

Therefore, I will speak to Bob Kensler himself, who, I am certain, is sitting here wondering what all the fuss is about, because a sense of humility is also a part of his makeup. I will say to you, Bob, that it was my pleasure to have had you as a student. I am overjoyed that you walked the halls of our school, participated in our activities, worked for student government as you did, and helped renew my confidence in a future world which would have people like you in it.

There are many people who would view your award tonight as outstanding new businessman of the year as a culmination or end result of your accomplishments. I am not one of them. Rather, knowing you and knowing that of which you are capable, I look on tonight as a ship's launching; as the countdown to a rocket's flight. Your future lies before you, Bob; it is in your hands; and, knowing you, it can be nothing but bright.

Special Data: *Time of speech: about four minutes. This speech in honor of a former student who "made good" could be made even more effective if you were to add some personal reminiscence of an incident in which you and the subject were involved in a manner that brought out the character or a particular quality of the subject. Make certain that the incident is not one that will be embarrassing to the subject—a good place to tell it would be just after the third paragraph. Since you will undoubtedly have known the individual in this situation for many years, your aim should be to sound warmly paternal (or maternal) without overdoing it.*

$$\boxed{81}$$

TOPIC: Testimonial for a Teacher.

AUDIENCE: Adults; educators, family, friends, colleagues.

Ladies and gentlemen, allow me to acquaint you with a few facts.

The kids know that Bernice Croft is a very special teacher; the parents know that she is special; her colleagues know that she is special; the administration knows that Bernice is special. What's more, each of these groups has known Bernice's special status for some time, and, now that she has been chosen to receive the Educator of the Year Award, everyone will know what we have known for a long time—that Bernice Croft is a very special woman, a very special teacher, and very worthy of this outstanding award.

Now, I promised myself that I would do nothing this evening to embarrass Bernice, but I really feel that I have to share one anecdote with you. . . . .

(NOTE: Here you would tell a personal anecdote that would bring out the subject's abilities and qualities as an outstanding educator.)

If I really wanted to embarrass Bernice, I could tell you about her educational accomplishments; of the letters of merit and honor in her file; of the praise that has been heaped upon her by her exstudents and their parents and the community which she has served so well; of my personal observations of her work with children—all children—of the hours of tireless and selfless work she has put in to ensure her students receive the best possible education while caring for their personal needs as well—far beyond the confines of the classroom.

All of this and more I could tell you, but you probably know most of it already, because there is one more thing that Bernice Croft has done for us that we all realize but don't voice often enough—that Bernice has served and continues to serve as an inspiration to us all. The love and care she manifests toward her students she also pours out upon her colleagues as well. Which of us has not received the friendliest of greetings to start the day; which of us has not had our spirits buoyed by

Bernice just when they needed lifting; which of us has not received counsel, sympathy, encouragement, and tons of very practical advice from this woman who gives so freely of her wisdom as well as her expertise.

We who are privileged to work with her know only too well her dedication, her commitment, her tireless efforts on behalf of her students. Not only do we in the school know this, but good news cannot be kept down, and the parents of this community literally shout for joy and telephone the school to affirm that joy when they learn that their child is to be in Bernice Croft's room.

This is the type of person Bernice is and has been for as long as I've known her. Always ready to help a student or colleague, always sensitive to the needs of her kids or her peers, always one to be the first to share with all about her, Bernice Croft has labored long and hard, given what was in her to us all, and we have found it wonderful.

Tonight, you receive the Educator of the Year Award, and that is, indeed, a well-deserved honor. Yet, for all of us who know and work with you day in and day out, know you have always been the outstanding educator of *every* year, and, yes, of every single day as well.

In a very real sense, it is we who have received an award this evening—the award of being allowed to live and work with someone like you.

Take pleasure in this honor, Bernice; we can think of no one who deserves it more.

Special Data: *Time of speech: four or more minutes depending upon the length and number of anecdotes used. This speech indicates a personal anecdote. When you tell one, make certain that it is on the warm side. It may be funny certainly, but may never be funny at the subject's expense. In fact, it is a good idea to clear the anecdote with the subject before using it if at all possible. Any audience composed of people who are there to honor the subject will only resent you if it becomes apparent that you have made the honored subject ill at ease. Keep the anecdotes warm and human, however, and the audience will really respond positively.*

$$\boxed{82}$$

TOPIC: Testimonial for an Administrator.

AUDIENCE: Suitable for any adult audience.

There is a very old and very poor joke that I'm about to tell you; so old it has all but become a cliché, but I'm going to ask you to bear with me for a moment, and we'll see if we can make something out of it together.

Briefly, the story is about the little boy who comes home from school one day looking extremely sad and defeated. His mother asks if anything went wrong at school; if school has begun to get him down. The child replies, "It ain't school; it's the principal of the thing!"

I know, I know, that was the million and first time you've heard that, and it has almost attained the status of cliché, but for a moment consider that a cliché has become a cliché because it has been used so often, and the reason that it has been used so often is that it communicates a basic truth to which most people can relate. "Haste makes waste," for instance, is used so often, because it is so true.

So, we come to the fact that, "It ain't school; it's the principal of the thing."

We have gathered together tonight in order to honor Patrick Connor, who, for ten years now, has served as the principal of our high school. This very gathering testifies to the fact that we admire him, care for him, and want him to know how much we appreciate the hard work and dedication he has put into his job as principal.

It's the principal of the thing—the principal of any school sets the tone of that school, both academically and as a place of personal growth for the students. Pat Connor has done that, working tirelessly to ensure that the high school be a place where the finest quality education a child could get was available to all students, at the same time making certain that students were allowed to grow and mature in a place that promoted positive values; a place that cared for its students, its teachers, and its staff. Pat Connor cares deeply, and, consequently, the school cannot help but reflect that nurturing and caring attitude.

It's the principal of the thing—the principal of the school is a leader, a guide, and the chief cheerleader for the institution. As a leader,

Pat has not only been innovative in curriculum and new academic programs, but is always there for those seeking advice. He is a guide without peer; a person who doesn't merely point the way, but shows it by walking it first himself. Look around at virtually every sport's event, play, concert, or get-together of any kind that involves his school and his students, and you may be certain of seeing Pat Connor as part of the crowd. If you listen for the loudest cheer within the fans, you can be sure it will be Pat's.

It's the principal of the thing—the principal of the school is the guiding light for that school. During his tenure as principal, Pat has lived through budget crunches, changes in policy, a school strike, the introduction of new programs, a building project, and the thousand-and-one "normal" pressures that beset a principal on the best of school days. Through it all, he has maintained a highly professional attitude; kept his sense of humor as sharp as it ever was; and handled each emergency and each crisis with calmness, concern, and an efficiency borne of the ability to look at a problem to see the best possible solution for all parties.

It's the principal of the thing—this principal, Pat Connor—who has made the high school a place where learning is truly a shining beacon, where students grow and learn and teachers teach, where this community can send its sons and daughters with pride and with the knowledge that they will be challenged and guided to achieve at their highest level.

It's the principal of the thing—Pat Connor, who is respected by all, admired by many, and acknowledged by us tonight as a person of merit who has done an outstanding job and is worthy of our respect.

It's the principal of the thing—in a very real sense, the essence of the school.

It *is* the school, and that school *is* the principal of the thing, and that is the man we honor this evening—Pat Connor!

Special Data: *Time of speech: about five minutes. Instead of the phrase "our high school" used throughout, you would, of course, substitute the name of the school involved. This speech shows a very useful technique. Take a phrase that applies to the situation and start each paragraph with that phrase, as we did with "It's the principal of the thing." Each paragraph expands a bit more on the meaning of that phrase relative to the subject. It is an effective technique that audiences remember.*

$$\boxed{83}$$

TOPIC: Testimonial for a "Friend of Education"

AUDIENCE: Basically members of business and the community.

> *(NOTE: This is a testimonial by an educator for a civic or community personage, such as a mayor or city commissioner that has been helpful to the schools or the school district enough to classify him or her as a "Friend" of Education.)*

What is a friend? There are many definitions, some meaningful and some frivolous, but one definition that has always struck me is that a friend is someone who sees you as you are and likes you anyway.

If this is an acceptable definition to us, then Mayor Mary Higgins is truly a friend; a friend to every parent and teacher and student in our community, for Mayor Higgins is, truly, a friend of education.

Administering a municipal government as large and complex as ours is a Herculean task. There are so many items that call out for attention on a here-and-now basis. Each item is of high priority, and each involves citizens of the community in pursuit of the interests of their constituency.

With all of these problems and duties and needs facing her, it would have been easy for Mayor Higgins to delegate the responsibility to others. One of the hallmarks of her administration, however, has been the intensive personal care she has given to each task before her. This has been true of municipal budgets, tax reform, and, most importantly for us, education.

Throughout her tenure in office, Mayor Higgins has taken pains to support our school system, taking a personal hand in helping to shape not only the direction of the future of our schools but aiding in practical ways in the funding and the development of community resources devoted to the education of our children.

She has not only manifested her care and concern at the conference table, but in the halls of the schools themselves. Our children, from elementary children through middle school kids to high school seniors, are more than familiar with Mayor Higgins through her frequent visits to our schools, her participation in township-wide events centered about our schools, and the personal help and counsel she has given so freely to so many of our students. Yes, our students know her, and they respond with true affection to one who continues to show genuine love and concern for their welfare, and for one who continues to work tirelessly to achieve for them the finest in education.

Mayor Higgins has worked very closely with us. She knows our strengths as well as our limitations. She has seen what we can and, yes, what we cannot do, and she has set upon the task of helping us grow to become the finest school system we can be, because she cares deeply for the children of this community and believes in what our school system has to offer.

In short, she has seen us as we are, and she still likes us, still cares about us, still makes every effort to help in whatever way she can.

That's an excellent definition of a friend—and Mayor Higgins is a friend to every child in this community and a true friend to education as well.

For this, we give her our heartfelt thanks and are exceedingly proud to be able to join in this well-deserved tribute to her today.

From students to teachers to administrators, all of your friends in education send you their best, as you have given us your best for so many wonderful years.

It gives us great pleasure to proclaim to all that Mayor Mary Higgins is a *friend* to *education,* and how happy we are that she is.

Special Data: *Time of speech: about four and a half minutes. Testimonials for business leaders and political officials are quite common, more common, we sometimes think, than those held for educators, and, as a school administrator, you may, indeed, be asked to speak at one. Remember that these affairs are held to honor the person designated, so this would obviously not be a time to voice any political opinions or lobby for some pending legislation. Indeed, such an action could well have a detrimental effect upon future support for you or the school. Think of the good qualities of the subject, and let that be expressed.*

$$\boxed{84}$$

TOPIC: **All-Purpose Outline for a Testimonial.**

AUDIENCE: **Suitable for any audience.**

NOTE: The following is not a speech per se, *but an outline for a testimonial. You fill in the blanks with material that is appropriate for your subject as indicated in the speech.*

It is inevitable, at a time such as this, that our minds and hearts turn to (*subject's first and last name*)._____When that happens, we are warmed by memories of the times we have shared together, and we smile as we remember.

There is one particular incident that I recall, and I am certain that (*subject's first name*)_____would not mind if I shared it with you. . . .

NOTE: Here you would tell an anecdote, a true one, that would in some way point out the special nature of the subject. Speak of a time when he or she was courageous, tender, loving, filled with integrity, etc. Remember this is a testimonial, not a roast.

Of course, that was then and this is now, as the saying goes, but I affirm to you that time has neither diminished nor dulled the fine edge that has marked *his/her* life and career. Indeed, the voices of those assembled today (*this evening; this afternoon*) are ample proof of the high regard in which (*subject's first and last name*)_____is held by us all.

Indeed, I can think of few people more worthy of honor.

Let me tell you just a little bit about this person we are honoring today. . . .

NOTE: Here you would insert between two and four paragraphs of material explaining why the subject is worthy of a testimonial. Make certain that each paragraph is complete in and of itself. If you can add personal highlights to each paragraph, so much the better.

These are reasons why I, personally, will always honor (*subject's first and last name*)_____in my heart, and why I am so overjoyed to be a part of this well-deserved honor.

(*Subject's first name*)_____, this honor is yours, and we take the greatest pride in giving it to you, just as you have given each and every one of us so much of yourself over the years.

Take this honor, (*first name*)_____, and with it take our gratitude, our respect, and, most importantly, our love.

Special Data: *Time of speech: as long or as short as you wish to make it. Please understand that this is a good, basic, and very, very solid base from which to build any testimonial speech. You won't go wrong with this one. If it needs to be reduced even further, the most basic outline would be: This is whom we are honoring; these are his/her good qualities; here are some reasons why he/she should be honored; we are very happy to honor him/her; we wish the best. Apply this outline to several of the speeches in this section, and you'll see how well it works.*

Afterthoughts

As you go through this section on testimonials, remember that there is nothing to stop you from taking a part from one speech and a part from another in order to make a speech to suit your particular purposes. If you do this, however, make certain that you go over it several times for continuity. It must "hang together" in order for it to be effective, and this may mean changing several of the transitional words and phrases. If it works for you, however, please go right ahead.

We are all a mixture of the good and the sometimes less than good. In a testimonial speech, remember the good points and concentrate on those until you can talk about them effectively.

NEW AND EFFECTIVE EULOGIES AND MEMORIALS

It is never easy to write a eulogy, and we, personally, find it difficult to deliver one. Even so, life is so constituted that you often do not have a choice, and such a task is yours, whether you may wish it or not.

Over the years that we have been active in education, we have found occasion to give eulogies and memorial speeches in a wide variety of settings, from a eulogy for someone who had retired years previously but had spent a life in education, to a student who met with a tragic death, to presenting a group eulogy at a class reunion. These are never easy; they are always necessary; they are always charged with emotion.

Above all, the eulogy or memorial speech must be presented with dignity and respect. Even if you knew the deceased well, and even if that person had asked you to "keep it light" and tell some of the "funny" things that happened during your time together, you would be well advised, we feel, not to heed that request. A eulogy is a time for sober reflection; a time to allow people to look within themselves to study their personal relationship to the deceased and their own feelings about mortality, faith, the transitory nature of life, and all else that goes with this particularly trying time.

A memorial speech, although it is presumably given some time after the death of the subject, is nonetheless charged with emotion as well, because these memorial services tend to rekindle emotions that many thought had at least cooled to embers. Consequently, this speech requires almost exactly the same approach as a eulogy.

In both cases, you should keep your speech dignified, respectful, genuine, short, and centered upon the positive qualities of your subject.

In the following pages, you will find speeches of this nature suitable for a wide variety of subjects. Hopefully, they will meet your needs during difficult times.

Eulogies

$$\boxed{85}$$

TOPIC: Eulogy/Memorial for a Class Reunion.

AUDIENCE: Adults who would attend such an affair.

Ladies and gentlemen of the class of 1961:

It has been thirty years since we left the halls of Rock Township High School and entered the world with expectation and promise.

In that time, the inevitable has happened, and several of our classmates have been taken from us.

It is fitting and proper, therefore, that we pause for a moment to remember them, each of us in his or her own way.

May we all stand, and let us, for a moment reflect on those that are here only in our hearts.

NOTE: When all stand, pause for a moment and then read the following poem.

How often when the shadows call
   In murmurs soft and deep,
Before we lay aside the day
   And put the world to sleep;
Before we close our weary eyes
   To leave behind our care,
Do we visit in our memories
   With those no longer here . . .
How often in that silent time
   Before our day's work ends,
Do we extract a silent smile
   Reflecting on our friends,
For in our minds we walk with them
   As we did once before
And share the thousand closenesses
   That friendship held in store.

We see their faces fresh and bright;
    We see them smile, and then
We watch with eyes of memory
    As they are young again.
We see those classmates whom we knew
    So many years ago,
Who never more the ravages
    Of time will ever know.
Once more we walk these students halls
    And hear the classrooms ring
With laughter and the joy of life
    That only youth can bring.
We see them as we saw them then,
    A story yet untold,
Who live within our minds and hearts
    And never will grow old.
Oh, silent classmates one and all,
    Although we are apart,
How cherish we the golden times
    We've hidden in our hearts;
How dearly do we hold you close
    Although you are not here,
And keep you safe in memory
    Until we join you there.

James A. Callerman, September 7, 1975
Maria C. Farnelli, August 22, 1982
Jeanette D. Grosse, March 27, 1985
Charles G. Marensen, May 1, 1989

Oh, silent classmates one and all,
    Although we are apart,
How cherish we the golden times
    We've hidden in our hearts;
How dearly do we hold you close
    Although you are not here,
And keep you safe in memory
    Until we join you there.

Ladies and gentlemen of the class of 1961, I give you our absent classmates . . . may they rest in peace and in love.

Special Data: *Time of presentation: between three and four minutes. In this particular speech, presentation is everything. You must find out ahead of time the names and dates of death of the deceased class members. When you ask the audience to stand, pause until everyone is standing and there is no further noise of scraping chairs. Then begin the poem and read it slowly and distinctly. When you get to the last line (Until we join you there) for the first time, pause for a count of two and then begin to recite the names and dates of death of your deceased classmates. Do this slowly, allowing a silent count of two between each name. After the last name, slowly and with great feeling recite the final eight lines again. At the conclusion of the speech, pause for a mental count of two or three and quietly say, "Thank you; you may be seated." Do not expect any applause, of course, for your audience will be too moved to respond in that way. This is a highly effective eulogy and memorial for those classmates who have left us.*

86

TOPIC: Eulogy for a Teacher.

AUDIENCE: Suitable for any audience.

Mrs. Greenwald, Joan, Members of the Greenwald Family, ladies and gentlemen. . . .

I have been twice honored. I am honored and deeply humbled that the Greenwald family has asked me to participate in these services, but I am even more honored to be able to say that in my lifetime, I knew a very special human being who brightened and enriched my life as he lit up the lives of the thousands of students he touched during an outstanding career in service to education.

Whether it was in the classroom that he loved so well, sharing knowledge and guidance with his students, or as an advisor and coach in which he gave so much joy and growth to others, Harold Greenwald was a man whom others looked up to, respected, and loved. The presence of so many here today as well as the outpouring of love that has come to the Greenwald family speaks eloquently of that. Harold Greenwald loved people, and those of us he touched so deeply could not help but respond in kind.

Of course there are no words truly appropriate to state what we feel in our hearts. We know that there is an emptiness that cannot be filled. We know that we will miss him, and that his absence leaves a palpable ache that cannot be soothed and must be left to time alone.

Yet, if we have anything in this hour, it is our memories. In our minds, we continue to see him smile and wave at us across a student-filled hallway. In our hearts, we recall with warmth and affection his wit, his kindness, his open and giving nature, the selfless way in which he gave of himself to his colleagues and his students. We remember this—what he was; what he said; what he accomplished in his own life and in the lives of so many others—we remember, and we cannot help but be inspired and uplifted by that memory.

We who will carry on realize that we will do so on the path that Harold Greenwald has prepared for us and illuminated with that special glow that was his alone.

And we realize something else as well—we realize that during our lives, we were privileged to have been touched by the life of someone truly outstanding, truly fine, truly an example of the finest that education has to offer and that humanity can become.

We have had the honor to know Harold Greenwald, and we are all the better for it.

Special Data: *Time of eulogy: about three minutes. This eulogy is one written about someone the speaker knew well. When this happens, we have a tendency to want to recall a hundred anecdotes and instances that reflect our friend. We must remember, however, the delicacy of the time and place as well as the emotions and feelings of the family. A eulogy—any eulogy—is better kept short. Brevity is preferred, while a ponderous or lengthy speech will be remembered for all the wrong reasons.*

$$\boxed{87}$$

TOPIC: Eulogy for a Student.

AUDIENCE: Family, educators, students.

Mr. and Mrs. Kenner, Tom and April, Members of the Kenner Family, ladies and gentlemen. . . .

I speak today with the voice of many, for I know that I represent every teacher, every administrator, and every person on the staff of Rock Township High School as well as every student, and, I firmly believe, the entire community, when I express the grief, shock, and deep sense of loss we suffer with you over the untimely death of Martin Kenner. He was known to us in school as Marty, and we knew him as someone very special, indeed; as someone whom we were proud to have as a student in our school, as a player on our teams, as a leader in our student government, as a friend. . . .

Teachers, coaches, and administrators alike, as well as the many people on our support staff such as cafeteria workers and custodians whose lives Marty's crossed, have asked me to convey to you their sorrow and the depth of the loss they feel. This I do, and I add my own deepest sympathies as well. We will all miss Marty.

No one needs to tell us nor need we belabor the point that the passing of someone vibrant with youth is a true tragedy. When we speak of someone as popular, talented, and respected as Marty Kenner, we know that it is a tragedy that affects us all.

Mr. and Mrs. Kenner, we are well aware of how meaningless words are at a time like this, but please know that you are joined in your grief by all of us who say with pride that your son has been a part of our lives.

Our sincerest sympathies and our fervent prayers are with you during this time of loss and sorrow.

Special Data: *Time of eulogy: about two minutes. No matter what you say or how you say it, there are no words that can in any way lessen the impact of the situation when one of your students dies. At such a time, it is the genuine outpouring of support to the family that will be meaningful. Say what is in your heart.*

$$\boxed{88}$$

TOPIC: Eulogy for a Coach/ Athletic Director.

AUDIENCE: Family and friends; colleagues; athletes.

Mrs. Aimsley, Annette and Tom, Members of the Aimsley Family, ladies and gentlemen. . . .

When the news of Don's passing reached us, his fellow teachers and coaches, it hit us with tremendous impact. We were saddened, for his death has left us with a void that can never be entirely filled. Everyone at the school, the team members, his fellow coaches, and I cannot help but respond to this loss.

Our only consolation during this time is the knowledge that we were privileged to know and work with Don over these years. During that time, we came to know him as a person of intelligence and integrity, always willing to help, whose life and career were, indeed, an inspiration to us all.

We also take comfort in the fact that a part of Don will continue to live, reflected in the lives of those young people whom he has coached, guided, and inspired over the years. Don was a man who gave unselfishly of himself, perhaps the greatest gift of all; and the student athletes who were fortunate enough to fall under his care will carry the ideals, knowledge, and moral principles he instilled in them into their personal lives as they enter the world. And the world will be a better place because of it.

Our hearts and our prayers are with you at this most trying of times.

Special Data: *Time of eulogy: about two minutes. This is an example of a very short and simple eulogy, merely detailing in general terms the deceased's contributions and the affection of those with whom he or she worked. Something simple like this can often be more effective than a longer, more drawn out speech that might become tedious during a time when feelings are "on the edge." Present a short eulogy, acknowledge the family, and then sit down. Everyone will appreciate this.*

$$\boxed{89}$$

TOPIC: Eulogy for a School Administrator.

AUDIENCE: Family and friends; educators; community.

Mr. Sanchez, William and Elizabeth, Members of the Sanchez Family, ladies and gentlemen. . . .

Over several decades in public education, I have been faced with many tasks that have needed to be done that I have not wanted to do. Today is just such an occasion. Gladly would I sing the praises of Julia Sanchez, outstanding educator and remarkable human being, yet to do so upon this occasion fills me with the deepest of sorrow, for in speaking of her passing, I must acknowledge my deep sense of personal loss as well.

Yet if Julia were here in person as she dwells among us in spirit, she would be the first, I am certain, to tell me to stop concentrating on what is *not* and look toward what *is*. Indeed, that was one of the qualities that marked Julia Sanchez as an outstanding human being; her ability to look beyond the present, beyond the circumstances, beyond the day—to see tomorrow as a shining possibility in which she would play a part.

Of what, then, should I speak? Should I speak of the woman who, from a background of poverty, sought to know and to learn; worked and financed her own way through school; fought against tremendous odds to become a teacher, to go on to graduate work in administration, to serve as vice-principal in one of the toughest schools in this state only to literally "turn the place around," to go beyond that to the principalship of our own high school, a position she filled with dignity and expertise for so many years? Should I speak of these things?

Of what, then, should I speak? Should I speak of the woman whom we came to know not only as an administrator of insight and intelligence but as a friend who was always willing to give direction when there was none, support at the precise spot where it was needed, encouragement when everyone else had given up, and unqualified affection to all people at all times? Should I speak of the woman whom faculty, staff, and students knew as a principal and also as a friend who was there whenever she was needed? Should I speak of these things?

Of what, then, should I speak? Should I speak of the woman whose insight into and knowledge of education made her an invaluable asset to the school system of this community; of the woman who could fight like a tiger when she thought her "kids," as she called them, were being shortchanged or slighted educationally; of the woman who sought change where it was needed while stressing the basic and traditional values of American education; of the woman to whom education was not a word to be spoken, but a commitment to be lived each and every day? Should I speak of these things?

Yes, I could speak of all of this and more, and still would not have touched the merest part of what Julia Sanchez was. She was all of this and one thing more—she was a friend. In the truest sense of the word, she was a friend to every administrator, every teacher, every parent, and every precious student in our school system. She gave of herself unstintingly, and when her life touched yours, you knew that you were dealing with someone very special indeed.

Finally, I will speak of the memorial that Julia Sanchez leaves behind; a memorial not of stone or steel, but a memorial that is carved into the lives of those who knew and worked with her; a memorial in the lives of the students for whom she labored so diligently and so well. It is we who are left behind that continue to be living memorials to a life that had the courage, the dignity, and the integrity to touch each of us on a personal and deeply meaningful level.

Julia Sanchez will be deeply missed, but her spirit abides with us still, and it is that spirit of love, faith, and hope that she imparted to us that will continue to encourage, to guide, and inspire us throughout those tomorrows in which she continues to play a part.

Special Data: *Time of speech: between five and six minutes. This is a full speech and much more what one would expect of a "formal" eulogy. This eulogy also uses a technique that is very effective; notice how the same topic sentence is used over and over again, adding to the dramatic impact. This technique is not to be limited to eulogies, and can be a very effective speaking tool when you have to present something that is dynamic, dramatic or something you wish to have a solid impact on an audience, such as would be your desire here in eulogizing this outstanding woman.*

$$\boxed{90}$$

TOPIC: Eulogy for a School Worker.

AUDIENCE: Family and friends; possibly some educators.

Mr. Bogner, Lois and James, Members of the Bogner Family, ladies and gentlemen. . . .

There are so many times when the facts fail to tell an entire story; when the data alone is insufficient to really express what has happened.

Mary Bogner served as a school crossing guard for seventeen years. For fifteen of those years, she was assigned to Crestview Elementary School. In that time, she served with distinction, being three times awarded the Rock Township Safety Citation for her work in educating school children about traffic safety. She was all but a permanent fixture at Crestview Elementary, having served every morning and afternoon with hardly an absence for the fifteen years she was there.

These are the facts, but as I said before, they tell only part of the story.

How can mere facts relate the wonderful, loving, and giving person Mary Bogner really was as we at the school came to know her?

To Mary, this was a job she took very seriously. She loved and delighted in children, and all you had to do was look to see that they returned that love to her. When we chanced to look, we would constantly see her with her arm around one of the children, tying a shoelace, wiping away a tear. Oh, certainly, she helped them in crossing the streets and taught them invaluable lessons in safety, but her concern went beyond that to the children themselves.

Time after time, Mary would spend extra time on the job to talk to a child or an anxious parent. To the children she offered herself as a loving and compassionate adult who could move to their level, listen while they poured out their concerns, and send them off again with a smile. To many a parent, she was a person who cared about children and who was there when asked to offer sage advice, support, or just good common sense.

Mary Bogner was like that—a person who truly loved people and was ready to give of herself whenever the need arose. Whoever met her, whether the kids or the many teachers who would make it a point to stop by for a word or two after school, knew that Mary Bogner went far beyond her job; from mere duty to genuine concern, and from mere responsibility to real love.

There will be other crossing guards, for that is a requirement of our school system, but there will never be another Mary Bogner. Her passing leaves an emptiness that we know will never be filled completely.

To the Bogner family, we extend our deepest sympathies. Mary was a very special and wonderful woman; we remember her fondly, we cherish her memory, and you may be assured that we will not forget.

Special Data: *Time of eulogy: about four minutes. Let us confess freely that sometimes, what with all the necessities of dealing with the educational process within the school, we may tend to take for granted those school workers who have so diligently served the needs of our students and us over the years. This is a fine tribute to such a person. While this speech has been designed for a crossing guard, there is no reason why it can not be adapted or altered to fit a cafeteria worker, custodian, or other dedicated school worker. Use the same factual approach, and simply change the details to suit your particular needs.*

Afterthoughts

We have not commented on the method of address used to start each eulogy. Simply put, you should address the surviving spouse (Mrs. Jones . . .), the children of the deceased (Bill and Mary . . .), the rest of the relatives (Members of the Jones Family . . .), any dignitaries who might be present (Mayor Smith . . .), and the general audience (Ladies and Gentlemen . . .).

When delivering the eulogy, do so in a straightforward manner, never trying to be "dramatic" about it; believe us, the situation will be dramatic enough as it is, and if you do shed a tear, it will be genuine.

Finally, don't forget to go over to the family and say a few words before you sit down. Be brief. A simple, "He was a wonderful person; we will all miss him. . . . " is sufficient.

Above all, only say those things that you mean from your heart; your eulogy will carry with it the comfort and sympathy you really wish to convey.

Memorials

91

TOPIC: **Introduction to a Memorial Ceremony.**

AUDIENCE: **Suitable to any adult audience.**

Good evening members of the Harris family, and ladies and gentlemen....

It so happens that within the duties of my position, I am often witness to many human dramas. I see people working toward a myriad of goals and striving to be the best that they are capable of becoming. Yet, even as I watch, often advise, and sometimes help, I am aware that while we may all share a common humanity, our individual lives vary greatly in a wide variety of ways. From the mass, a few people are singled out in our minds as being exemplary. These are people who live their lives with such dignity, morality, and honor, that we realize at once that we are associating with someone who is very special. Not only in the work setting, but certainly in life as well, this is a truth that our experience affirms. Now, when such a person is taken from us, we know in our hearts that it is altogether fitting and proper to stand up and proclaim for all to hear that this was a life so well-lived that it is worthy of note; worthy of respect; worthy of honor.

When a life shines forth as a bright beacon and symbol of what can be accomplished in our imperfect world, we know that somehow we must extoll that life's virtues and hold it up as a shining model for those to come after. When a life is that outstanding, humankind is shaken by its loss, and we can do no less than speak out about it.

That is why we gather together this evening. Our dear, valued friend and colleague, Ralph Harris, has been missing from our ranks for some time now, but we who are left remember what his life entailed as a teacher and administrator, and what his life meant to us and to all with whom he came into contact. We know what he gave; we know what he did; we know what he was. We remember so well, and this evening we gather to express not only our sorrow that he is gone, but, more importantly, to express our thanks and our deepest appreciation for the legacy of honor, selflessness, dedication, commitment, loyalty, and honorable service that he has left us.

Our first speaker this evening. . . .

Special Data: *Time of introduction: about two minutes. This is an example of an introduction to a memorial program where you have been asked to serve as "moderator" for the ceremony. You would be expected to give a memorial speech, but you would also be expected to introduce other speakers, get the ceremony started, and keep it moving throughout. The preceding speech would be an appropriate introduction to such an affair. Following it, you would introduce the other speakers, saving your own speech for last. Following your speech, there would either be a short benediction or you would be expected to close the program. In that case, you would sum up the ceremony's activities and bid everyone a good evening.*

92

TOPIC: Memorial Ceremony for a Tree Planting,

AUDIENCE: Suitable for any audience.

Ladies and gentlemen. . . .

We are gathered this afternoon to pay tribute to the memory of someone we all knew and held dear.

Lois Lasser served as a special education teacher in our district for over twenty-three years. For the last ten of those years, she was a part of our faculty. I do not think that I exaggerate a bit when I say that she was admired and respected by administration and faculty as well as students and parents.

Indeed, the many commendations she received, plus the support she engendered for her beloved "special" students, provide ample testimony to her abilities and talents as a teacher. The genuine outpouring of grief from the community in general and our faculty and staff in particular stand as a tribute to her affability, her concern for others, and her indomitable spirit that has touched and enriched us all.

Now, Lois Lasser has been taken from us, and we who are left gather in tribute to her memory. Of course, it is inevitable that each of us will remember Lois in his or her own way, but for a moment, we have some people who would like to share briefly some of their memories of Lois with us.

Therefore, allow me to introduce. . . .

NOTE: At this point, you would introduce the speaker(s) for the afternoon. There should be only a few, certainly no more than three, and their memories of the deceased should be short, recalling a single incident only. Thank each speaker as he or she is finished, and when the last speaker has concluded, you should step forward. . . .

Thank you, Mrs. Thompson, for that beautiful memory of Lois.

While the spirit of Lois Lasser will continue to live within the minds and hearts of us all, we, her friends and colleagues, have thought it appropriate to purchase this tree in her memory. Today, with the full knowledge and approval of the Board of Education, we plant it here on the grounds of the school in which Lois worked with us and touched us for so long.

This tree that we plant today will take its nourishment from the ground of this school, just as this school was nourished by the presence of Lois Lasser; this tree will partake of the same cooling rains and warming sunshine that fell upon our school, just as our school was refreshed by her vibrancy and warmed by the affection she showed to student and colleague alike; this tree will grow and spread its arms to provide shade and shelter for all, just as Lois provided a covering and refreshing shelter for those under her charge; this tree will bud and blossom every spring and fill our hearts with its beauty, just as the memory of Lois Lasser will bloom in our hearts and fill us with the fullness and beauty of her memory.

NOTE: At this point you would proceed with whatever ceremony you had planned. One very lovely ceremony we attended had the tree planted with loose earth forming around its base. The audience was invited to come forward one by one and add a small spadeful of soil to the base of the tree. It was quite touching. Whatever you choose to do, instruct the audience accordingly, and when the ceremony is over, come forward for the last time.

Before we leave this afternoon and allow this tree to settle in to its surroundings, let us pause for one final moment, to bow our heads in silence and pay tribute to Lois Lasser. All mortal things decay and perish, but the spirit—yes, the spirit—will continue; it is *free.*

Let us bow our heads and remember. . . .

NOTE: Count to ten silently.

Thank you, ladies and gentlemen. As Lois gave so much to so many of us, may this tree be a fitting memorial to her as it continues to thrive and grow and give of itself to all future generations.

Now, *that* is a monument fully worthy of the spirit of Lois Lasser. Thank you, again, and good afternoon. . . .

Special Data: *Time of ceremony: between five and fifteen minutes depending on the length of the actual tree-planting itself. Planting a tree in the memory of the deceased is an excellent memorial. Planting it on the school grounds is particularly appropriate for anyone who was involved in education. In order to be effective, make certain that this activity is well-planned. Will there be a plaque? Will it be attached to the tree? Will it be placed on a stand beside the tree? Will the tree be planted ahead of time, or will it be planted during the ceremony? These details will vary according to individual tastes, of course, but make certain that they are worked out prior to the actual ceremony. Also remember that you need the approval of the School Board to plant anything on school property (we have never heard of any school board ever refusing the planting of a memorial tree). Know what you are going to say, make certain that all needed materials such as spades and/or plaques are in place, and then speak from your heart along the lines given here, and it will be a memorable ceremony, indeed.*

$$\boxed{93}$$

TOPIC: Memorial for a Mass Tragedy.

AUDIENCE: Suitable for all audiences.

Ladies and gentlemen. . . .

Life is filled with questions that have no answer. It is part of human nature to seek out the hows and whys of that which we experience, and humankind has filled libraries with explanations of all sorts of issues—why the sun rises in the east; how thunderstorms occur; even how the heart functions. The world has amassed a treasury of knowledge and explanation, but there are times when this is not enough; not nearly sufficient. Life is filled with questions that have no answer.

We may know the "how" of the workings of this world, but we seek more answers. Within each of us there lies a part that goes beyond the mechanical workings of our worldly wonders and seeks an answer to a far more poignant question; we seek to know the *"why"* of life as well.

Facts speak for themselves. We know, only too well, the facts—almost fifty fourth graders; the bubbling anticipation of children; the frenzied supervision of the teachers and parents; the last-minute details to be worked out; the exhilaration of boarding that train . . . the switch that was not thrown . . . the crash . . . the teachers . . . the children . . . the children . . . the children.

Facts speak for themselves, and grief cries out on its own. There is no one in our school who will ever forget that day. There are some who would say that then was the time to carry on as usual, but to these I say that there was nothing usual about it. Students and teachers, the office and the custodians—there was not a person, adult or child, in the school who was not immediately reduced to the basic frailty and weakness that is our common lot. There was little we could do, save hold on to each other and allow the burning emptiness and sorrow within us to be expressed. Grief cries out on its own.

A little more than a year has passed. Now, school continues as it has for decades; one class has gone on to the middle school, and another class has entered into its first experience with classes and teachers. On the outside, to the casual observer, there is no difference between this school and a thousand other elementary schools throughout our nation.

But that would be for the casual observer, indeed. We who are a part of this school realize oh so well that the memory of our classmates, of our students, of our children is still here—it sits in the empty seats; it gathers around the vacant lockers; it gleams from the eyes of teachers and classmates who stop for a moment as they pass what was the fourth grade classroom and stare at the door behind which silence reigns. No difference? Yes, that would be a statement for the casual observer, the very casual observer, indeed.

For still, after this year has passed, after the ceremonies and the speeches, after the investigations and the articles—still it remains, and it haunts me as I know it stirs the hearts of others. Facts speak for themselves, but in our very souls, we seek the why, and there are so many times we simply do not understand.

Ralph Waldo Emerson wrote, "Nothing is at last sacred, except the integrity of your own mind." Perhaps it is in the mind that we must all begin our journey. The question of "why" is one that cannot be found in libraries; cannot be found in monuments; cannot be found in memorial services such as this. Rather, "why?" is a question that may find its answer only within the individual human heart. It is there, in the "integrity of your own mind"; in the sanctity of the individual human spirit that we must seek to come to terms with what has happened; where many find a resolution and a peace that goes beyond our abilities to understand; where some find the fires banked with time but glowing embers that may spring to flame when touched. We speak to each other; we comfort each other; we say a thousand words to touch and soothe and cool, yet each of us must of a time retreat inside and seek the answers with what we find there. In the end, "nothing is at last sacred," except the integrity of what each one of us may find within himself individually.

And if there is one thing beyond the grief that has come out of this great tragedy, it is a firmness and resolve that these children and teachers shall not be forgotten, nor shall they have died in vain. In this year following the event that has changed all our lives, the outpouring of support from parents and the entire community has been unprecedented. Not only will the plaques and statues serve to prod our memories and our hearts for as long as this school stands, but the educational programs and trust funds that have been set up in memory will continue to enrich the lives of those students who follow; the students who will know that they learn and grow and step forward to build for the future in the name of those who have gone before. They shall not be forgotten; they shall not have died in vain.

Our colleagues and friends, our sons and daughters, our children—we reach out to you. How we would long to take you in our arms once more, but the arms we stretch out to you are not arms of flesh, but arms of faith. The eyes with which we see you now are not eyes of flesh, but eyes of memory. The hands with which we would caress you are no longer hands of flesh, but hands of longing and desire; hands that join with other hands in prayer and rise in supplication for the understanding we so desperately seek.

And this we promise you—that our arms will work for the good of those you have left behind; that our eyes will continue to see you live in all of those the love of you has touched; that our hands will not cease to touch others, to comfort others, to build your memory into something living and glorious and nurturing for all.

And in our hearts and in our minds, we will continue to see you as we remember you; we will continue to hear your laughter; we will continue to honor your living memory. We will continue to hold you close in our hearts and minds as one day we with faith affirm that we shall hold you close to us once more, beyond time and sorrow, in Love . . . and in Truth.

We love you.

Special Data: *Time of speech: about eight minutes. How incredibly sad is a mass tragedy such as the one detailed here. How we would all wish never to have to give a speech such as this. Nonetheless, tragedies such as this happen time and again, and there is never a way to prepare for the impact of them. The tragedy that happened in Newburg, New York, where the cafeteria wall collapsed on the children, for instance, affected the entire nation, and brought all of us into close contact with our own mortality. The memorial service detailed here would be one that would take place some time after a tragedy itself, but you would be unwise to suppose that time would lessen the grief. Indeed, memorial services, of themselves, tend to stir memories. If you must give a speech of this type, don't think that you have to be a pillar of strength. Rather, let your heart go, and say what you really feel; be the voice of those people and put into words what they are feeling and the questions they have in their minds and hearts. And, if you should weep during your presentation, don't give it a second thought; there will be plenty of people joining you.*

$$\boxed{94}$$

TOPIC: **Poem for a Eulogy/Memorial.**

AUDIENCE: **Suitable for all audiences.**

Oh, God, so much is difficult
   For us to understand,
And so, in faith, we look to You
   And seek to take Your hand.

Sometimes it seems as if the sun
   Has melted in the rain;
We cannot understand the dark;
   We shudder from the pain.

When in the midnight hour it seems
   Eternity till dawn,
In faith we must believe that You
   Will lead us ever on.

For though we do not know what lurks
   Within the fearful night,
We trust in faith You'll see us through
   And lead us to the light.

And, if we cannot understand
   Why certain things must be,
Then let us look with eyes of faith,
   That looking, we may see.

And seeing, may we realize,
   Though causes be unknown,
There is a hand that fits in ours
   And leads us gently home.

Special Data: *Time of poem: a little over one minute. Faith is a wonderful thing—it has built civilizations and raised humankind out of emptiness to reach for the stars. It has also provided comfort and* *rest during very difficult and trying times to many. There is never a need to apologize for your faith, and we have found overwhelming positive reaction for a statement of belief, particularly in times of trial such as would occasion a eulogy or a memorial speech. This type of statement might well have been used, for example, in the last speech, or anywhere where an affirmation of faith may seem appropriate.*

$$\boxed{95}$$

TOPIC: **Benediction for a Eulogy/Memorial Ceremony.**

AUDIENCE: **Suitable for all audiences.**

Ladies and gentlemen. . . .

May we bow our heads for a moment, and may each of us remember Jeff Fisher in his own way.

As we conduct our personal journeys through life, at times we cannot help but be touched by someone who has exhibited that extra kindness, care, or concern that marks he or she in our minds as a special human being, worthy of our attention. We are here today, because we realize that Jeff Fisher was just such a person. We have, each of us, been touched in some special way by his presence, and it is only natural that we are equally touched and stirred by his loss.

So it is that we join our hearts now in prayer for comfort for his family and for ourselves. We each seek out a power higher than ourselves and seek for understanding in the days to come. But, more than that, we each offer our thanks that in our daily lives, we were privileged, if only for a little while, to know and live and work with someone as special and as wonderful as Jeff Fisher.

And, we make a silent vow that we will pass on to others the kindness he has shown us and will share with others the love he so deeply manifested in his life.

We remember; we cherish; and we will keep him with us in our hearts.

So be it, and so say we all.

Special Data: *Time of benediction: about one minute. If you are asked to deliver a benediction either for a eulogy or a memorial, please remember that it is not supposed to be a major speech. Keep it short—about a minute will do—and keep it simple. Basically, a benediction is a blessing on the gathering, and your aim should be to draw things together and to draw the ceremony to a close.*

$$\boxed{96}$$

TOPIC: Closing for a Memorial Ceremony.

AUDIENCE: Suitable for all audiences.

In every endeavor, there comes the time when we must close the book, shut our eyes, and pause to rest in order that we may begin again.

We have gathered here today to pay tribute to the memory of someone special; someone whom we knew and admired and cared for deeply. We came to honor our friend, Don Hesser.

That is what we have done. There is not a one of us here who has not been touched deeply by what has been said this afternoon; there is not a one of us here who has not remembered Don within his heart and relived those days when he was with us; there is not a one of us here who does not cherish the spirit of Don Hesser in a very special way.

Indeed, we have remembered, and we have found that memory to be good.

As we leave today, we leave with the knowledge that Don is far from forgotten, and that his spirit continues to live reflected in the lives and hearts of all those who knew and cared for him.

That, I am certain, is a tribute that Don Hesser would have loved. Thank you for coming. Good afternoon. . . .

Special Data: *Time of closing: a little over one minute. The closing of a memorial service should be short and to the point. Without reiterating the points made, there should be some very general summation of what has gone on during the ceremony, and it should end with a suggestion of looking toward the future. Finally, the audience* *should be dismissed, and the first line of this closing is as good a way as any of doing this.*

Afterthoughts

If ever you are asked to host or to speak at a memorial service, the one thing you really must do is to make certain you have all your facts straight. We can think of few things so embarrassing as, let us say, referring to the deceased's two lovely children Kathy and Billy, only to have someone tell you later that the children are named Connie and Willy. This *has* happened, much to the consternation of the audience, the family, and the speaker.

So, be sure of all facts, times, dates, awards, degrees, and all other information, and *double check* these for accuracy before your speech.

Other than that, be genuine, be caring, and keep in mind the feelings of the family and close friends and treat them as you would wish to be treated in a similar situation, and your eulogy or memorial will be one that will pay true honor to everyone involved.

New Speeches for Special Events

Just as there are special individuals in this world who persistently defy classification, so there are speeches and sometimes written efforts which will be required of you that simply do not fit into a given classification.

Take, for example, something that is quite popular right now called the "roast." Here, you are asked to get up, usually at a dinner of some sort, and say things, usually derogatory in nature, about the guest of honor that will make everyone laugh heartily, especially the subject of the roast. It is all in fun, of course, and everyone knows it, but how would one classify that kind of speech? It's hardly a testimonial, is it?

What about an administrator's speech for a graduation, with several hundred young people and their parents bursting at the seams to get out and get on with it, as the June temperature nears ninety-five degrees? That, certainly, is a "special" occasion that requires a special speech and special handling of the situation.

All sorts of times, places, and circumstances call for special speeches, and that is what you'll find in this section. From a humorous poem about work and the workplace to the "roast" for a school official to that special graduation speech for a warm June evening, these are speeches and parts of speeches that will fill the bill. Most of them are short, and all of them are to the point and ready for use.

Remember, as with all the speeches in this book, your key to their effective use is how well you adapt them to your particular situation. Be certain that you rewrite the speech for your audience and your subject. Moreover, be sure to add whatever additional, personal information you consider pertinent.

Finally, relax and enjoy yourself, and your audience will share your experience.

97

TOPIC: Humorous Poem on the Trials of the Job.

AUDIENCE: Suitable for any audience.

There are few things in life that will give you more strife
    Than working in school, I would say;
There is just no relief from the mountain of grief
    You must climb on your job every day.

When I came in this morning, without any warning,
    Computerized woes quickly met me,
For the terminal wouldn't, or possibly couldn't,
    Recall who I was—that upset me!

So, in my deep terror, I made a slight error,
    Pushing one button slightly too soon;
And the thing, in reaction, erased all transactions
    Of attendance reports back through June.

The report which I know was assigned weeks ago
    Is due today just before noon,
But it's still on my desk; an incredible mess;
    And I really must get to it soon!

Now, my coffee is cold, and I start getting old,
    When the morning mail comes in a sack;
And as I read each letter, things do not get better,
    But just turn a little more black.

For I have a meeting that came in a greeting,
    Officially stamped and impressed,
For a personal audit (I think I have bought it!)
    With the friendly folks at IRS!

Now, I know my frustration's the justification
    For my wish that it disappears some way,
But despair without hope is stuck here in my throat,
    Because, blast it all, *it's just Monday*!!!

Special Data: *Time of poem: about one minute. This poem should hit a responsive chord in anyone who has ever had to handle the myriad of problems and situations that fill the modern school day. It bespeaks the fact that things do not always run as smoothly as we would have them. You could use this alone, as a humorous poem, perhaps in a flyer or newsletter, or as part of a speech, let us say one on overcoming daily problems or managing your workload. If used for a speech, you might like to start with the poem, comment about how everyone feels this way sometimes, and then go into the speech itself.*

$$\boxed{98}$$

TOPIC: "Roasting" an Educator.

AUDIENCE: Adults; educators, friends, community.

Ladies and gentlemen. . . .

When I was asked to talk about Charlie Martin, I didn't know what to say, so I thought I would make a list of his good points and his bad points and see what I could come up with. I made a list of all Charlie's faults (**hold up several sheets of standard typing paper**), and I made a list of all of Charlie's outstanding qualities (**hold up a scrap of paper about the size of a postage stamp**), and since I'm expected to speak longer than five seconds, I'll have to tell you about the *real* Charlie Martin.

What do you say about a man who has absolutely nothing to recommend him? I tell you, it's difficult. I could tell you about how warm and loving a person he is, but my mother taught me never to lie. So, let me talk to you about Charlie Martin, the educator.

Charlie is an example to the students of this community. He doesn't smoke; he doesn't drink; and there is positively no evidence that he has ever taken a mind-expanding drug. In fact, I have never known anyone to even question Charlie's intelligence. Come to think of it, I've never even heard anyone mention it. In elementary school, he was the teacher's pet, because she couldn't afford a dog. In high school, the class voted him the man most likely to go to seed. For a while, Charlie tried correspondence school, but he kept playing hooky and sending in empty envelopes. Finally, he went to (college). The only difference between that school and a mental institution is that Charlie would have had to improve greatly to get out of the mental institution.

But, Charlie finally graduated in a mere seven years. They finally gave him his degree when he convinced the English Department that he had read the complete works of Shakespeare in the original German. He went on to get a B.A., an M.A., and a Ph.D. He asked his father what degree he should get next, and his father told him, "Get a J.O.B.!" All the colleges were unanimous in their praise, claiming that they had educated Charlie far beyond his intelligence.

Now, of course, Charlie holds a position of responsibility in our school system. In fact, whenever anything goes wrong, Charlie's usually the one responsible. Charlie never has to worry about being replaced by a computer, because no self-respecting computer would ever work that little. Why, when it comes to integrity, Charlie is one of the most suspected people in education.

Charlie really excels as (position). Last week, he got a phone call from a man who asked, "Is this the Natural Gas Company?" Charlie answered, "No, this is Charlie Martin's office." The guy said, "Well, I didn't miss it by much!"

But, Charlie came up with an idea, even though it hurt, that will endear him to educators throughout this community. According to Charlie, every teacher or administrator who applies to this district will be given an intelligence test. The top five percent will be allowed to teach in our schools, and the bottom five percent will join Charlie in Central Administration!

Yes, where Charlie works, it's like a snowstorm, no two flakes alike. Charlie himself is like a cyclone, a vacuum surrounded by a lot of hot air. Charlie's computer is the only one in the place that has to be sent for personal counseling, but that computer is better now. In fact, it's learned so much from Charlie that it's now blaming its mistakes on the computer it replaced.

Well, I guess we'd better get on with this, because we're all missing the "Brady Bunch" reruns. Besides, Charlie's really not looking himself tonight—and that's quite an improvement. In a few minutes, Charlie will be addressing us all, so I have to find something urgent to do elsewhere. We all know how Charlie can take a dull and boring subject and somehow make it dry and lifeless. In fact, Charlie puts a lot of fire into his speeches, and if we could just find a way to put Charlie's speeches into the fire, we'd be fine.

In conclusion, however, I'd like to say something positive and uplifting about Charlie Martin. However, since I couldn't think of anything over the past week, I guess I'll just have to close by wishing Charlie the best of luck and hoping that somehow, in some way, after a great many years have passed, Charlie may, with hard work and diligence, finally gain some small measure of respectability.

Thank you, ladies and gentlemen, and thank you, Charlie.

Good night.

Special Data: *Time of speech: between five and six minutes. We think this is a fairly funny speech. It can fall flatter than a crêpe, however, if it is not delivered properly. Your delivery must be "upbeat," keeping a good pace throughout. If you deliver it slowly, with long pauses, it will not be effective. Keep it moving. When there is laughter, wait until the laughter starts to subside, and then continue. Remember also, that all of this is to be done in a spirit of good-natured fun. Your audience must be aware that you are never serious about what you are saying. Therefore, keep that smile on your face and that grin in your voice, and everyone will have a good time, including the subject of the "roast" who should, if it's done properly, be laughing the loudest of all.*

99

TOPIC: Speech for a Graduation.

AUDIENCE: Students; parents and family; educators; community.

Ladies and gentlemen, and the graduating class of (year).

For decades now, on a certain night in June, someone like me has been getting up before a class like this and talking about graduation. This is well and proper, because your graduation this evening is a true milestone in your lives. Indeed, it is a time that you will recall over and over again in the years to come, hopefully remembering it with fondness.

In all the speeches over all those years, it is inevitable that the speakers have told of the significance of calling a graduation a "commencement" exercise. Commencement means a beginning, and in a very true sense, that's what tonight is, the beginning of your lives in the adult world.

If your years of education have been meaningful, then you don't need me to tell you what that means; to tell you of the responsibilities that you now accept; to tell you of the contributions to our society that are now expected of you; to tell you of the trials and the triumphs that await you. This you should already know.

Rather, let me tell you that tonight is also an ending. Tonight is the closing of your books, and the ending, for a number of you, of your formal education; it is, for those of you who will continue your education, the ending of the time when you were guided and reminded and led through the process; it is, for all of you, the ending of those days which have been referred to as childhood.

When you were babies, a rattle occupied your attention for hours; when you were small children, a new doll or a toy truck filled you with unbounded joy; as preteens, perhaps you discovered the telephone, and your parents wondered if they would have to have that device surgically removed from your ear; then, as teenagers, new interest and a new consciousness began to form within you, and those things of your former years seemed somehow less important than they once did.

Tonight, you take a major step. Tonight, you put aside those trappings of childhood and turn your eyes to the future, eyes that now see with a wider scope and a deeper perspective than those of the boy or girl who ran unchecked across the playing fields of this school.

But, do not lay aside all child within you. Take with you the learning and the growth you have experienced in this school; take with you the excitement and the joy that marked your process of discovery of yourself and the world around you; take with you the childlike wonder that allowed you to reach out toward the unknown and make it yours; take with you the spirit that has guided you through these years and allow it to guide you through the years that are to come.

Tonight is both an ending and a beginning. Laying aside that which is no longer needed, and taking up those tools that have led us to this spot, now take a step into your future with anticipation and delight.

Congratulations to the Class of (year)!

Special Data: *Time of speech: about four minutes. A graduation speech should be kept short. Graduates want the affair over and done, and parents want to see their children receive their diplomas. Even so, the graduation speech often sets the tone for the entire ceremony. A short, dynamic graduation speech that reaches both the graduates and their parents will always make for a memorable graduation ceremony that will be appreciated by all.*

$$\boxed{100}$$

TOPIC: Humorous Lines Acknowledging Your Introduction.

AUDIENCE: Suitable for all adult audiences.

Thank you, Jim, for that marvelous introduction. Actually, I'd be more impressed if I didn't know that the only reason I was asked to speak tonight was because Buffo the Clown couldn't make it.

* * * * * * *

Thank you, Jim. That was a marvelous introduction. You know, Jim, I've always admired your talent, your skill, and your decided ability to exaggerate. . . .

* * * * * * *

Thank you, Jim. After an introduction like that, I don't see how I could possibly go wrong—but I think I'll give it a try anyway.

* * * * * * *

Thank you, Jim, for that wonderful introduction. I just hope now that I don't have a great many words left when I run out of ideas. . . .

* * * * * * *

Jim, I want you to know that that was a fantastic introduction, and those of us who are still awake want to thank you for it.

*   *   *   *   *   *   *

Thank you, Jim, for that fine introduction. Now let's see if I can make a speech that's immortal without being eternal.

*   *   *   *   *   *   *

Jim, these audience members are certainly very polite and mannerly. I was watching them while you were introducing me, and every time they yawned, they covered their mouths.

*   *   *   *   *   *   *

Jim, I know that introduction was right from the heart, and I want you to know that I appreciate the way you read it—exactly the way I wrote it.

*   *   *   *   *   *   *

Jim, I'm really taken with that speaker you just described. Do I know him?

*   *   *   *   *   *   *

Thank you, Jim, for that very kind introduction, but I don't think you realize how long my speech is going to be.

Special Data: *Time of lines: a few seconds each. These ten lines are clever ways of acknowledging your introduction, but should only be used under certain circumstances. These lines would not be used for a formal speech, such as a speech before a legislative body, a Board of Education, or the like, and certainly not in any situation that is extremely serious such as before a hostile audience or at a eulogy or memorial. When, however, you are speaking before a receptive audience or before colleagues or friends who know you well, then a line or two along the lines given here goes a long way toward establishing a favorable rapport.*

$$\boxed{101}$$

TOPIC: Speech About an Injured Student Athlete.

AUDIENCE: Press; administrators; colleagues; community members.

Ladies and gentlemen, I would like to begin by making a statement.

Last Saturday, during a regularly scheduled football game, Douglas Arnold, a player on our team, was seriously injured during one of the plays. As he carried the ball, Doug was tackled by one of the defensive players on the opposing team. When he failed to rise following the tackle, Coach Hartnett and his assistants ran on the field and were at his side immediately. It was apparent that Doug was injured far more seriously than merely having the wind knocked out of him. Within seconds, Dr. Ferris, our team physician, was there along with several trained members of the First Aid Squad. Coach Jenner, the coach of the opposing team, immediately asked their team physician, Dr. Lyle, to assist in any way possible. When it was determined that Doug had suffered an injury to his back, the ambulance was brought on to the field, and, using all the proper techniques, Doug was transported to St. Luke's Hospital.

At present, we know that Doug has suffered a traumatic injury to the spine which has left him incapable of movement from the waist down. The full extent of Doug's injury as well as the effect it will have on him in the future are still being evaluated by the medical team in charge. I can tell you that I have been assured by several medical authorities that Doug's life is not in jeopardy. As far as the paralysis is concerned, we do not know at this time whether this is a temporary or permanent condition.

That is basically what happened last Saturday. If I were to leave it at that, however, I feel that I would be doing a great disservice to many people, including Doug himself. Therefore, I am going to ask you to indulge me for a few more moments.

We have had a chance to view the films of the incident. Coach Jenner, our own Coach Hartnett, the entire coaching staff, several league officials, and the entire administration of this school have run those films several times. We have studied the incident, talked about it, rerun it in slow motion, backwards and forwards. After hours of study, everyone involved has come to the same conclusion.

Basically, neither of the players involved was at fault. The young man who tackled Doug did so in a legal and proper manner. He was performing his function as part of the team. He performed that function as he and every other athlete in his position had been trained to do. He tackled in the legal, prescribed manner. The films offer clear proof of that and of the fact that there was no—I repeat, *NO*—undue violence or evidence of vindictiveness in the action. In other words, this young man tackled Doug the same way that he has tackled dozens of other players throughout all the games in which he has played. There is no doubt in our minds of this.

Nor is there any question that Doug was at fault in any way. Doug was carrying the ball properly, as he had been trained to do. He was running in a normal manner such as we have seen him do on many occasions. His body was in a proper position for running, and there is nothing to indicate that he was doing anything other than what he should have been doing at the time. In short, Doug was performing his task correctly. Doug was in outstanding physical shape. I spoke to him personally on the day of the game, and can testify that he was as bright and alert as ever. Doug's mind was clear, and his body was strong. He had been tackled many times the same way he was tackled on Saturday. There is no doubt in our minds. Doug is completely without fault in this incident.

Yet, it happened. Doug now lies in St. Luke's Hospital paralyzed from the waist down. Tests to be performed shortly will determine whether this is a permanent or a temporary condition. It is the deep and fervent prayer of everyone—coaches; players on both teams; the school faculty and administration; the fans who watched the game; everyone to whom I have spoken—that Doug's injuries may be temporary and that he may soon be back with us. With every part of our beings, we pray for this.

I was with Doug on the field shortly after it happened, and I was allowed to see him later that night at the hospital briefly. He had been given a sedative, and was groggy when I entered the room, but he recognized me. We spoke for a while, and I can tell you that while his body may be injured, there is nothing wrong with his spirit. Time and again, he would tell me, "I'm going to beat this; I'm going to make it."

I want to tell you now that I believe him. He *is* going to beat this;

he *is* going to make it. I have known this young man for three years now. I know what a talented, intelligent, and determined person he is. I have seen him commit himself to a goal both on the playing field and in school and then work long, hard, and demanding hours in order to reach it. I have seen the sweat that went into this; I know the will that kept him at it until he reached those goals.

If his condition proves to be a temporary one, as we all hope and pray that it will, then I know that Doug Arnold will win. He will do whatever is necessary in order to come back. He will not be alone. Every coach, every trainer, every physical therapist, every athlete on the team will be there at his side. If he needs training and therapy, these people will be there. We will be there when he needs us, whenever he needs us, wherever he needs us. We will take our inspiration from Doug himself. We will not give up; we will never let him down; we will, whatever the cost, work until we have achieved our goal. Doug taught us this by his example when he was with us, and now it is our turn to apply those principles in his case. No one forces us to offer this; no one forces us to do this. We offer and will do this gladly, willingly, with pride and with joy, because Doug has been, is, and will continue to be a prized and valuable member of this team and this school.

And, if the worst should happen . . . Well, Doug told me personally that he was going to beat this; that he was going to make it. I firmly believe that this will be true no matter what happens. To some, a handicap is a crushing blow from which they never rise. To others, it is a setback to be dealt with and overcome. I know that Doug is one of the latter. Whatever happens, Doug will rise above it. It may take him time; it will certainly cost him pain and effort, but it will *not* keep him down; it will not crush him. We all know Doug as a person of intelligence, insight, wit, and ambition. We have no doubt but that his future, whatever his physical condition, will be filled with success. A physical handicap could never keep a person of his caliber from rising in the world.

To Mr. and Mrs. Arnold, Doug's parents, we want to say that you have our deepest sympathies for this tragic accident. We join you in your concern. We also want you to know that we are here for you. You have our support not only in terms of prayers and good wishes, but practically as well. When Doug needs us, you have our promise that we will respond in any way that we can. You also have our belief in Doug; a belief based on our knowledge of him as a teammate and fellow student, an outstanding human being, and an inspiration to us all; a belief that *nothing* can beat him, subdue him, or tie him down for long.

Working together, there is nothing but hope for whatever the future may hold.

Thank you for listening, ladies and gentlemen. Now, if you would care to ask some questions, I'll do my best to try to answer them for you....

Special Data: *Time of speech: about six minutes. We think this is an effective model of a speech about a tragedy that has happened. It details what happened precisely; it offers a calm and positive appraisal of the situation; it offers hope for the future. Although the circumstances of this speech are particular to the athletic field, there is no reason why whole sections could not apply to any accident anywhere where future help is needed. Throughout this book, we have stressed honesty in delivery. Well, a speech such as this has a great need for those qualities. This would be an extremely emotion-filled time, and to deliver this with a stony facade would not reap the reaction you would hope for. There doesn't have to be weeping and gnashing of teeth, but* do *show that you are genuinely concerned.*

102

TOPIC: Speech on Emergency Procedures.

AUDIENCE: Teachers; administrators; staff members.

Ladies and gentlemen....

I know that we're all anxious to get home or to our next activity of the day, but there really are some things I want you to know; that I think you have to know. So, if you'll bear with me for a few moments, we'll get this taken care of.

As you know from this morning's bulletin, the state has mandated that all—that's *all*—schoolchildren be given a certain amount of practice in evacuating a school bus in a safe and efficient manner.

Certainly you are aware of the tragedies that have necessitated this directive. Knowing how to evacuate the bus in an emergency situation safely can save an untold number of student lives. This emergency procedure practice is a good idea, and even if it wasn't, it is a mandate of the state, and we are under obligation to comply.

Therefore, tomorrow we are going to hold just such a practice for the entire school. Let me preempt a few questions by stating that this means *everybody*. If Johnny doesn't take the bus—that doesn't matter; Johnny practices. If Mary's mother drives her to school and has sworn that Mary will never set foot on a school bus—too bad; Mary practices.

I believe that I cannot emphasize too strongly that this is extremely important. If what we do tomorrow saves the life of one child, will it have been worthwhile? I know the answer, and so do you.

You have already received the instructions detailing when each cluster will report to the cafeteria as well as procedures for going outside to the actual bus. I know you as professionals, so I know that you have already gone over these procedures, and I merely ask that you take a moment further to review them again before tomorrow. In order to keep things running smoothly, please remember to wait until you are called via the public address system.

I'm certain you realize how extremely important it is that the procedure we will go through tomorrow is taken seriously by our students. Please impress this fact on your class, and remember that your class will take its lead from you. Your personal conviction as to the importance of this procedure as well as your close supervision and guidance will make this practice a profitable one for your students, and, without exaggeration, may help to save a child's life someday. As educators, this is an extremely worthy goal; one that we will achieve together.

I know that I will do everything in my power to make this emergency practice a success, and I also know that I can count on you, as I have so many times in the past, to be the outstanding professionals you are; to make tomorrow's practice the worthwhile activity it was intended to be; to give your students the knowledge that may one day save their lives.

Thank you, have a good afternoon, and I'll see you tomorrow on the bus!

Special Data: *Time of speech: three or four minutes. Bus evacuation practice is a part of New Jersey School Law, but this speech could be adapted easily to any situation in which you wished to enlist the aid and support of the faculty for some procedure around the school. Of course it is true that the attitude of the teachers involved* *has a great deal to do with the behavior of the students, and enlisting their support as well as emphasizing the seriousness of the activity goes a long way toward ensuring success.*

$$\boxed{103}$$

TOPIC: Speech on Parental Conferences.

AUDIENCE: Teachers; administrators; staff.

We all know what time it is. Next Monday, parental conferences begin. Yes, that time has rolled around again.

I am well aware of how taxing these parent conferences can be, both physically and mentally, but I also know that they are extremely valuable, not only to the parent, but to we as educators as well. I have witnessed children who were headed for failure completely turned around after the help of the home was enlisted and given, and I am certain that I am not alone in that. You all know the many benefits of a positive home/school relationship, and I will not belabor that point.

Therefore, I'd just like to take a few moments to review some of the basics that can help make that conference the positive force that it can be in the partnership between home and school in the education of the child.

We should start by remembering that it is our attitude that will set the tone for the conference. We want the parents to understand that we share a common goal of working with them to meet the needs of the children.

We try, therefore, to make the parents feel comfortable; to establish a rapport with them. Greet the parents at the door. Be positive and friendly. Don't sit at your desk, but put some chairs together and establish a neutral ground where you can work as equals. Throughout the conference, remember that these are their children you are talking about, so try to be considerate of their feelings.

We should understand that parents want what is best for their children. There is no parent who does not want their child to be a success in life. Of course we've seen exceptions, but the vast majority of parents are more than willing to take responsibility in order to achieve this goal.

Begin by encouraging parents to share information about their children. As they talk, you listen, because we can all learn a great deal this way, without having to bombard parents with questions. Accept everything the parent tells you about his or her child, and try to listen to what is truly *meant* as well as to what is being said.

Understand that parents will have questions, so be prepared with all the information they may need. This might include information on your grading or homework policies, class projects, a child's behavior, how he or she gets along with others, and a host of other topics that you know only too well. Try to answer each question as politely and thoroughly as you can.

Always be supportive. Toward that goal, be willing to share your ideas and suggest possible courses of action should they be called for. Try to come to a mutual understanding on the course of action needed, and make certain that everyone knows the role they are to play. Certainly, take notes during the conference, but be willing to share those notes with the parents in order to achieve consent on whatever plan is suggested.

Before the conference ends, make certain that you summarize what has occurred. Keep it positive, noting the areas that need improvement and the recommendations for implementing that improvement.

If such a plan has come out of the conference, make arrangements for some follow-up activity. When will you call the home? When will they call you? What's going to happen next? All of this should be established clearly.

Above all, try to smile. It has been the observation of many that a positive attitude begets a positive attitude. Put another way, treat each parent as you would want to be treated. Now, where did I hear that before?

Basically, it's a series of do's and don't's. *Do* be pleasant, listen, avoid arguments, be prepared, be flexible, be specific, be encouraging, and be honest. *Don't* criticize, place blame, jump to conclusions, give commands, talk down to parents, or compare their child to others.

Finally, realize that parents are individual human beings. As such, there will be a wide diversity in types of personalities and approaches to each subject. If we understand this and do our best to accommodate the individual differences of the parents as well as their children, then we are headed for successful conferences.

It can't be called a "challenge" to have a conference with the parents of a student who carries an A+ average, is president of the class, and takes time every day to tell you how nice you look. That is no challenge at all.

It is quite another thing to conference with the parents of the student who hasn't handed in the last three homeworks, daydreams during every lesson, and delights at throwing wads of wet tissue at the ceiling of the lavatory. Now that *is* a challenge.

Yet, both conferences can be handled successfully, because both conferences can be handled in exactly the same manner. Keeping a positive attitude, listening to what the parents have to say, being prepared with facts rather than opinions, suggesting viable courses of action, establishing a rapport where home and school can work together for the ultimate growth and benefit of the child—this is the road to real success in both instances; this is how everybody wins.

Let your parent conference be the start of a positive relationship, and it will be the start of the student's future success as well.

As educators, that's a goal we can all accept, and toward which we must all strive.

Special Data: *Time of speech: about five or six minutes. If the individual teacher's attitude sets the tone for the conferences, then the school administrator's attitude sets the tone for conference procedure. We feel that there is good, sound advice in this speech, with which few would disagree. It is coupled, hopefully, with an enthusiasm for the conferences themselves. This is meant to set the tone for a series of positive and fulfilling parent conferences to follow.*

$$\boxed{104}$$

TOPIC: **Opening Speech for a Debate on Grouping.**

AUDIENCE: **Adults—teachers, parents, administrators, community.**

There is an expression that I am sure you have heard. It states, "What goes around, comes around." I'll tell you this, whoever wrote it originally *must* have been in education. I think you know that I have spent my entire adult life in public education, and I can assure you that there are issues in education that tend to rise and fall so frequently, you'd swear you were spending a day at the seashore!

We deal with the education of the child. That is not a "product" that can be stamped or placed in a box or measured with a ruler. Indeed, there are so many variables that go into each individual child's schooling, that I think it impossible to list them all. Because of that, there are precious few issues where we can say, "This always works," or "Children must be taught in this way." It simply does not work that way, as anyone who has been around education knows exceptionally well.

What am I talking about here? You are familiar with almost all of the arguments. There's the "new" math versus (What else?) the old math; departmentalization versus the self-contained classroom; the giving of letter grades or the giving of number grades; the list goes on and on.

Chief among the issues on the "hotly debated" list is the topic of heterogeneous versus homogeneous grouping. I honestly cannot remember a time when this issue was not being debated. I can picture Aristotle or Socrates arguing the issue in classical Greek, and I'm positive it was being discussed when I went to elementary school—in the days when dinosaurs roamed the earth.

In fact, seldom has an issue so involved everyone connected with education in such a passionate manner. The question of grouping for education is one that is tremendously important, as we are all tremendously concerned about and involved with our children's education.

Why don't we just do what is best for our children? Aren't we concerned about meeting the needs of our students? Oh, come now; of course we are, but that does absolutely nothing toward solving the problem. For as many as espouse heterogeneous grouping and can offer their reasons for it, there are just as many who will tell you of the obvious benefits of homogeneous grouping as they see it. Indeed, this program tonight will offer you a vast field of opinion, research, fact, and projection on both sides of the issues.

This is a necessary part of any decision-making process, and that is why we are hosting this series of discussions and debates. It may well be that this issue will never be decided to everyone's satisfaction and that schools will continue the practices that have worked for them in the past. Nonetheless, when we listen, we learn; when we learn, we understand; when we understand, we are one step closer to making the informed decisions that are required of all those involved in the task of educating our children.

Therefore, let us begin this evening by hearing from a woman who has great experience in the field of. . . .

Special Data: *Time of opening speech: about four minutes. It may well be that there is no solution to the "grouping" problem; i.e. you show me your expert, I'll show you mine, and we'll debate forever. This may also be said of a number of other topics in education. Yet, to stand still and debate the issue forever while our children languish is wholly unacceptable. Therefore, debates such as the one introduced here go a long way toward clearing the air. You could also adapt this as a speech to parents for a topic currently under consideration in your school system.*

$$\boxed{105}$$

TOPIC: Speech to Parents on Communicating with the School.

AUDIENCE: Parents; teachers; a PTA gathering.

If I wanted to borrow a dollar from you, maybe you'd give it to me and maybe you wouldn't, but one thing is certain—I wouldn't know until I asked you. What's more, if you didn't speak English too well, and I asked you for a "buck," I might look pretty silly trying to carry home the male deer you produced.

As the cliché goes, "What we have here is a failure to communicate!"

Throughout the school year, it is only natural that there will be times when the home and the school must communicate. Sometimes this is pleasant communication; sometimes it deals with problems. Especially in the latter case, where problems arise with the child in school, it is essential that both parents and teachers clearly understand what is being said. When there exists good, solid, understandable communication between home and school, then everyone benefits—the child, certainly, but the teacher and parents as well.

Let's begin by understanding that there is no problem that can be solved unless it is acknowledged and discussed first. If you feel that there is a problem developing, then make certain that you let us know about it, just as we will let you know if we see something starting to go astray. Let both the school and the home do this in precise, clear, and understandable language in order that everyone knows exactly what is being said.

It is also essential that there exists an atmosphere of mutual respect. That respect will produce better understanding and allow the problem to be discussed calmly and evenly, with a free interchange of positive ideas. Of course it is understood that opinions will vary—we are, after all, individual human beings—but that mutual respect will help all of us arrive at a common ground.

Both sides also need to keep an open mind, realizing that what the teacher has heard from the child about the home may be only as true as what the home has heard about the teacher and the school. This is the time to discuss real concerns, not hearsay or personal feelings.

Remember also that we are human beings, and human beings are fallible; we make mistakes. I would like to think, however, that we can keep an open mind as well. We understand that everyone involved with each child is trying to do their best. With that understanding and a willingness to listen and learn from each other, real progress can be made.

Therefore, let both sides speak the truth. Of course everyone wants to be tactful; that is understood. Truth, however, must come first, and if we appreciate the fact that we are working for the ultimate good of the child, then truth should be a welcome part of the process.

Finally, let us dedicate ourselves to finding a solution to our problems. In a school such as ours, no one person can handle everything. It may take you a while to find the person who can best help you, but it will be worth the effort if you do. A child's neglect in handing in homework to one particular teacher, let us say, may be best handled by communicating with that teacher, but if the same problem extends to all classes, you may find it necessary to involve all the teachers, or the guidance counselor, or the child study team, or any combination thereof. Of course it is frustrating if a problem continues despite your efforts to remedy it, but don't get discouraged. Keep at it, don't give up, and we will find an answer—together.

If both the home and the school can keep these guidelines in mind, then real and meaningful progress can be made for any adverse situation. When we communicate, we understand; when we understand, we can seek solutions together; when the home and school work together in close cooperation, the student stands an overwhelming chance of success.

Let us remember how important communication is in the home/school liaison; let us work at it as partners, with willingness and conviction; let us always keep in mind the goal for which we work, the education of your child.

If we can appreciate that, then I may, indeed, have communicated something worthwhile to you this afternoon; something that will benefit the teacher, the parents, and, most importantly, the student.

Thank you, and good afternoon.

Special Data: *Time of speech: about five minutes. While this is a speech for "special" occasion such as a forum on parenting or on "how to get the most from your child's school," it also provides basically true and very important basics for home/school communications. Shortened to a list, it could provide a basis for a parental "hand-out," or, lengthened a bit (which could be done by giving some concrete examples of the points made in each paragraph) it could serve easily as a featured speech at a regular PTA meeting.*

$$\boxed{106}$$

TOPIC: Speech on State Monitoring of Curriculum.

AUDIENCE: Administrators and supervisors responsible for each school.

Ladies and gentlemen. . . .

As we are all aware, there are twenty-one days of state monitoring coming up during November and December of this year. Monitors will review documentation in the Central Administration Office for two days, and will also look for documentation from you and teachers during visits to the schools. You may certainly expect all monitors to visit each classroom and talk to all teachers in small groups. At present, these monitors plan to schedule three days in each high school, with one day in each middle school and elementary school.

The objective of these discussions is to document and certify that the district's curriculum is, indeed, being implemented. Consequently, each teacher should have a course of study for each preparation. When a course of study can serve as a plan book or working support document for classroom planning and activities, please encourage teachers to use the material as it applies. We will be happy to run off additional copies of courses of study at your request; please do not be shy in asking for them.

Lesson plans can be used as one of the sources to document implementation of curriculum. Understandably, there have been several questions as to precisely what expectations you should have for lesson plans. Let me share with you the following guidelines which have been carefully reviewed and are within the guidelines of the current contract as well as provide for the district monitoring objective of documentation of curriculum implementation.

First, every professional employee shall plan lessons within the guidelines and framework of the existing curriculum or course of study.

Next, these plans are to be submitted to the building principal or the supervisor designated by that principal on a weekly basis. Indeed, it may even be more frequently than that should the need arise and the requests be made.

Finally, the lesson plan is to be written, and is to contain objectives, procedures, and evaluations.

As far as the objective part of the lesson plan is concerned, it can be written as it appears in the course of study. An alternative would be to have references in the lesson plan by unit, objective number, or other citation specific to that course of study, with the objective summarized in a topic phrase or sentence.

Please, do what you do best—work with the teachers to use this course of study to the teachers' advantage. Since our goal is implementation of the curriculum, the lesson plan should support the tested curriculum style.

We have a fine school system; we have nothing to hide; let's make every effort to present our practices to the monitors as succinctly, logically, and completely as possible.

Let them see just how good we are.

Special Data: *Time of speech: about four minutes. The appearance of State Monitors on the scene always heightens tensions. It is not that we are not doing what is required, but everyone is anxious that the schools be shown and presented in a manner so that all will* *know what a fine job we are doing. Invariably, preparations for the visit begin well in advance, as indicated by this speech. Notice that this speech is extremely straightforward, presenting what has to be done in a one-two-three manner. The objective here is to inform, and rhetoric becomes secondary in this instance. If details are spelled out clearly, people will respond positively.*

Afterthoughts

There are, of course, many other occasions in the career of any educator that could qualify as "special." We have given you many of them here. This text, along with our first book, will provide you with formidable reference material suitable for all occasions.

When writing a speech for any "special" occasion, remember that special occasions require special speeches. First, you should determine precisely what is required for the occasion. Does the audience want straight information? Is your speech meant to inspire? Will the gathering be confrontational? Are you serving as an authority figure or is your task to entertain?

Next, you should write your speech according to what is required. On a "hot" topic such as the opening for a debate on grouping, you would never want to use any of the material given in the "roast," even if you or one of the participants were best friends. Keep your audience and your purpose in mind, and all will go well.

Finally, deliver your "special" speech as you deliver all your speeches: with enthusiasm, conviction, and a love and respect for your audience.

ORIGINAL SPEECHES FOR HOLIDAYS AND OTHER JOYOUS OCCASIONS

If you talk to some educators about the time they spend in school, you might come away with the impression that education is little more than one headache after another. To be sure, there are enough headaches in professional education to send every educator scrambling for aspirin, but to leave it at that would be to neglect the full picture. Along with the trying times and situations, there are also those times that delight us; those times that lift our spirits and give us the encouragement to carry on; those times when we speak to students or teachers or parents not about problems but about topics that are interesting, positive, and filled with joy.

In our first volume, we included speeches for every legal holiday the school celebrates, and we even included the Fourth of July (just in case you held a summer session). Here, we are offering several new speeches about some of those same holidays, but we are also including speeches on those situations which may be described as "joyous."

There is so much in which we do take joy. We love giving awards to students who have excelled; what a joy to be able to speak to students and parents about a *winning* sports season; how grand it is to acknowledge an upcoming spring break with the realization that we've gotten through another winter. There are many happy occasions during the school year.

In this section, we have tried to include speeches on many of them. From a welcoming speech acknowledging the successful settlement of negotiations, to a speech on the start of the baseball season, to a happy send-off for students and teachers at the end of the school year, there are many speeches for those occasions where your audience is behind you one hundred percent, you are brimming with good news, and everyone's spirits are in celebration.

It's a winning situation—ripe for your winning speech.

107

TOPIC: Settlement of Negotiations.

AUDIENCE: Educators; those affected by negotiations.

Ladies and gentlemen. . . . Welcome back!

If that sounded a little enthusiastic, let me assure you that it is. I am overjoyed to be welcoming you back to school after the summer hiatus.

It occurs to me that I say that every year, and I hope you'll believe me when I tell you that I mean it sincerely, every time I say it. I have always found the school building to be a bleak and lonely place during the hiatus. It needs the human touch that our students and you supply so well. Therefore, when I welcome you back, I am really welcoming life and vitality back to a place where we spend such a grand proportion of our lives each and every year.

What makes this year so special, for myself, and I am certain for you as well, is the fact that negotiations between the Board of Education and your professional association have been concluded; the contract language has been worked out; and, as I understand it, two days ago the membership ratified the contract. Personally, I am delighted!

We are all aware that these negotiations were not as smooth as we all hoped they would be. Certainly there was conflict, and very often that conflict manifested itself in rhetoric that was trying on both sides, a seeming intransigence and unwillingness to budge, and a perceived need to take measures beyond what was being done at present.

I speak, of course, of the strike vote that was taken back in May and the passage of the authorization to strike. I'm sure you will recall that at that time, a strike at the start of school in September seemed a very real possibility. I hope you will also recall that I let it be known to anyone who asked me, that I deeply respected this faculty as a group of outstanding educators, and I respected their integrity. I believed then, and I believe now, that the decision to participate in the strike, had it been called, was an individual decision that would be respected by me, whatever the decision might have been. I was of the opinion, voiced openly, that a strike would have a devastating effect upon our school and our students, but I always added that when the strike had finally come to an end, I would make every effort to pick up from the place where we had left off, with an eye to the future, with no enmity for the past, and with trust in the professionalism of the teaching staff.

I thank God that both sides were able to meet over the summer and come to some degree of understanding. Your own association president has commented publicly that he thinks your new contract is a fair one. The president of the Board of Education has stated that she feels the Board can work within the boundaries of the contract. If it is good enough for these people, let it be good enough for us.

It is time to put behind us any vestiges of concern or rancor that the turbulence produced; it is time to rid ourselves of any personal feeling which might, in any way, bear upon the process of education in this school; it is time to recognize the fact that we are all human beings, and that the essence of growth is conflict, with diversity of opinion playing a significant part in any developmental process; it is time to look toward the future; it is time to pull together into the tightly-knit unit that provides the children of this township with the best education possible.

If every beginning implies an ending, then it is also true that every end implies a beginning as well. The contract has been signed and ratified; negotiations are finished; both sides are resting from their labors.

It is time for us to begin.

Welcome back!

Special Data: *Time of speech: about four minutes. Like any traumatic experience, negotiations seem to bring out the best and worst in all people. I do not have to tell you that negotiations that are going badly are hardly pleasant for anyone. Add to that such variables as strike votes, variations of the "blue flu", and other "job actions", and it can become an absolutely horrendous situation. The successful settlement of negotiations, therefore, is quite joyous. This speech acknowledges that fact and makes an attempt to bury the past and regroup in order to press on toward the future. The respect, both implied and stated in this speech, cannot help but be returned to everyone's benefit.*

$$\boxed{108}$$

TOPIC: Thanksgiving.

AUDIENCE: Students; teachers; administrators; community.

Good afternoon. . . .

Were I to ask you the history of Thanksgiving as a legal holiday in the United States, I wonder how many of you could give me the facts. Oh, don't worry, I'm not going to ask you. Indeed, if you are like a majority of people, what you know about Thanksgiving is that in a few hours, school will be over and a four-day weekend will begin.

To most people, and I include in this myself, your teachers, parents, and most people in the community, Thanksgiving is a wonderful day off. It's a day when we don't have to get up with the alarm clock; it's a day when we get together with our families, perhaps with brothers and sisters and parents or perhaps with grandparents and aunts and uncles and cousins; it's a day when we are all busy preparing a special meal that will draw ooos and ahhs from the folks who sit at the table; it's a day when we all overeat a little bit; and some of us a whole lot; it's a day when we can enjoy our family, joke and laugh with each other, and come away with a good feeling of warmth and satisfaction.

This is fine, because this is definitely a part of what Thanksgiving should be, but is only half of what the holiday was intended to be. Thanksgiving was also intended to be a day when each of us spent some time in reflection, in looking over our lives and our situations and in thinking about those things for which we are thankful.

Tomorrow, many of you will attend religious services; many of you will pray with your families before the big meal; and, all of us can afford to spend some time thinking about the many things for which we may be thankful.

For what am I thankful on this day before Thanksgiving? Well, it may surprise you to know that one of the things I'm most thankful for is this school, and that means I'm thankful for you, all of you, both those who come to my office for honor roll recognition and those who have seen the inside of my office under less-than-happy conditions.

Truly, this school would not exist were it not for you. A school is not merely brick and wood and glass and stone—a school is the body of people who study and teach and learn in it, and who fill its halls every day.

You are this school. There are some of you who have no trouble and others who experience trouble at every turn; there are some of you who are so smooth you glide through the school year and others who have a lot of rough edges that need to be sanded down; there are some of you who fill us with anticipation and others over whom we have poured out a great deal of time and worry. Wherever you fit, you are a part of this school, because it is a part of your life that will always have an influence on you, always be a part of your memories, and always be the starting place of your adult life.

That I and your teachers can play a part in that adventure is something that gives me joy, and something for which I am very grateful. Tomorrow, on Thanksgiving Day, I will give special thanks for the students and teachers of this school, as I do in my heart all year long.

It is my fondest hope that some of you will pause for a moment, reflect on this, and come to the conclusion that this school and the people in it are grateful as well.

Have a wonderful Thanksgiving!

Special Data: *Time of speech: about four minutes. This is the type of speech that a principal might give to a student body (with attendant teachers, parents, etc.) on a preholiday occasion such as a pep rally for the big Thanksgiving Day game. Note that the language is different from that used, let us say, in the speeches for fellow educators. It's a simple message, short and to the point, and that seems to be exactly what is needed in circumstances such as these. You know your student body; tailor your speech accordingly.*

TOPIC: The Winter Break.

AUDIENCE: The student body; teachers; staff.

Did you ever hear an adult, particularly an older adult say, "The winters aren't the same as when I was a kid . . . "? Perhaps you have. Well, I think these people are right, because everything changes, particularly the way in which we view our surroundings.

Today, winter is, for the most part, just another season. If a foot of snow should fall tonight, the snowplows will have it cleared by tomorrow. If the temperature drops to five degrees, perhaps we will turn up the thermostat or the control on the electric blanket. If the day is dark and threatening, perhaps we'll take the bus or train instead of driving or walking. No matter what the conditions, life will continue as usual; we will make plans as usual; we go to school, go shopping, go to the movies, and visit each other . . . as usual. It would take some really bad weather to interrupt that routine, and even then, it would be for a few days at most.

It wasn't always that way. Even through the last part of the nineteenth century, most of autumn was taken up in preparing for winter. Foods were cooked, salted, and preserved in jars for use during the winter when no one would be able to leave the immediate vicinity of the house for days. Supplies were bought in quantity and stored for the long and lonely winter ahead. It was expected and anticipated that a month or perhaps two might go by during which you would be separated from your neighbors by the snow and cold. Needless to say, firewood was stacked to the rafters, because oil and gas heat were decades away.

Even so, the winter for these, our ancestors, was not a waste at all. Those winter months that, of necessity, were spent in the home, were a time when people worked at repairing what needed to be fixed and in preparing for the spring that was certainly to come. These people reviewed what they had done and the progress they had made over the past year and made plans for what they would be doing in the year to come.

You know, that wasn't such a bad plan. In a few hours, you'll be out of school and the winter break will have begun. Of course, we all look forward to that. In fact, I'm sure you realize that your teachers are probably looking forward to it every bit as much as you. I'm also sure that everyone has plans as to how they will spend that time.

I'd like to remind you, however, that this winter break comes in the middle of your school year. As far as this year in school is concerned, half of it is the past, and half of it is the future. This winter break is the "mountain peak" between the two "valleys."

It just might be a good time, along with all the rest of your plans, to spend some time in copying the procedures of the people of those winters long ago. It would be to your advantage to look at the past of this year and see what repairs are needed. What have you done or not done; what progress have you made or not made; what areas need the most "repairs"? Then, look forward to the half year that still remains. What are your plans? Are you going to repeat the actions of the past? Will you resolve to create a new future for yourself?

Our ancestors knew that spring followed winter, and that spring is the season of renewal.

Your winter break begins today, and the spring will follow in its own time. Will you take a part of this "winter" break to decide what type of renewal this spring will bring to your school life?

Have a wonderful winter break. Don't overlook the past, and please don't forget to plan for your "personal" spring!

Special Data: *Time of speech: three or four minutes. Again, while there is nothing earth-shattering or philosophically profound in this speech, it speaks of a sound truth that everyone should inculcate. If the winter break falls around your midterm exams, you might want to make mention of them as a turning point as well.*

110

TOPIC: **Christmas/ Hanukkah.**

AUDIENCE: **Suitable for all audiences.**

Soon it will be what generations of writers, poets, and philosophers have referred to as the most wonderful time of the year. You are all aware that I am referring to the very special holidays of Christmas and Hanukkah.

Some of us here tonight will be celebrating Christmas, which many have spoken of as a "celebration of Love"; some of us will be celebrating Hanukkah, which is also known as the "Festival of Lights." All of us will be taking part in this time of year that fills each and every one of us with Love and Light and is a time that is dearly cherished.

Each of us may look inside and find there a number of precious memories of a Christmas or Hanukkah of the past that fills us with the joy of remembrance. Perhaps, in our mind's eye, we see grandparents, mothers and fathers, brothers and sisters, or other relatives who exist now only in the love of those memories. Perhaps we see them around the Christmas tree or lit by the light of the Hanukkah candles, and for a moment they live once more in our hearts. The memory may be bitter-sweet, but it is a prized possession with which none of us would ever willingly part.

And, whether we realize it or not, we are well on the way toward building a set of memories for our own children; memories of this special time; memories of the warmth and security of a family together; memories of love—memories that will stand up to the ravages of time as a golden legacy for our children and their children yet to come.

This is a time when the love that exists flames into the light that brightens all the dark corners that the year has brought with it. Certainly, there will come tomorrow, and with tomorrow will come the hardships and the hardness of the day and the thousand darts that chip away at our human frailness, but now, for a moment, we are safe. See the lights that glow upon the evergreen tree; look at the dancing glow of the candles in the menorah—in that warm and beguiling light, all hard edges become smooth; all troubles scurry away to hide in the darkness; all challenges become possibilities. We reach out and touch the faces of the ones we love and find their love caressing us in return. For a moment, we are safe.

If it is illusion, as some hardened skeptics claim, then it is an illusion that is magnificent; it is an illusion that we would gladly trade for the brightest reality; it is an illusion that is borne of the heart and nurtured in the soul.

But, let us not believe that cynic's view. Let us leave that view to them. Let us believe that love is real and never need be relegated to a single day; let us believe that light can flow within the deepest dark as long as that light burns within us as a true beacon in the night. Let us believe that the spirit of Christmas and Hanukkah are not for one day only, but instead that which we may carry into life each and every day, as long as its passion burns within.

Let us understand one other thing as well. Let us understand that from these special times we have all received a legacy of Light and a legacy of Love which is ours to pass down to our children in order that they may follow, their feet guided by the light and their hearts warmed by the love.

This is the miracle of Christmas and Hanukkah; this is the gift that we receive; this is the treasure that we keep by passing it on.

In this most wonderful of times, whether it be "Happy Hanukkah" or "Merry Christmas," may Love and Light be yours in abundance—now, and throughout this bright year.

Special Data: *Time of speech: about four minutes. Both Christmas and Hanukkah are religious holidays, even though they have been secularized a great deal. This speech gets to the essence, we feel, without going into particulars. Consequently, we feel it is suitable for any audience. Indeed, you won't find many who will object to anything said here, since it is so universal. This might also be typed and published as part of a "Preholiday" newsletter or parent bulletin. Either way, we think this speech will be very effective and appropriate.*

TOPIC: Martin Luther King Day.

AUDIENCE: **Suitable for either student or adult audiences.**

January 15th is a day designated as a holiday. Its official name is Martin Luther King Day. It is named in honor of a man of courage and conviction, a man who fought through peace, a man who sought freedom, even for those who would oppress him. On this day, we honor the memory of Dr. Martin Luther King, Jr., a true leader in the cause of freedom for all people.

Martin Luther King, the son of a Baptist minister, was born into a world where equality was a concept that had not yet been realized. As a child and later as an adult, he would face tremendous prejudice. Discrimination against him and the people whose cause he championed would be based not on personality, not on achievement or lack of it, not on what they had or had not contributed to society—not on any of these factors. No, Dr. King would face discrimination as would the people of his race on the fact of their color.

Sometimes this discrimination would take the form of being forced to use a separate restroom facility, or to shop only in a certain store; in sitting in a certain section of a theater, or in being allowed to ride in the back of a bus only. Sometimes this prejudice resulted in denying an education to someone with the ability and desire for it; in the burning of homes, schools and churches; in the murder of innocent people whose crime was nothing more than that they were black.

Dr. Martin Luther King, Jr. fought against this evil. Like his father, he was a minister; a man of God and of peace. The means he used to fight were not the trappings of the hatred and violence that had been used against him and his people. Rather, he used the principles of nonviolent resistance to achieve the equality of opportunity that should have been a part of our society in the first place. In spite of tremendous hardships, violence, and untold aggression aimed at him and the people with whom he worked, Dr. King stood by his faith in God and his belief in peaceful, nonviolent protest in order to bring the injustice to the forefront of public attention.

He worked not for personal glory nor for personal gain, but he labored because, as he would later tell a nation, he had a dream. He dreamed of a nation where individuals were judged solely on their individual merits and not on the color of their skin; he dreamed of a nation where people of all colors and all races could live and work together in harmony; he dreamed of a nation where black and white children could play together and walk hand-in-hand together into a future that would hold the best for each child based only on the individual potential of the little boy or girl.

Dr. King's life was ended by an assassin's bullet, but even that could not end his work or the indomitable spirit that had been his inspiration and his guide. Thanks in a large part to his efforts, the fight for equality continues; the fight for a nation where race and nationality play no part in an individual's ability to achieve; the fight for a place where we can live side by side in peace and in love and in hope for a future where prejudice and discrimination will be facts relegated to a history book, with little bearing on the society in which we live.

This is the legacy of Dr. Martin Luther King, whose memory we celebrate and honor on this holiday.

Let us honor that legacy in our spirits, and in our deeds.

Special Data: *Time of speech: between two and three minutes. This speech is appropriate for any school program honoring the holiday as well as any program on civil rights and/or its history. We think this would also be appropriate for a school newsletter. If a more de-*

tailed speech were desired, you may certainly find a great deal more information about Dr. King in any library.

$$\boxed{112}$$

TOPIC: A Winning Sports Season.

AUDIENCE: Suitable for all audiences.

Let's start by acknowledging something we all can agree on—it's good to win! The season has ended, and our record stands for everyone to see. We have every reason to be proud of it. We worked for it. We fought for it. We sweated for it. It is ours!

Perhaps we should just accept it for what it is, an outstanding tribute to the dedication, diligence, and hard work of a superb group of young athletes and their coaches. Certainly, this is what that record shows. We see reflected in it countless hours on the practice field, sore muscles, infinite patience, and a fierce determination on the part of our players to be the best they are capable of being.

Perhaps, also, we should take a closer look at our record and see in it something else. Perhaps we can also see the untiring efforts of everyone who supported these athletes, from the cheerleaders who spurred them to victory to the young men who collected the towels after the games. All—and I mean this sincerely—all of them have played a vital and necessary part.

No machine works well if even a single part has broken down. Let one belt break in the motor of your car and see how well it runs. So it is with this team. Without the complete and total support of everyone who contributes to the team, it will—no—it cannot—be the excellent, functioning, winning team that we have been privileged to see this past season. So to these, the support personnel, this victory is your victory as well.

But, there is something else that I see in our record. Yes, our players and our support people are vitally important, but there is one other group, just as important, just as vital, and just as necessary to the total victory. It is to them that I speak now.

I am speaking of you—our student body; our teachers; our parents—the people who sat on the sun-baked bleachers and huddled inside blankets in the freezing cold; who shouted with the team in the joy of triumph; who kept the faith when things looked bad; who willed the team to win; who lifted their hearts; strengthened their resolve, and gave every ounce of energy in filling their souls with support, determination, and love. Without you people, defeats would have been crushing, and victories would have been but hollow experiences.

So, you see, this is your victory also; this record is truly your record. Therefore, yours is the record of which we are so proud. Yours is the honor of our team as well. I know that I speak for every member of the team as well as for every coach and every member of the support staff in saying that we are grateful to you—you are our support and our inspiration. In all honesty, we could not have done it without you.

Yours is the spirit that uplifts; yours is the spirit that tells us to press forward when all circumstances say to quit; yours is the spirit that picks us up when we are too tired to move and puts us in there for one more try. Yours—yours is the spirit of victory.

Let us take a closer look at that winning record and see in it our victory, the victory of everyone who is a part of this team. Players, coaches, team workers, cheerleaders, the people who took tickets at the home games, the teachers, the fans, parents, friends, all those who worked, hoped, prayed, cheered, supported, laughed, wept, and raised hands in triumph—this is *our* record!

We have been victorious. We have had a winning season. *We* have worked; *we* have striven; *we* have won.

We may all be justly proud of it.

Thank you . . . and wait 'til next year!!!

Special Data: *Time of speech: about four and a half minutes. If you are giving this speech before your student body, then the minute you utter the first sentence, there will be an uproar that may last for some time. Wait for that to die down before you continue. If you wish to elaborate on the individual season's records, a good place to do so would be after the second paragraph. We think that the ending is fairly powerful as it is, and should be delivered vigorously and with conviction and enthusiasm. This speech could be used effectively in any postseason gathering, and it might be particularly effective for a press conference, awards dinner, or a team postconference dinner where parents and/or members of the faculty and* *administration are present as well as team members. It is a very good feeling to have a winning season. Since these don't come along that frequently, we think it justifiable to make the most of it when it happens.*

113

TOPIC: Spring Break.

AUDIENCE: Students; faculty; administration; school staff.

> The Spring has sprung;
> The grass has riz;
> I wonder where the birdies is?
> The bird's on the wing—
> Ain't that absurd—
> I thought the wing was on the bird!

I don't know who wrote that poem, but in spite of its bad grammar, all we have to do is to look around us to see exactly how true it is.

The snows of the winter are melting into memories of snowballs and ski trips, the summer has become a vision that we can see looming on the horizon that marks the end of the school year. In between here and there lies that season called spring.

Everyone knows that spring is a time of rebirth. The trees that have bent in the winter's wind are beginning to produce those little green buds that, in a few short weeks, will become the leaves that will shade us from the summer sun. Underneath the frozen ground the roots and bulbs of flowers that have slept their winter sleep are pushing upwards and will soon be exploding in color all around us. In a like manner, many people who have moped and lagged and dragged themselves through the winter months are starting to perk up; starting to gaze at the blue skies; starting to get out those shirts and blouses they put away late last fall. Everywhere, there is a new excitement, a new anticipation. Spring is here.

Shortly, we will begin what we are calling our "Spring Break." For ten days, we will lay down our books and put aside our routine of daily classes. Most of us, I am certain, will be out in the predicted pleasant weather; many will be on vacations with family; even those who stay at home will be touched by the rest and beauty that spring and this spring break affords to us all.

Undoubtedly, this is good and fitting. It is right that after the struggle of winter there should be a time when we can enjoy the promise of spring. It is right that we can pause for a moment to reflect.

But, just as spring carries with it the promise of summer, so this spring break carries with it the certainty of the final leg of the school year to come. Of course, all we want to concentrate on right now are these few days to come shortly, but there are none of us, I think, who do not realize that the final marking period of the school year still lies before us.

So, just as spring is a time of rebirth for trees and grass and flowers, I'm going to ask you to consider it a time of rebirth for yourself as well. I'm going to ask you to think of this spring break as a time when, like a general on a battlefield, you pull together your forces for a battle to come.

Pause for a moment and look back at the school year you have left behind. Ask yourselves what you have done and what remains for you to do. Take a look ahead at the time that remains and what there is yet to accomplish. Stop for a little while and see if you can make decisions that will aid your academic goals in the time remaining. Take a moment to be like the spring itself, something that places the past into memory and takes a step toward the future, bringing with it light, hope, and expectation for every future day.

Enjoy your spring break, to be sure, and marvel in the yearly miracle that we call spring, and remember that the rebirth of spring can also be a rebirth of mind and spirit that will carry you through the remainder of the school year.

Have a wonderful spring break!

Special Data: *Time of speech: about four minutes. We have always found that everybody, not only the kids but the faculty and administration as well, needs the spring break. Your audience for this speech will probably be all but jumping up and down to get out and get going, so it is best kept short and to the point. The speech also carries a small reminder that they have to consider the final weeks to come and that the school year is far from over.*

$$\boxed{114}$$

TOPIC: Start of Baseball Season.

AUDIENCE: Suitable for all audiences.

Did you know that baseball started in controversy? Of course, we are well aware today of the controversial players and activities of players that often bring the sport to front-page prominence, but did you know that there was controversy from the moment it first started?

It seems that throughout the late 1700s and early 1800s the people of the towns and villages of the colonies and later the United States, would play a game with a ball that was called "Rounders" or "Town Ball." Teams of men were chosen by various towns, and they played each other. They played on a field laid out in the form of a perfect square with sixty feet between each base. The "batsman" stood on a line halfway between first and fourth base with a catcher standing behind him but outside the square. Any ball that was hit was considered to be fair and playable. When he hit the ball, the batsman would start to run around the bases. He was considered "out" when he was hit by the ball after it was caught.

Town Ball became so popular that clubs were formed. In 1833, the Olympic Town Ball Club was formed in Philadelphia, and in 1825, the Rochester Baseball Club was founded in Rochester, New York.

Then came the summer of 1839. In Otsego County in central New York State, in the small village of Cooperstown, an instructor in a military preparatory school who would later become a general in the United States Army, set up a field of new proportions, changed the rules of Town Ball somewhat, called it "Baseball," and began what has come to be known as "America's Pastime." His name was Abner Doubleday.

The popularity of baseball in America grew and grew, and Town Ball and Rounders were replaced by baseball. It really caught on. Originally, all players were amateurs who played for the love of it, although it was accepted that certain players of great talent might accept fees for their services to play for one particular team. By the late 1800s, however, professional baseball teams had been formed and were playing schedules of games with complete team competition.

It was at that time, during the 1880s and '90s, that a controversy arose that would rise to a fever pitch and never really be resolved to anyone's satisfaction.

Many people believed that Abner Doubleday had "invented" baseball. Others argued that it was merely an outgrowth of Town Ball and Rounders and pointed to the fact that originally, Doubleday still had a man go "out" by being hit with the ball. In fact, it wasn't until 1845 when a commission was established to formalize the rules of baseball that "tagging" out of a player rather than having him be hit by a thrown ball was adopted. Reports flourished, and people began to divide into camps. Then, as passionate as the controversy had been, it simply cooled down. Perhaps people grew tired of arguing about where baseball came from and just wanted to play the game. Whatever the reason, criticisms died down, and if people had objections, they stopped voicing them. Baseball itself, unperturbed by arguments about its birth, kept gaining popularity and expanding in scope.

So it was that on June 12, 1939 at Cooperstown, New York, the National Baseball Hall of Fame and Museum was dedicated. There you will find a memorial to Abner Doubleday, along with memorabilia and commemorative plaques and statues for the greatest players and personalities that American baseball has produced.

Whether baseball was wholly of American extraction; whether it was Doubleday, or a commission, or someone lost to history who formulated the rules—whatever the case, baseball *is* America's favorite pastime. It is the sport played by more Americans than any other. It does engender more arguments, give more pleasure, and provide a greater source of recreation and enjoyment to the American public than any other sport. Let historians talk. Baseball will not mind; for the game, wherever and however it developed, has captured the minds and hearts of America.

With such an audience, what can it do but grow and flourish as a mainstay of American culture.

Special Data: *Time of speech: about four and a half minutes. Everything in this speech has been researched and documented, just in case you were wondering. Of course, whole books could be written on this aspect of the sport alone, and this speech carries only highlights. There is much material available should you wish to expand the speech or merely know more for yourself. This speech might be good for a sports dinner or "sports night" affair as well as any assembly program relative to spring sports.*

$$\boxed{115}$$

TOPIC: **Memorial Day.**

AUDIENCE: **Suitable for any audience.**

In 1868, the Commander in Chief of the Grand Army of the Republic, General John A. Logan, ordered that May 30, 1868 be designated as a day when people would decorate the graves of their fallen comrades. He wrote that it was his hope that this practice would be "kept up from year to year."

Of course we cannot go back and ask General Logan what occasioned him to issue such an order, but it is neither difficult nor inappropriate to speculate. The Civil War had ended but three years earlier, and the nation was in the process of trying to heal its wounds. Many brave men on both sides of the conflict had given their lives for the cause in which they believed. Now that the war had come to a close, the memories of absent fathers, husbands, brothers, and sons were still vivid and burning.

It was altogether proper and sensitive of General Logan to issue such an order, and, as he hoped, the practice and the sentiment did catch on and has been repeated year after year until this present day.

For many years this day was known as "Decoration Day." I remember, as a child, going to a cemetery with my parents and placing flowers and a small American flag on the grave of a relative who had died during World War II. I also remember the place being filled with people on those "Decoration Days." Many of them wept openly.

Over the years, that term has changed until today we refer to it as "Memorial Day." Whatever the name, the sentiment is the same. It is a day to remember; it is a day to reflect; it is a day to honor the memory of those who have sacrificed their lives and futures for the imminent causes and expectations of their world. It is a day worthy to keep and honor.

From the fields of Lexington and Concord to the sands of Desert Storm, brave men and women have gone forth to fight for and defend the way of life we in America have chosen. Certainly, there are those voices who decry the violence as irrational, but let us be mindful that we would not be here, today, doing what we are, if some American had not shed his or her blood for that purpose; if men and women of integrity had not given their lives that others might live.

Let cynics scoff; let radicals harangue; let the well-meaning continue to plead—nothing can ever detract from the fact that these brave souls went where others would not go; they fought in the belief that what they were doing was right and just; they gave their lives in the hope that others would not have to give theirs. There is no rhetoric that can lessen the fullness of their contribution; there are no words that can possibly tell how much they are missed; there is no speech or speech-maker who can do justice to the sacrifices they have made.

Therefore, on this "Memorial Day," let us indeed remember. Let us remember them as individuals; let us remember them as heros; let us remember them as sons and daughters and husbands and wives whose memories continue to burn within us.

Let us decorate their graves with flowers; let us honor their memories with prayer and reflection within the sanctity of our human hearts; let us provide a memorial for them by vowing that they will not have died in vain, that we will follow after them and be free to work toward establishing that freedom for every child that takes breath within this precious country.

That will be a memorial worthy of them, indeed!

Special Data: *Time of speech: about four minutes. Again, this might serve as a speech for an assembly program, for a Memorial Day ceremony at which you were asked to speak, or even for a patriotic civic affair where the purpose was to honor those who had made this supreme sacrifice. This can be modified into a longer speech, if desired.*

116

TOPIC: Award Ceremony.

AUDIENCE: Students; parents; faculty; administration.

There are many fine and insightful writings about point of view. People are always telling us that an optimist is one who sees the glass as half full while the pessimist sees it as half empty; one sees the doughnut while the other sees the hole; one sees roses surrounded by thorns while the other sees thorns surrounded by roses. Any way you would care to express it, the difference lies in point of view.

That's why I am so delighted to be at this award celebration this evening.

You see, quite often, my position forces me to deal with the negative. I see students who are failing—not only failing in a class, but many times in that larger class called life. I become acquainted with those who have problems that often deter them from reaching goals; I see those who have been alienated and who alienate others.

Please don't mistake me. These are not the majority of the students I see, any more than they are the majority of the students in our school, but we tend to remember those that stick out for the wrong reasons. The vast majority of the students I meet as part of my duties are fine young people who lift my day and my spirits, but I would be less than honest if I did not also tell you that I meet students who try my patience and trouble my very soul. Sometimes, it is they who cross my mind during the midnight hours when sleep is slow in coming and responsibilities pile up around my bed.

That is why an occasion such as this one fills me with such joy. Here, I am reminded of the young men and women who will truly be tomorrow's leaders as they are the leaders here and now in our school. Here, I can take a look at people who have worked hard and given of themselves and put in effort in order to achieve. Here, I can look at you, and I can believe that tomorrow will be a very fine day, indeed.

Make no mistake about it. The awards you will be receiving this evening are not "handouts," meant to appease. Rather, they are meaningful and real representations of an effort beyond the usual; of work that excels beyond the ordinary; of effort and work and time and spirit that go well beyond what is expected of people of your age. These awards bespeak the fact that we acknowledge that you are very special to us, and they tell the world that, as far as we are concerned, the world should sit up and take notice of you, for you are well worthy of being noticed by it.

Moreover, these awards are symbols for which you have worked. Tonight, no one will *give* you anything. Rather, these will be awards which you have *earned;* awards which are your due, because you have fulfilled the requirements and high standards they represent; awards that bespeak your abilities, your efforts, and your integrity as leaders in our school and soon-to-be leaders in our community.

I know that your parents and teachers are proud of you, and I want you to know that I am proud of you as well. It is you who represent what this school is really all about, and it is you who will carry on after we are gone.

You are to be congratulated.

Now, let's get on with the awards. . . .

Special Data: *Time of speech: just about four minutes. The students who attend these ceremonies because they have won awards are, most often, the backbone of your school. It is good, therefore, to concentrate for a while on these outstanding young people, and this speech does just that. You could use this speech as the opening of an awards ceremony, as the closing of such a ceremony, or anywhere in between. With adaptation, this might also be used at a dinner to honor the recipient of a single, prestigious award.*

$$\boxed{117}$$

TOPIC: **End of the School Year.**

AUDIENCE: **Students; faculty; administration; staff.**

What a year this has been!

I think every one of us may look back on this past school year with justifiable pride, for it has been a year of accomplishments. Whether it was our award-winning teams or our award-winning plays or our award-winning chorus or our award-winning chess club, this has been a year of accomplishment and honor for you, our award-winning students.

Now, it has all but come to an end, and in a few short days, the summer hiatus will be upon us. Some of you will be leaving this school to rest and renew yourselves in order to return next year; some of you will be leaving this place to enter into the world at large, returning as alumni when you do decide to visit. All of you take with you the memories you have made for yourselves during this time; all of you take with you whatever learning you have achieved during this time; all of you take with you the very best wishes of your teachers, your counselors, and everyone in the administrative offices that your summer will be a healthy and enjoyable time filled with laughter and wonder, and that your futures may be filled with all the good and wonderful things that life has to offer.

You have learned, and you have expanded your minds; you have grown, and you have taken another step towards adulthood; you have met with happiness and sorrow, triumph and failure, pain and pleasure, and because you have gone through these experiences common to all mankind, you are that much closer to attaining the status of a caring and competent adult who will function in society to the betterment of society. It is the world that will be the better for your being in it.

The school year is all but over, but your lives are just beginning. May you have a wonderful summer, and may it be but one of many wonderful summers to come, both in your years with this school and throughout your entire lives.

Special Data: *Time of speech: about three minutes. This, we feel, might best be used as a concluding speech for an end-of-the-year assembly, although it could also serve as a written notice in a year-end bulletin. You might also find whole paragraphs of it to be useful for a graduation speech or something of that nature. It is also a fitting conclusion to the school year, since it looks back and then looks forward, which is not a bad formula for a speech of this type.*

Afterthoughts

It is good to give a speech on a happy occasion. It is wonderful to have before you a happy audience anticipating the happy occasion. Under circumstances such as these, it is difficult to make a mistake. Nonetheless, it can happen.

Even if you are enthusiastic and quivering in anticipation of the speech you are to give, don't make the error of supposing that you don't have to prepare for it but will just "wing it" off the "top of your head." That's a sure way to get up there and give a disorganized and chaotic speech that will be remembered for all the wrong reasons.

Every speech needs to be prepared, polished, and practiced if it is going to be effective and memorable. This includes those speeches that you may feel are so easy that they will not tax you at all.

Treat each speech as if it were the most important one in the world, and every speech you give will be truly excellent.

SPEECHES THAT DEAL WITH TROUBLESOME TOPICS

Wouldn't it be wonderful if we breezed through our school careers and never had anything worse to concern us than on what day we should hold the PTA picnic? What if the worst thing that happened all day was that the electric pencil sharpener broke down and all the pencils had to be sharpened by hand? What if your worst academic problem were a student who could not see Shakespeare's use of light and dark as metaphor in *Romeo and Juliet?*

Well, for one thing, you surely wouldn't be in our school! More than likely, you'd awake to find the morning had arrived and you were due in a *real* school in an hour or so.

Indeed, anyone in education knows that while there are certainly bright spots and happy times and great achievements and causes for rejoicing, along with these positive events there occur dark spots and sad times and underachievement and cause for weeping.

True, this may be said of life in general, but it may also be said of virtually every school in particular. Just as there is not a corner of society that does not have its problems, so the modern school faces problems of its own.

There are troublesome topics and areas that arise in every school and school district, and these areas must be addressed before they become overwhelming and threaten to engulf us all. The rumor that threatens the morale of the school; the negative editorial in the local paper; the feeling and beliefs of various groups as well as parents that are offended by movies shown in a classroom or in sex education classes, or the use of live animals in science—all of these and more threaten to grow beyond either reasonable or manageable proportions unless they are addressed quickly, efficiently, and thoroughly.

Public education is not a place for "faint hearts," but it requires conviction, courage, and determination. Hopefully, the speeches in this section will reflect these qualities, for they deal with all the topics listed above and then some—topics that may only be described as "troublesome."

From handling a rumor to a speech for your own retirement, here's hoping that all *your* troublesome topics will lead only to happiness and growth.

$$\boxed{118}$$

TOPIC: **Dealing with Rumors.**

AUDIENCE: **Faculty and staff—those involved.**

Ladies and gentlemen. . . .

I'm going to ask you to indulge me for a moment, because I'm about to tell you a story. That's right, a story. Like all stories, this one has a moral and is being told to make a point. Therefore, since I will not be asking questions later, I'd appreciate it if you could give me your full attention now, thank you.

Here's the story. There was a man who had a large feather-filled pillow. You know, one of those large, very soft affairs just crammed with feathers. Well, one night, this man went to the highest place in town, which happened to be the steeple of the local church. He climbed up into the bell tower with his feather pillow under his arm and stood, at last, overlooking the great city as it stretched away below him. Then the man took a knife from his pocket,opened it, and proceeded to slash open the pillow. It was a windy night, and the wind howled through the side of the bell tower in the steeple, catching feathers here and there and blowing them out over the city. Had there been anyone to see, it would have seemed that a great snow flurry had started, but soon the cloud of feathers dissipated as it scattered the feathers over the sleeping city and blew them out over the surrounding countryside.

The man climbed down from the steeple and went home, where he spent a restless night, because his big, comfortable pillow wasn't big and comfortable any more. The next night, he took the empty pillowcase and set out into the city to see if he could retrieve the feathers he had set loose the night before. He found one or two of them and put them back, but the vast majority of them were gone forever, blown who-knows-where by the winds. There was no chance of getting back what he had loosed.

I hope that it is obvious to you by now that I am not talking about feathers. I'm talking about rumors; rumors and gossip that have spread through this school as if they were feathers from a pillow spilled into the night breeze.

To start or to pass along a rumor is exactly like opening a feather pillow, and just as it was impossible to retrieve all the feathers, so it will be impossible to take back all the damage that will be done by rumors; to reclaim all the hurt that will be caused by gossip.

Of course, I know the rumors that revolve around the recommendations I will make for head guidance counselor. I shall not dignify these rumors by repeating them, since most of you know them already, nor shall I take your valuable time and mine to defend myself or anyone else.

Rather, I will tell you very honestly that I am both shocked and hurt that such rumors have begun and, most especially, that they are being passed around. I would like them to stop, but I more than realize that that power is not within my hands.

How long have I served with you? How long have you known me? When have you known me to lie to you—to any of you? When have you seen me deny a request without very good reason that was fully spelled out to you? When have I failed to treat you as professionals of the highest quality? These are questions I would have you ask yourself; this is the appraisal I would have each of you make in the integrity of your own mind.

When you get the answers that I hope you will, then I'd like you to evaluate these rumors in the light of your answers and tell me what substance you found there!

If you want to know something, ask me; I will tell you. I will tell you completely and with as much understanding as I can possibly muster.

Truly, you have a choice. You can listen to rumors, or you can listen to me. That's your decision, but I'll tell you this: If you come to me, I can guarantee that you won't go away with an earful of feathers!

Special Data: *Time of speech: about three minutes. Rumors and gossip can devastate a school, and totally do away with morale and productivity. They need to be addressed aggressively. As in this speech, it does not hurt one bit if you become righteously angry over a rumor; in fact, it could be the best thing for stopping it immediately.*

$$\boxed{119}$$

TOPIC: Rebuttal of a Negative Editorial.

AUDIENCE: Adults: teachers, parents, community.

Ladies and gentlemen. . . .

Last evening I, along with many or perhaps even a majority of the citizens of this community, settled down to read the newspaper that serves us. In that newspaper, in the column that is headed, "From the Editor's Desk," I had the unpleasant task of reading an editorial entitled "Is School a Safe Place for Children?"

I was incensed by what was written. It pointed out four recent instances across the nation where schoolchildren were seriously injured while in school. It pointed out that "lack of proper supervision" was responsible for these injuries and decried the "obviously unsafe and negligent" conditions that are a "threat to every child everywhere."

I feel that it is necessary to point out that four instances out of the thousands of public schools throughout our land hardly constitutes a radical departure from the norm.

Shall we say conservatively that in the United States there are four thousand public schools? (There are many more, but let's just use that figure for a moment.) Four out of that number comes to *four one-thousandth* of the whole. Is this number significant enough to engender such a cry of outrage? Certainly, even one child who is seriously injured is one child too many—there can be no disagreement on that. However, by these percentages, a child is more likely to be injured seriously at home than at school. I think that common sense tells us that those four children being injured, though a deplorable circumstance, hardly constitutes a basis for the rising tide of indifference on the part of our school.

Indeed, this editorial has proven nothing except that there are ways of making almost anything look bad and engendering bad feelings where none should exist.

Yet, if that were all there was to the editorial, I might have given it the sincere lack of attention which, in my opinion, it so heartily deserved. As part of the editorial, however, one indictment that was mentioned was (and I quote from the actual editorial), "Since September of this year, there have been sixteen cases of broken bones in our own middle school."

That is why I am here this morning. As the principal of the middle school, I know full well that we have had *no* instances of broken bones this year—*none.* I did some checking, and I found out where the figure came from.

Each time a child comes to school with an injury such as a broken bone, this fact is reported to the school nurse who subsequently takes time to check on the progress of the student. There were, indeed, sixteen cases of broken limbs so far this school year, but *in each case,* the limb was broken outside of school, either at home or in the vicinity of the child's home. In no case was the arm or leg broken either in school or on school grounds.

Simple inquiry should have sufficed here. A slightly different slant would have shown the fine safety record of our school, placed the number of injuries in a proper perspective, and would not have outraged and prejudiced the public against our school.

Frankly, not only do I demand a full retraction of the entire editorial, but for the sake of decency, I think that a public apology is in order.

For the sake of schools throughout our nation as well as the sake of our own good name that we have built through hard work, dedication, and the professionalism of our staff, we can accept no less!

Special Data: *Time of speech: about three minutes. If you are going to rebut anything in a speech, start by stating the incident or accusation; then tell why you think it is either unfair or untrue. If you have any evidence, such as the mistaken interpretation of data mentioned in this speech, save it for last and then use it for all it is worth. During the first part of the speech, your attitude should be one of sorrow and hurt. When it comes to the part where you have the proof, your attitude should change to one of righteous indignation. These things must be felt sincerely. A negative editorial can cause a school some very serious damage, so it is best to be aggressive in your rebuttal of it.*

$$\boxed{120}$$

TOPIC: Animals in the Science Class: Some Guidelines.

AUDIENCE: Teachers; supervisors; possible community.

I want to start out by giving you a personal observation. I love animals. I have two black cats at home named Beau and Arrow, and I am very fond of them. I detest, to my very soul, seeing any animal suffer. I do believe, however, that the use of animals in the development of drugs, surgical techniques, and the like is not only justifiable but necessary.

I say all this in order to let you know where I stand personally.

I am also issuing a directive that will be in your mailboxes tomorrow morning to the effect that there will be no live animals allowed in science classes or in any class in the school. I feel that this in no way impedes the learning process in science, since biological supply houses continue to supply specimens that are fully ready for dissection and study. There is no need to keep any live specimens in the class.

I am also aware that there are times in regular classes when students wish to bring in pets for various reasons, some of them frivolous and some of them legitimate. However, if this ruling is to apply to science classes, it must apply to all other classes as well.

This ruling has been occasioned by two instances that occurred in nearby schools. In one case, a science teacher brought in a live chicken for dissection and killed the animal in front of the class. Not only did this action cause one child to become physically ill to her detriment and embarrassment, but several children became what may be termed upset psychologically over the instance. This took place in an elementary school, and I make no judgment as to the rightness or wrongness of the decision, since that is still being adjudicated in a neighboring school district. We will not, however, even give it the chance to happen here.

In a second instance, a child was badly scratched and bitten by a "gentle pet" that had been brought in to use as a model in art class. Suit has been filed by the student's parents, and I make no further comment about that case, either.

We are all aware that nature has provided many animals with very sharp teeth and claws to use as a defense in the natural environment. A classroom full of children who act out their natural curiosity by touching and prodding may hardly be considered a "natural environment" for any animal, even the most docile and lovable of house pets.

In either case, the most logical course of action, as I see it, in avoiding these unpleasantries is to ban live animals of any type from the science classes and all other classrooms in the building.

I am certain that, in the months to come, there will be people who will seek exceptions to this ruling. Of course you are always free to discuss these matters with me, but I tell you quite frankly that I will be hard pressed to set a different precedent due to the circumstances that I have just described to you.

Certainly, you are free to disagree with my decision, and I respect your opinions as professionals, but as professionals, I ask that you respect this decision, and see to its implementation immediately. Should you really feel strongly about it, I know you are aware that there are procedures in place for seeking redress.

In the past, I have counted upon your cooperation, and have never been disappointed. I know that this is another occasion where that cooperation will be manifested.

Thank you for your obvious care, your understanding of the problem, and your cooperation.

Special Data: *Time of speech: about four minutes. Instances such as the ones mentioned in this speech do happen. There are times when we must take a stand; this speech does just that. It also presents your personal point of view without apology. At no time, in any speech, should you apologize in word or in tone, for what you honestly believe. A basic summary would be, "This is what I believe. This is what happened. This is what I'm doing. You don't have to like it, but I expect it to be done." There are times when this approach may be necessary.*

$$\boxed{121}$$

TOPIC: **PG and R-Rated Movies in the Classroom.**

AUDIENCE: **Faculty; supervisors; staff.**

Audio-visual aids and education have gone together probably since the first teacher picked up a twig and made symbols in the dirt. No one denies that these tools have a decided impact upon the learning of the student. Indeed, there are many audio-visual supply houses that publish huge catalogs of filmstrips, tapes, transparencies, reproduction masters, and films of an educational nature to be used for every subject and grade level. Each department in this school has a number of them, and I know that they are used to the benefit of our students.

With the advent of the video cassette recorder and videotape, the showing of movies in a class has been greatly simplified, and tapes of movies for rental abound on practically every street corner and in every shopping mall.

I suppose it is only natural, therefore, that teachers will want to show some of these movies to a class, particularly when the theme of the motion picture fits into the curriculum. On the surface, it sounds like a fine idea.

At one time in the history of cinema, this would have posed little problem. The only concern would have been seeing to it that the film really was relevant to the curriculum being taught. That point established, one could go ahead and show the film, content in the knowledge that the worst thing to be shown would be some "bad guy" who said, "Aw, rats!"

Times have changed; movies have changed. Language that was once relegated to the gutter now floods from the screen in stereophonic sound. It seems that no movie can exist without an obligatory "nude scene." Violence is often portrayed for the sheer sake of the violence itself. At least, to my sorrow, it seems that way to me.

Recently, a teacher from another district, let me hasten to add, showed a videotaped film to the class. The teacher had not previewed the film, nor had he checked its rating, I am told. When the children came home telling of the unique language and explicit scenes of sex and violence, the phone calls began pouring in to the school.

Now, please, no arguments on "artistic merit." I don't care if the film won 147 awards and was the greatest thing since *Hamlet.* Children lack the maturity, the perception, and the cultivated taste to be able to project over the basest impressions that the language, sex, and violence provide.

Therefore, I am directing (and this shall become part of our policy book), that only G-Rated films or those specifically approved by the board of education be shown to any students. Under no conditions may PG or R-Rated movies be shown at any time.

Now, if this ruling offends you, and you are about to shout about academic freedom and your right to show something like "The Secret Love Life of a Blood-Sucking Vampire" to your seventh grade class, then I'm going to ask you to first consider the rights of our parents to instruct their children in moral values, and then to consider that I personally find no way—that's *no way*—in which I could either approve or support that decision.

If we all stick to the G-Rated movies, the movies that are sold or rented through the approved educational supply houses that service our district, and the approved movies that we carry in our own AVA center, then there will be no trouble, and the education of our students will continue unabated and, most importantly, undisturbed.

You do not have to agree with this decision, but it is an administrative decision and as such will be implemented in this school starting immediately. If any of you take exception to this, then you know what grievance procedures to follow.

I thank you in advance for your cooperation.

Special Data: *Time of speech: about four minutes. If you have an opinion and you feel that it is justifiable and right, then go on the side of your conscience and see to it. When the directive detailed in this speech was delivered originally, there were no grievances filed, and better than forty percent of the faculty saw the principal privately to tell him that it was about time someone took a stand on this issue. There are times when you have to go out on a limb. Do so with honesty, and you will always be in the right.*

$$\boxed{122}$$

TOPIC: **The Abused Child and the School.**

AUDIENCE: **Faculty; staff; community; parents.**

Ladies and gentlemen. . . .

You are about to hear from several distinguished members of social agencies that serve the children of our community. These are people with a great deal of experience in the topic they will address today. They will be telling you many things of which you may not be aware; they will be telling you some things you may wish you never learned when they are finished; they will be telling you things which, as professional educators, you absolutely must know.

They will be talking to you about the abused child and the school.

My first exposure to child abuse cases came when I was a young teacher, barely out of college, on my first teaching assignment. At that time, I dealt with a child who first came to my attention when I noticed that she was having difficulty writing in class. Later, I was to learn that the child's mother punished her by placing the child's hand on the burner of the electric range and turning on the unit.

It has been decades since that incident, ladies and gentlemen, yet I want you to believe that I can still close my eyes and see that girl. I will not go into details; suffice it to say that the case was handled, the child was placed in a foster home, and it all took place over twenty-five years ago. Even so, I still see her from time to time in my mind; I still wonder; I still care.

Yet, if the horror of that abuse had such an effect upon me that I can remember the victim of the abuse almost thirty years later, what effect must it have had upon the victim herself? What horrors must her mind still contain? What must those experiences have done to her in her teenage years? In young adulthood? Today?

If you are like me, these things fill you with the deepest sorrow and fire you with righteous anger. There is sorrow for the child, the victim of the abuse, and a longing desire to cool the pain and tell the child that everything's going to be all right. There is anger aimed at those who could knowingly perpetrate such abominations against anyone, much less a helpless child.

There is also an overwhelming sense of frustration, where the desire to come to the aid of the child comes dead upon the limits of our abilities as teachers in the legal system. If only there was something we could do.

Well, the good news is that there is something we can do. This afternoon we are going to hear that there is a great deal that not only *can* we do, but that we are required to do as professional educators when child abuse is suspected.

We shall learn to look for signs of child abuse, and we shall learn what to do if we suspect that a particular child may be being abused. We shall be told of procedures to follow that will ensure that the case of every child is handled swiftly, discreetly, and with total efficiency in order that, should the child truly be a victim of abuse, that abuse will stop immediately.

As we listen this afternoon, let us pause for a moment to recall the reasons we became teachers. Wasn't it because we felt that somehow we could make a difference in the lives of children? Wasn't it because we felt a special affinity for children in our hearts? Wasn't it because we wanted, above all else, to help and guide the children with whom we would come in contact? Weren't these some of the reasons why all of us entered teaching in the first place?

Today, we will learn that, for the abused child, we *can* make a difference—a difference in some cases between life and death, and for all of them a difference between fear and a future filled with possibilities.

This is truly worthy of our time and our attention.

Special Data: *Time of speech: about four minutes. This speech would be useful as the opening speech for a conference or panel discussion on Child Abuse. It could also be used as an introduction to a single speaker on the subject, particularly if the speaker were an expert in the field. Child abuse is a topic that strikes at the very core of most teachers, since most teachers enter the profession for the ideals detailed in the speech. We are certain that you will have a very attentive audience.*

$$\boxed{123}$$

TOPIC: Sex Education and the AIDS Tragedy.

AUDIENCE: Educators; parents; community members.

Ladies and gentlemen. . . .

I wish to begin by stating that it has been and continues to be my opinion that sex education is primarily the responsibility of the home.

I truly believe that statement, just as I truly believe that sex education has a valuable place in our curriculum and our schools as well.

If you think that these two statements seem diametrically opposed to each other, I would suggest that you are mistaken. I would ask you to remember why sex education was originally included in your child's curriculum.

I could give you incident after incident from my personal experience as a teacher, of children and adolescents who became pregnant, destroyed their potential careers, and went through tortures no child should face, because they had no information, the wrong information, or the twisted information of the street instead of knowledge based on truth.

I have neither the time, nor the inclination to bombard you with tragedy after tragedy based on lack of knowledge concerning one of life's basic functions. The point is that every single one of these students *should have known;* they should have been told at home; they should have received instructions from Mom or Dad or even the family doctor—but they didn't.

I have believed and continue to believe that sex education is the province of the home, but when the home doesn't teach properly, then the school must. Sex education came into the schools not to surplant the home as conveyor of information, but because, in the majority of the cases we had seen, the home wasn't performing its function.

It is not, however—definitely not—the time to sit back and assess blame. Rather, it is a time to look at what we have and is happening and seek for ways in order to cooperate in building toward the future.

There is, for instance, the AIDS epidemic, and it is, indeed an epidemic. AIDS is not going away in the forseeable future. Medicine may develop ways in which to cope with the symptoms, but it is generally agreed that a cure for AIDS is years, if not decades away. In the meantime, your children and mine will be entering that world where the AIDS threat is real and present. It is essential that they know the facts—that knowledge is power, possibly the power of life and death.

We are not speaking here of morality. Certainly, we all have moral codes and religious beliefs, and just as certainly, you have the right to educate your children in those moral beliefs. Whatever the belief, however, the fact remains that experience has taught us that we are far from perfect, and the tragedy of AIDS is a terrible price to pay for a moment of deviation from any moral code you may think your children hold.

Therefore, I feel that it is essential that students learn about AIDS—the facts, and not the fantasies. Even if a person never engages in high-risk activity relative to AIDS, that knowledge could prove invaluable in helping others as well as himself or herself.

I am a strong advocate of the rights of parents and the home, but I am just as strong an advocate of knowledge as a preventative factor. For the very best of reasons, the future of our children and this nation, AIDS education must continue in our schools as an adjunct to the instruction that should continue to be given in the home.

As always, working together, the home and the school will become partners working toward the best possible future for each and every child.

Special Data: *Time of speech: about three and a half minutes. We would suggest that you cross-reference this speech with the opening and closing speeches on a program of AIDS information found in the section on openings and closings. Few topics engender more or hotter controversy than sex education in general and AIDS education in particular. This speech could be used as is, or it could become part of a longer speech in which you may want to go into precisely what is taught in the curriculum for this topic. We have found that being honest is a great deal better than trying to sit on both sides of an issue. Try to please everyone, and you end up pleasing no one.*

$$\boxed{124}$$

TOPIC: Getting Tough with Drugs in School.

AUDIENCE: Educators; parents; community members.

Ladies and gentlemen. . . .

If, by now, there is anyone sitting in this audience who does not know, who is not aware, that drugs are a scourge that threaten the very fabric of our society, then that individual must have spent the last twenty years locked in a closet.

Indeed, through the mass media, we have been personal witnesses to tragedy after tragedy centered around drug abuse in our nation, in our state, and in our very home town. We have seen crimes increase, homes and careers destroyed, and lives wasted by this vicious specter that looms over us all. We have seen drug dealers and suppliers living in regal ease while drug users huddle in filth and die in forgotten corners or refuse laden gutters. We have been first-hand witnesses to tragedy that makes the "Black Death" of the Middle Ages seem all but trivial and insignificant by comparison.

We know, also, that drug abuse strikes every segment of our society, from the inner city streets to the tailored lawns of the most exclusive sections of suburbia. We know that the problem exists not only with people in situations of poverty but in people who work in gleaming buildings of steel and glass and are part of corporate structures. We know, to our deepest sorrow, that the problem has even reached into the halls of schools, not in isolated locations, but across our entire nation.

Of course we are concerned; of course we feel the frustration of trying to rid ourselves of this problem; of course we raise our fists in anger at this demon that plagues our souls—these are our children; these are our hope for the future; these are the people we love most in the world; and, these are the targets and the victims of this menace.

I am not qualified to speak for other public agencies, but I do know the school—I have spent my entire life there. The thought that drugs could enter our school infuriates me. The thought that there may be drug dealers waiting to entice our children into the slavery of addiction fills me with wrath. The thought that in the school, a place that should be a safe haven for children to learn and grow, there are those who would pressure others into the first steps toward slow suicide makes me resolve to do everything in my power to rid the school of this scourge; makes me resolve to get tough, very tough, with any drug use, sale, or possession in this building; makes me resolve to make this school so uncomfortable and so unbearably painful for those in the drug culture that they will run screaming from the scene and leave this school alone.

We are serving notice that we have had enough! Anyone caught selling drugs in or around the school will be prosecuted; anyone caught using drugs in school, will be prosecuted; anyone caught possessing drugs of any type, *will be prosecuted.* I mean everything, from heroin down to a marijuana cigarette. If you have it; if you use it; if you sell it—you will be prosecuted to the fullest limit the law allows. This applies to every single person in this school, every staff member and every student without exception.

Of course we understand that justice must be tempered with mercy, but we also understand that we are all—every one of us—answerable for our actions. If school is for learning, then learn this lesson now. There will be no exceptions.

I know that these are tough rulings, but I want you to consider that you don't look at a person whose appendix is about to rupture, give him two aspirin, and wait to see how he'll do by the next day. Of course this is ludicrous; you would take that person to a doctor at once; have he or she operate on an emergency basis; and take whatever aggressive measures are needed in order to save that person's life.

I see no difference between that situation and the one of drugs in our schools. A burst appendix can mean death for the afflicted individual; drug abuse does mean death for our children. Halfhearted efforts will not cure appendicitis, and slaps on the wrist won't take the disease of drugs out of a school either. We need aggressive methods in both cases.

Yes, we are going to get tough with drugs in school by getting tough with the sellers, the users, and even the holders. We will be ruthless in our prosecution, just as we will be relentless in our efforts to heal the patient before death comes to bear claim.

For the sake of our children; for their future; for their lives—how can we do any less?

Special Data: *Time of speech: a little over five minutes. Over our years in education, we have seen too many students destroyed by the drug menace. This speech could be used as a closing speech in a*

*program on drug abuse, or it could be adapted to whatever mea-
sures you may be taking in your school. There are sections of this
speech that are applicable to any speech an administrator would
give about drug abuse and the school, for whatever reform might be
being inculcated.*

$$\boxed{125}$$

TOPIC: The School Administrator and the Public Image.

AUDIENCE: Fellow educators; teachers and administrators.

Ladies and gentlemen. . . .

I would like to speak to you for a while this afternoon on the topic
of image. More specifically, I want to speak to you about the image of
the school administrator in our community.

I know, I know—the first time I heard the word "image" applied to
a professional educator, it conjured up pictures in my mind of rock stars
and movie idols. For one, panic-stricken moment, I had a picture of myself in dark glasses, dressed in a suit made of spangle-studded Mylar℗ ,
walking a Russian wolfhound down the street as hoards of adoring teenagers squirmed over me, begging for my autograph. The perspiration
started to form on my forehead. To my relief, as well as to yours, that
was definitely not what was meant by the term.

Think of it this way. In this imperfect world in which we live, we are
dependent upon our senses for knowledge of that world. We form opinions, and we learn based upon what we see, smell, hear, taste, and touch.
Knowledge doesn't come to us in any other way.

Now, add to that the fact that we live in a community which, quite
literally, supports our schools through taxes and support of local budgets. Certainly, were it not for the children of this community, there
would not be schools for us to work in. For better or worse ladies and
gentlemen, we are a part of this community.

Now, let's create a character—we'll call him Mr. X, isn't that
clever? Mr. X, let us say, works in a nearby town and lives in this community. Of course he knows that his children attend school, and that

schools have something called a "principal" who lives in a small room off the main office, but except for the most cursory and rudimentary knowledge, he, for the most part, hasn't the slightest idea of what that breed called "administrator" is like or what these people do all day. He can look in the local newspaper around budget time each year, however, and find that they may make a better salary than he.

Mr. X, like all of us, is dependent upon his senses for information. He looks; he listens. He watches TV news; he listens to the news on the radio while driving to work; he reads the newspaper every night after supper. He may not know a thing about us, but he can see us; he can listen to what we say; he can find out what others have said about us.

The opinion that he forms about us—an opinion, incidentally, that will pass for knowledge in a majority of cases—and the opinion that he forms about our schools will come almost exclusively from what he may see us do and what he hears others say about us.

If that opinion is formed around positive images, you will have a parent and a community member who is supportive of our schools; who feels that he is involved with "good people"; who will give his loyalty and his support to the schools of this community as well as to the budgets that support them.

If that opinion is formed around negative images, for whatever reason, you have a parent and community member that is convinced that the schools are horrible places; that educators get paid high salaries for baby-sitting; that the principal does nothing and gets paid for it. This will be a community member whose support of education and the schools has been virtually nonexistent.

It is up to us, therefore, as administrators who are deeply involved in the growth and development of our schools, to help promote *positive* images. Please understand, I am certainly not suggesting that any of you should go out and kick a small dog at high noon in the town square, but I am telling you that it is not enough that we don't do anything wrong; we must also project the image of competent and concerned people who always strive to do what is right and good in the eyes of society and work to provide the very best in education for our schools. In other words, we want the people of this community to know the great job you are doing day after day in the schools of this community.

Do you coach Little League? Teach a class at the college? Do volunteer work at the hospital? Serve in your church or temple? Sponsor any cultural activities? Engage in any cultural activities? If so, send it to our public relations office, and let us make it known!

As far as your school goes, are you engaged in any innovative educational programs? Are any of your classes giving any special performances? How are your teams doing? Do you have any true stories from school that would warm the heart or stir the imagination? Are any of your teachers up for special awards? What are you doing around the school that is new and exciting and will benefit your students? We want to know these things in order that we may let the community know as well.

This is the image of which I spoke a moment ago. This is the image we wish to project. This is the image we want Mr. X and those like him to receive day after day. We are well aware that you are good people and outstanding educators with a wealth of talents and good deeds to contribute to the schools and the students of this community. We want others to know that as well.

And if, because your selflessness, contributions, and educational endeavors are made known and the public image soars; and the members of our community gain a new appreciation for our schools and become supportive of them; and we can go on doing our jobs with passed school budgets to the benefit of untold numbers of students; then that's not boasting; that's an investment in tomorrow.

It is an investment which I know each and every one of you can make happen.

Special Data: *Time of speech: about six minutes. More and more schools that do not have them in place already are adding public relations officers to their central administrative staff. Since schools are dependent upon the consent of the public, and the image the public has of us plays a major part in whether or not school budgets get passed and in who gets elected to the school board for what reason, then a speech such as this is extremely useful. You might even want to designate a public relations person for your individual school.*

$$\boxed{126}$$

TOPIC: Speech on the Media in the School.

AUDIENCE: Members of the faculty and staff and all concerned.

Ladies and gentlemen. . . .

As everyone is only too aware, tomorrow the governor of our state will be coming to our school. There will be an assembly program, and by now you have all received written instructions as to how and where this will take place. As I'm sure you realize, the governor's time is rigidly scheduled, and all times mentioned in the instructions must be adhered to faithfully. I know that I can count on your cooperation as I have so many, many times in the past.

Along with the governor will come members of his staff, some security personnel, and, of course, the media. I have been told that there will be two camera crews from the major TV networks, a camera crew from our local TV station, several members of radio news crews, and an unspecified number of reporters from the press, both local and from nearby major cities.

It is about these members of the media that I wish to speak to you for a brief moment this afternoon.

They are here to record the governor's visit. Even so, it is inevitable that the cameras and microphones will be turned upon our students and on you. This may be in the form of "panning" the audience, or it may mean asking a student or one of you for a stand-up interview. There is also the possibility that a camera crew may show up at your classroom door and ask if they can tape something that is going on. Later, this footage might be edited into a story about the governor's visit. Also, newspaper reporters may come up to you and ask anything from what you thought about the governor's speech, to your opinion of the president of the board of education.

Under no circumstances would I even think of telling or suggesting to you how you should respond in these instances, if, indeed, they happen at all. You are professionals. I have repeated and repeated that I have the highest respect for your judgment, and I do.

What I want you to know this afternoon are your rights in terms of this onslaught of media.

And you do have rights as regards the media. You have the right *not* to be interviewed if that is your desire. If the cameras come to the door of your room, you have the right to refuse to allow them in. It is *your* class, and you will determine what constitutes an interruption of that class.

If you are interviewed, you have the right to say whatever you wish. This is, after all, a democracy. Certainly, we have nothing to hide in this school, and we are all proud of what we do here. What you say is up to you.

I will ask of you only one thing. I will ask you to remember that what is said will reflect upon this school, for better or for worse. I would ask, therefore, that whatever you say, especially if it could be construed as a negative reaction, that you qualify it as your personal opinion. I think that this is only fair.

Enjoy the governor's visit, and who knows; I may be watching you on my TV set tomorrow night.

Special Data: *Time of speech: about three minutes. This could be part of a longer speech preparing the faculty and staff for some occasion where there will be media present in the school. This speech is a very gentle appeal to temper what is said to the TV cameras with some understanding and perspective. Under no circumstances would you tell people what they can and cannot say to the free press. This speech suggests a rational appraisal, and it will probably work as well as any.*

$$\boxed{127}$$

TOPIC: Acceptance of Your Own Retirement.

AUDIENCE: Those who would attend such a function.

Ladies and gentlemen....

I'd like to tell you that tonight has been one of the most exciting and meaningful nights of my life, which just goes to show you what a truly boring and meaningless life I've led up to now. Given my choice, I think I'd rather have gone through root canal; at least there they give you an anesthetic before the drilling begins.

One of the best things about having your bosses speak at your retirement is the fact that this is the last time I'm going to have to sit here and pretend that they're intelligent.

Ok, so I couldn't possibly leave without throwing a few barbs here and there, and I'm glad you laughed with me. You see, I feel rather like the man who was just told that he owed ten thousand dollars in back taxes. The man started to laugh like mad, and his friend said, "What's the matter with you? You get news like that and you start laughing? Are you crazy?"

"It's not that," answered the man. "You see, I just paid thirty bucks for this silk tie and I don't want to get it wet. That's why I'm laughing, because if I don't, I'll be crying all over the place!"

And, that's why I am happy to join you in your laughter tonight. This is, after all, a joyous occasion, and so many of the speakers this evening have pointed out that I deserve a little rest that I think I'm beginning to believe it. I am, indeed, looking forward to spending time with this lady by my side; I am looking forward to working in an advisory capacity to our school system; I am looking forward to bashing that alarm clock right across its face with a baseball bat. I am looking forward to my retirement.

But I would not be honest if I did not tell you also that there is a part of me that is on the verge of weeping. One cannot put thirty years of his life into something without having it become a part of him. Yes, I am leaving, but a part of me is staying on and will remain in the buildings, in the programs, in the methods of instruction, in the smiles of the students and the grins of the teachers. I'll be there when the school opens and when it closes; I'll be there in the concern of every educator for the learning of every child; I'll be there in the hopes and dreams of every child, every teacher, and every administrator in the system. For thirty years I have lived and worked with them. They are a part of me, and I a part of them.

So, I'm not really leaving; I'm simply making an adjustment, one of many I will make until it comes time for the final adjustment of all. But, I won't be gone. You look for me, and you'll find me there, as I will find each and every one of you in the place where you'll be living in my heart. . . .

Special Data: *Time of speech: about three minutes. You may have noticed that this speech seems incomplete. That's because it is. We* *assume that there would be some personal things that you would want to say publicly to people with whom and for whom you have worked. If not, then its fine the way it is; if so, then they could be placed in the middle of the speech. We think the final two paragraphs create a very strong conclusion, and state a touching truth about an educator who has endured.*

Afterthoughts

As we said, not all that happens in school revolves around situations that run smoothly; troublesome times and issues are bound to arise. When they do, your conviction that they can be handled coupled with your willingness to take a stand on a controversial or "troublesome" issue will be the way you will best handle and get through them.

One thing to be said about speaking your mind is that everyone knows where you stand, and no one can later complain that they were unaware. It also gives you the justifiable reputation of a person who stands up for his or her beliefs. People may not agree with your position, but they will respect you for taking it.

*   *   *   *   *   *   *

IN CONCLUSION

How wonderful that there's a place
    Where folks in freedom come
To share ideas and in the process
    Find that they are one;
How marvelous, that you'd consent
    To let us speak our minds;
We thank you for that privilege,
    So very rare to find;
But, every dawning sun must set,
    And everything must end,
So shortly we will go our ways
    Yet leave, we think, as friends;
And if, perchance, we've learned and grown,
    Then we'll both find it true;
You'll keep us living in your heart
    As we'll remember you. . . .
                    —Sue and Steve Mamchak

We could write a book ten times the size of this one and place in it every speech ever given in a school or school-related situation, and there would still occur that inevitable time when the educational speaker would have to compose an individual speech on his own.

Invariably, special circumstances or special events will dictate that a particular speech, perhaps containing specialized information, be composed by the administrator. At such a time, preparing a speech can be a very trying occasion, unless some special rules are followed in its composition; rules that have been developed to make the composition of that speech a painless and efficient process.

Even if, to save your valuable time, you can adapt or deliver one of the speeches in the first part of this book, you are still faced with delivering that speech. Most of the time, everything goes well, but if you speak frequently enough, you are aware that there are some pitfalls that await speakers that can disrupt any speech, unless the speaker is prepared to deal with them effectively.

Presented here is a step-by-step guide that has proven effective for us in the preparation and delivering of a speech. You will find practical advice for avoiding the pitfalls of public speaking, gleaned from years and years of practical experience; a guide that will serve you well in every speaking situation.

With these two guides to serve you, you will find it a relatively easy procedure to compose and deliver, free from any drawbacks, an exciting, appropriate, and memorable speech.

We know that these guides will continue to serve you, as they have served us, for a long time to come.

A STEP-BY-STEP GUIDE FOR PREPARING AND DELIVERING A DYNAMIC SPEECH

When presenting an effective, stimulating, and memorable speech or presentation, we have found a proven and dependable success formula that has served us well under all conditions. We call it the P R E P A R E formula. Each letter stands for one building block in the foundation of a good speech.

P—Preparing and Pinpointing Your Topic

If you were asked to speak on "education", your first question would be, "What phase or aspect of education?" Giving a loose, rambling speech makes an audience restless. Make every effort to limit your topic and pinpoint a specific area that you can cover in depth within your allotted speaking time.

Whenever asked to speak, you should ask certain questions:

What is the composition of the audience?

How many people will you be addressing?

Where will your speech fit into the total program for that afternoon or evening?

What event, activity, speech, etc. is to proceed or follow you?

What speaking facilities (microphone, podium, dais, head table/audience, stage/audience, etc.) will be available?

How much will the audience know (or think it knows) about the topic before you speak?

How does the program coordinator perceive your speech? (Entertaining? Persuasive? Informative?)

What is the maximum and minimum time you will have to speak?

In short, ask any question that you feel might have a bearing on the physical environment and/or content of your speech. This attention to detail will help you prepare the right speech for the right audience at the right time. For example, would you give a forty-five minute speech if you were speaking just *before* dinner was to be served? Would you give a serious speech at a parent-child dinner where Santa Claus' appearance was to follow yours? Pinpointing your topic and preparing for the physical surroundings of your speech is your first step on the road to success.

R—Researching for Success

Obviously, you need to *know* what you are talking about. Few speakers deliberately try to mislead or misinform the audience, but trusting to memory is risky at best and disastrous at worst. It is at this point that you begin to prepare yourself to meet your audience. Consequently, you will need some information:

What will your audience want to know?

What kinds of questions will it ask?

What kind of humor would it find best?

What would antagonize an audience?

What would please an audience?

Once you have determined the answers to these questions, you can begin your research.

Compile the information you need. If you are going to speak about a person, find out about him or her. If it is a current issue, review the local newspapers. Use Part I of this book and other speech books to select appropriate anecdotes, stories and humor. Remember that the *quality* of your research will pave the way to a successful speech.

E—Examples and Their Use

Good speakers use examples to prove or clarify their points throughout a speech. To get the most out of the examples you use, follow these rules:

1. The example should be appropriate. It must make the point you want it to make. To use an anecdote, however clever or delightful, that has no bearing on what you are saying will only confuse your audience.

2. The example should be understood by everyone. To describe two fellow educators as "the Castor and Pollux of the educational world" is fine—providing that everyone in the audience knows who Castor and Pollux were. Otherwise, the analogy is lost.

3. Avoid "inside" jokes. Every profession has its "inside" humor—those anecdotes and stories that are amusing only to those persons in that particular profession. To use such mate-

rial before a "mixed" audience could lead to confusion and antagonism. Therefore, such material is better left untold.

P—Presentation and Poise

Once you have written your speech, you will eventually have to give it before an audience. This phase of preparation is vital. Whether this is your first speech or your hundred-and-first, you should rehearse it thoroughly before you set foot before an audience. Sequester yourself, if need be, and stand in front of a mirror. See yourself as others will see you. Pay attention to your gestures, your eye contact, how you use your notes, your posture. Record your speech and listen to it with an open mind. Are you speaking too slowly? Too fast? In a monotone? Are your words distinct? Finally, decide what you will wear that day. You already know what type of function you are attending, so you won't be wearing a leisure outfit to a black-tie dinner. Make an effort to select clothes in which you look best and feel best. If you feel good about your appearance, you will project confidence to your audience.

A—Analyzing Your Audience

When you have arrived at the place where you are to speak, you will have an opportunity to analyze your audience. Look at its members, listen to them, and particularly pay attention to their reactions. Is the atmosphere formal or informal? Are they quiet and respectful or noisy and restless? If there were other speakers before you, how were they received? Your analysis of the audience will tell you what approach to take when it is your time to speak. Even a prepared speech may be delivered in several ways. It can be formal, conversational, or even intimate, as friend to friend. Your approach will be determined by your perception of the audience.

Finally, once you begin speaking, you will *feel* your audience. There is no way to describe this; it must be experienced. Through this rapport—this psychological bond—the audience will tell you what it thinks of your speech. You must take your cues and adjust accordingly.

R—Relaxing and Enjoying Your Self

In most cases, your audience *wants* you to succeed. It is on your side. If you have done everything in your power to make your speech entertaining, informative, clear and concise, then you need do only one more thing to ensure your speech's success—relax and enjoy yourself. If you are nervous, your audience will be nervous. If you are uncomfortable, your audience will be uncomfortable. But, if you are enjoying yourself—so will your audience.

Speaking before people can be a truly enjoyable experience. If you really believe that and learn to enjoy speaking, then you will be a good speaker. If you don't believe that, if speaking is nothing more than a task, and an arduous one at that, then don't worry about it—you won't be asked to do it often. Be at ease, enjoy your audience, and you will be in demand.

E—Enthusiasm and Empathy: Keys to Success

Be enthusiastic—believe in what you are saying. If you are, then even if your audience does not agree with what you are saying, it will still respect you as a person of knowledge and conviction. Your enthusiasm can build a lasting positive impression in the mind of your audience. If your speech is to be followed by a question and answer session, you will find that enthusiasm is your greatest ally.

When dealing with those questions from the audience, empathy is the keynote. Put yourself in the position of the questioner. If you do this, you will never slough off a question or make light of it or the person who asked it. There will be no need to become defensive, and, because you have done your research, you can answer the question straightforwardly and comprehensively.

This, then, is the P R E P A R E formula. As we said, it has served us well for many years in the preparation and delivery of numerous speeches. May it bring you similar success.

AN ADMINISTRATOR'S SURVIVAL GUIDE FOR AVOIDING THE PITFALLS OF PUBLIC SPEAKING

Public speaking can be an enjoyable experience, but it can also have its pitfalls. What, for example, is the best way to answer a question from the audience so that everyone understands the answer? What if you are faced with a hostile audience? How can you ensure that your charts or graphs will be seen by everybody? What happens if you are asked an obviously hostile question?

These are some common pitfalls of the public speaker, but they can be handled to the speaker's advantage. This section offers proven suggestions that will help you to overcome them, to deliver a memorable and enjoyable address.

How to Use Visual Aids to Advantage

You can have the best, most thoughtful, most interesting presentation in the world, but it will count for nothing if it remains unseen.

Consider it from the audience's point of view. How frustrating it is to have your attention called to a map, chart or diagram only to find that visual aid blocked, either wholly or partially, by the speaker's body. What makes it worse is that frequently the speaker is unaware of the problem.

Obviously, this is no problem when you are addressing a small, intimate group where everyone is afforded an unobstructed view of everything, or where they may move themselves or their chairs in order to obtain that view. It is when you are appearing on a stage or dais, before a larger audience, that this may prove a difficulty. Surprisingly enough, it is within the physical layout of the stage that your solution to the problem lies.

Most halls or auditoriums are set up so that the chairs for the audience are placed in rows, from just before the foot of the stage backward to the far wall of the room. The chairs on either ends of these rows are usually set up in line with the proscenium arch on either side of the stage.

Therefore, if you will conceive of your shoulders as pointers, it will become obvious that your audience will always be able to see you and your display if, when you are facing to your left, you keep your right shoulder pointed at the right proscenium arch and, when you are facing to your right, you keep your left shoulder pointed at the left proscenium arch. This affords every member of the audience, in every seat, a clear line of sight to what is happening on the stage.

You will also find it useful if, when gesturing, you gesture with your *upstage* hand, the hand closest to the back wall and furthest from the audience. If you will keep this in mind, you will never "reach across yourself" when gesturing, which is very unattractive from the audience's point of view, and can also block your speech and your display.

Certainly, everything you do to make your presentation as pleasant, clear, and intelligible as possible will aid in establishing rapport with your audience and leaving them in a receptive mood. You will find that the gratification your audience displays will make any effort on your part well worthwhile.

How to Answer Questions from the Audience Effectively

One of the severest tests of a good speaker is the ability to answer questions from the floor in an efficient and effective manner. If a question from the floor is handled in a halting, stammering, erratic manner, the audience may begin to suppose that the speaker is either unsure of his material or trying to mislead them in some way.

Fortunately, there is a tested and proven way of answering questions that not only conveys to the audience exactly the information that their questions require, but does so in such a precise and effective manner that both the answer and the answerer are remembered.

The method involves two steps. When a question is asked, you:

1. Repeat the question.
2. Use the A R E A formula of response.

Let's examine each of these steps.

When you are asked a question from the floor, the first thing you ought to do is to repeat the question. This serves two purposes. First, it ensures that everyone has heard the question and heard it exactly as the questioner intended. Second, it gives you time to think.

Quite often, the only one to hear the question is the speaker and a few people in the immediate vicinity of the questioner. This may be due to the acoustics of the hall or the soft-spoken manner of the questioner, but it happens more often than not. Therefore, your repetition of the question gives the rest of the audience the chance to hear what has been said. It also ensures that what you have heard is what the questioner indeed asked, so there will be no confusion later or claims that the question was not answered.

Repeating the question also provides you with time to think and organize your answer. You will be surprised at how even a few seconds provides you with time to get your material in order for presentation.

When it comes to actually answering the question that has been asked, there is no better or effective way of presenting your viewpoint than the use of the A R E A formula. Each letter stands for one step in an effective answer. They are:

A—Answer

R—Reason

E—Example

A—Answer

First, give your *answer*. Make the point you wish to make. Tell the questioner the answer that his question engenders.

Next, tell the *reason* for your answer. Tell clearly and concisely why you gave the answer you did.

Third, give an *example* that shows why you gave the answer you did. There is nothing like a concrete example to get across a salient point. Almost anything can be put into the form of an anecdote or story to which the audience can relate, no matter how intelligent you may think its members are. Everyone profits from a solid example.

Finally, repeat your *answer*. This time it should be a natural outgrowth of your reason and example. Also, leaving the questioner and, by projection, the audience with an answer gives it something to think about, and something which will be remembered for some time.

Let's look at how the whole method would be used in an actual situation. Suppose you were speaking, and it came time for questions. The person you call upon asks, "Which do you feel are better: heterogeneously or homogeneously grouped classes?"

"The question has been asked," you state to the audience, "which I feel are better: heterogeneously or homogeneously grouped classes. Is that correct? It is. I assume you mean 'better for the students involved,' is that correct? It is. Thank you."

You have been addressing the questioner. You now turn and give your answer to the audience as a whole.

"I personally feel that heterogeneously grouped classes are better for students than homogeneously grouped classes, because they allow for more flexibility in teaching methods and greater student-initiated help. When a teacher uses a variety of methods, as he or she must in a heterogeneously grouped classroom, *all* children benefit, because the material is covered from several different angles. Furthermore, the students who get the material more slowly can benefit from the aid of those children who get it more quickly, while at the same time reinforcing the knowledge in the quicker-learning child.

"For example, let's take a math problem—five times three equals fifteen. For some, just the explanation of the mechanics and techniques of multiplication is enough, but in a heterogeneously grouped classroom, the teacher might also use three sets of five children walking to the front of the room. He might also let students come up with their own examples which they would 'share' with others, thereby ensuring their learning and others' learning as well. Everyone participates and grows from the interaction. Therefore, I believe that heterogeneously grouped classes are much more beneficial in education."

Notice how, in the example, the question was not only repeated, but a potential area of misunderstanding was clarified before it caused any concern. Then notice how the question was answered in strict accord with the A R E A formula. Notice, too, that the entire answer was concise and did not ramble.

The next time you watch a televised press conference with any politician, pay attention to how he or she handles the questions asked by reporters. You will see them repeating questions, and, if you pay particular attention, you just might see the A R E A formula staring back at you from your TV screen.

While a huge factor in an audience's acceptance of an answer is the personality of the speaker, still, a decided factor is the way in which the answer has been presented to them. Repeat that question, give your answer, state the reason for your answer, use a solid example, and then repeat your answer, and you will have answered that question with effectiveness and dispatch.

How to Deal with the Hostile Audience

That you may one day be faced by a hostile audience is not a far-fetched assumption, particularly for the educator who may find himself addressing groups of citizens suspicious of "new" programs and wary of tax increases. There may, indeed, come a time when you must face an audience that is not willing or eager to accept what you have to say; that may, indeed, be hostile.

It will not be easy, but it can be made bearable and antagonism can be kept to a minimum if you keep a few rules in mind:

1. Acknowledge in the beginning that there are differences of opinion: "You might not agree with what I have to say to-night...."
2. Do not apologize for yourself. Say: "I believe in what I am about to tell you, and all I ask is that you hear me out...."
3. Base what you say on hard, cold *facts:* "As I see it *these* are the facts of the matter...."
4. *Never* get personal: To attack an audience's personal beliefs or opinions is the surest road to complete alienation. Let the weight of your argument win its members' support.
5. Be aware of the possibility of hostile questions. Handle these questions with tact and by stating provable facts, never opinions.

Under any circumstances, facing a hostile audience is a far from pleasant experience. Fortunately, ninety-nine percent of your public speaking will be before receptive audiences, but it is well to be prepared for an unpleasant possibility. In such cases, you will survive if you follow the rules above and make every effort to project an image of confidence, assuredness, and calmness.

Effectively Overcoming the Hostile Question

Does the term "hostile question" really need a definition? It is any question so stated that it is designed to put you on the spot. Please understand, we are not talking about a difficult or intricate question that is honestly asked. We mean the "When did you stop beating your wife?" variety that begs the question and the sole intent of which is to put you in an unfavorable light.

You can deal effectively with a hostile question if you:

1. Remain calm and treat the questioner with respect and courtesy.

2. Break a question into its simplest parts, both stated and un-
stated, and then answer each part separately.

Now, let's examine both steps.

First, it is essential that you remain calm. You can think more
clearly and you will gain the respect of your audience if you stay rational
in the face of hostility. Treating the hostile questioner with courtesy
and civility will further aid in swinging the audience's support to your
side.

Next, make certain that everyone knows exactly what is being
asked. Let's assume that someone has asked this question: "What
makes you so superior that you have all the answers?" (We think you'll
agree that that's a hostile question.) Here is a response that exemplifies
Step Two: "I'd like to answer that question, but, as I see it, you have
asked several questions. I think you're asking *if* I feel superior; *if* I do,
then what makes me feel so; and *do* I have all the answers? The answers
are 'no,' 'it doesn't follow,' and 'most certainly not.' Now, let's examine
each one of them in turn . . . "

By handling the hostile question in this manner, you have turned a
potentially embarrassing situation into one that will be advantageous
to you by gaining the respect of the audience and perhaps the hostile
questioner as well.

How to Learn to Love It

Finally, let's deal with the single biggest drawback faced by the
beginning speaker—nervousness.

Actors call it "stage fright"; radio announcers call it "mike fright."
You may call it what you will, but it is that feeling, just before you are
introduced, that your knees have turned to jelly, your spine is made of
water, your voice has just departed for parts unknown, and you would
rather be anywhere—from an arctic iceberg to the middle of a desert
sandstorm—than where you are. It is something that happens, and it is
something you must deal with. If it is any comfort to you, Helen Hayes,
that marvelous veteran actress of thousands of public appearances,
once reported that before every public appearance she made, she would
get so nervous she would become physically ill. Yet, anyone who has
ever had the honor of watching her perform will know that never once
was that anxiety communicated to the audience.

What is the solution to this problem? Many have been suggested.

We were once told to picture the audience sitting there in their underwear. The picture becomes so ludicrous that you can't possibly be nervous. Another speaker told us that he never looks at the audience, but focuses on the hairline of audience members. This gives the impression of looking directly at them without having eye contact.

Each of these solutions worked for the person who used them. We have never had to. Yes, we have been nervous, but a matter of philosophy has always been our salvation. You see, we have always expected to love every audience to whom we spoke, and we have expected them to love us. We have not been disappointed. Nervous? Certainly, but the minute the first words come forth, we get interested in the audience—and we forget ourselves, our problems, and, most importantly of all, our nervousness.

Try it; it works!

Appendix

LOCATOMATIC INDEX OF SPEECH TOPICS AND OCCASIONS

USING THIS INDEX

The numbers that you will find following each topic are *not page numbers*. You have undoubtedly noticed that each speech or anecdote in the book has been numbered. The numbers in this index refer to the *speech number*.

Think of the topic on which you are to speak and look it up in the following pages. There, you will be directed to a speech in this book that either covers or touches on that topic. This will help you to automatically find precisely the topic you had in mind. That's why we call it "Locatomatic" index.

If you should not find what you had in mind, try looking under topics that are related to your original topic. The chances are good that you might find something of use waiting for you.

AIDS
for a program on: 44, 50
and sex education: 123
ANECDOTES
attitude: 56
cleverness: 3, 14, 21, 23
kindergarten: 5, 8
parents: 23
pregnant: 5
quotations: 19, 20
responsibility: 62
roasts: 1
trust: 4
ANIMALS IN CLASS: 120
AUDIENCE
class reunion: 85
community/media: 14, 24, 26,
27, 29, 31, 35, 36, 37, 40, 57,
58, 60, 62, 63, 69, 74, 75, 77,
80, 83, 87, 101, 119, 122, 123,
124
educators only: 4, 32, 33, 34,
47, 53, 59, 61, 76, 78, 81, 90,
102, 103, 106, 107, 118, 120,
121, 125, 126
hostile: 25, 60
parents and students: 67, 99,
116
parents and teachers: 26, 27, 36
parents only: 5, 8, 20, 23, 28,
31, 37, 45, 46, 51, 52, 55, 56,
57, 58, 105, 122, 124
receptive: 30, 51, 119
students only: 36, 37, 68, 87,
108, 109, 111, 113, 117
AVA: 121

AWARDS
ceremony: 116
teacher: 24

B

BENEDICTIONS
all purpose: 41
inspirational: 42
"moment of silence:" 38, 39
volunteers: 40
BUDGET: 60

C

CHALLENGES: 66
CHANGE: 45, 104
CHILD ABUSE: 122
CHILDREN
general: 8
kindergarten: 5
noise: 23
CHILD'S VIEW: 5, 6
CHRISTMAS: 110
CLASS REUNION POEM: 85
CLEVERNESS: 1, 2, 3, 14, 21,
23
CLOSERS
general: 49, 50, 51, 52, 53, 54
inspirational: 72, 73
memorial service: 96
poem: 73
COMMUNICATION: 19, 65, 105